A Smuggler's Guide to Fine Dining

"Oh Captain Kenny, I love the book. It is such a jaunty yarn. I would love to read the second one."
Professor Katie Kane

"This is what it looks like out past the edge."
5.0 out of 5 stars

"Most 9-5 typical folks can't even imagine what the carefree, live-by-your-wits world is like. Many people would be uneasy reading this book, let alone living in this world. Very well written and with an excellent story line, this book will have you reading fast to get to the next page. Wish the writer was more prolific. I could read a dozen stories like this and never slow down."
Reviewed in the United States on January 2, 2021
Verified Purchase

"Ranen was the master at what he did. No comparison! Real deal."
Mike Leddy
5.0 out of 5 stars

"I read this book in 7 hours. I could not put it down and didn't want to! I wish I could have been there every minute…I can relate and was just a few years behind Kenny doing some of the same things but I didn't go around the cape! Or sail into the Middle East. Great story! One of my favorite Ocean going reads ever! What a sailor and true adventurer as well as a romantic. Total Pro! You are the MAN, Ranen! Hats off! Love the reflection on what weekend sailors thought when they saw the real deal.

Dropping Anchor with Sails up! GOOD STUFF!!"
Reviewed in the United States on February 3, 2018
Verified Purchase

"Brilliant!"
Patrick Waldron
5.0 out of 5 stars

"WOW. I loved this book. From the first page to the last, it is one heck of a ride. For just a while, we get to be a part of an extraordinary adventure, within one man's extraordinary life. For me, this book has what it takes to be a classic, up there with Tough Trip Through Paradise and Been Down So Long It Looks Like Up To Me, or Jack London's finest. A real, honest, authentic journey in another person's shoes, who has lived life to its absolute fullest."
Sam Stier, author of Engineering Education for the Next Generation: A Nature-Inspired Approach

COPYRIGHT © 2021 BY KENNY RANEN

ALL RIGHTS RESERVED.

NO PART OF THIS BOOK MAY BE USED OR REPRODUCED BY ANY MEANS, GRAPHIC, ELECTRONIC, OR MECHANICAL, INCLUDING PHOTOCOPYING, RECORDING, TAPING, OR BY ANY INFORMATION STORAGE RETRIEVAL SYSTEM WITHOUT THE WRITTEN PERMISSION OF THE PUBLISHER EXCEPT IN THE CASE OF BRIEF QUOTATIONS EMBODIED IN CRITICAL ARTICLES AND REVIEWS.

ISBN 978-1-7349568-6-3

FOREST CITY PUBLICATIONS

1658 MILWAUKEE AVE # 100-16118

CHICAGO, IL 60647

HTTPS://FORESTCITYPUBLICATIONS.COM

Library of Congress Cataloging Data

A Smuggler's Guide to Fine Dining / Kenny Ranen

ISBN 978-1-7349568-6-3

A Smuggler's Guide to Fine Dining

A Sailor's Hunger and the Ravenous Sea

Kenny Ranen
Cover Art by Tracey Fedor

Table of Contents

Tortola, British Virgin Islands, 1977 ············· 5

Jerome, Colorado, 1970 ······················· 29

Steamboat Springs, 1970 ····················· 38

Ranen's First Voyage, 1971 ··················· 45

Turks and Caicos Islands, 1977

Goodbye to Jerome ·························· 70

Maria, Nassau Harbour, 1977 ················ 78

South to Jamaica ···························· 93

Scoring In Jamaica ·························· 104

Load and Leave ····························· 113

Beating Out Of The Caribbean ·············· 119

"We're Going To Have To Take Some Chances" ······ 127

Stowaway ··································· 136

A Few Nervous Days in Virginia ············· 150

Onward to Cape Cod ······················· 157

The Other Dangerous Moment	166
A Sojourn in Boston	170
Marblehead	177
Key Largo, 1975	184
Crawling Away From Key Largo, 1976	205
The Pirates and the East Coast Yachting Establishment	216
Hood Sails, 1977	224
Rhode Island	235
Storm	244
Due South to Provo	265
North Again	275
Back in the USSR	286
Hugo and Adrienne	302
Marketing	312
A Rocky Mountain Hideout	318
Epilogue, beyond, 1979	330
About the Author	334

CHAPTER 1

TORTOLA, BRITISH VIRGIN ISLANDS 1977

Someone was knocking on Misty's steel hull. At first, I was merely annoyed to have to put down Sterling Hayden's Voyage, pull my shoulder-length, sun-bleached curly hair out of my face, and return to reality.

I was lying in the cabin of my sailing boat during the hottest chunk of the day, taking my usual siesta in the shade down below, while the cool, cleansing tradewinds blasted in off the wind scoop.

I've always been really small, only five and a half feet, but I was ropey and strong from years of skiing, climbing, and living in the mountains. I had a bit of an attitude. I never cared who came knocking on my boat's hull, friend or foe: let 'em come, I'm ready.

But I was anchored pretty far off the beach, on the far side of the coral reef in Cane Garden Bay, and I hadn't heard another boat approach. So the idea that someone swam all the way out here, uninvited, quickly transformed my annoyance into surprise.

As I heard the thump on deck of a bag being thrown on board, my first thought was, who the hell would swim out here to find me?

The boat rocked, announcing the unexpected guest climbing over the rail.

My second thought was, Where's my nearest pistol?

There was no time to search for the answer. I looked up to see the face of Jerome, my partner-in-crime and mountaineering, hanging upside-down from the open companionway[1] hatch. Jerome, a product of eastern U.S. prep-school culture, was handsome, smart, and much like myself–an adrenaline junkie.

"WHAT THE HELL?! How did you find me? You swam out here...? Nevermind. Come down. Let's smoke one."

Jerome flipped through the hatch as he spoke. "Dean said you'd be here. He said Maria's gone? Again?"

I shot him a knowing look.

"Right. Well, I flew in yesterday, started looking for you at West End. I met the boatyard carpenter."

"Fred," I interrupted, handing him the joint and lighter.

"Right, I met Fred. He thought you'd be anchored here. So, I hitched a ride to the hotel and swam out." He stopped talking to light up. Through a fragrant cloud of smoke, he exhaled the words, "I've got a job for us."

"Oh yeah? What kind of job?" I asked.

"A doctor." He replied.

---

[1] Companionway: a raised and windowed hatchway in the ship's deck with a ladder leading below and the hooded entrance-hatch to the main cabins.

This time I shot him an unknowing look.

"He's with Médecins Sans Frontières. Right now he's under house arrest. In Haiti. He needs an exit strategy."

I let Jerome take another long pull, and took the joint from him as he swallowed. "Let me guess, we are the exit strategy. What'd he do to piss them off?"

"He runs a free clinic. Everything the people need. He gets it, he treats them–everything. All the medicine, everything is free."

"I know what Doctors Without Borders is, Jerome. Where does this go wrong for him?"

"The government." Jerome spat out the words. "They see an opportunity. They start intercepting the medicine shipments. Start selling it to the people instead. So what does our good samaritan doctor do? Goes to some European news outlet, gives an interview, criticizes the president, Baby Doc himself, and voila..."

I commented, "Voila, he's under house arrest. Dictators don't take kindly to critics."

We both nod.

"So do we even know where he lives?"

"Atlantic coast, not far from the Dominican Republic border."

"Okay." I shrug, already decided, and pull out a mask and snorkel from a hatch, tossing them to Jerome. "Unhook my anchor and chain from the coral. I'll pull up the slack as you do. We'll motor over to West End. I want to pick Fred's brain and stock up. I just might know how to get him out."

"Okay..." Jerome hesitated, staring at the mask and snorkel.

I wasn't sure what he was pondering. He knew me well enough to know I'm always ready for the next gig. If I had business in Tortola, that would be something, but I don't. I'm ready, and that shouldn't come as a surprise to Jerome.

It's something else. I just let it hang between us until he found some way to voice it himself.

Finally, he asked his question, as casually as he can force himself to muster, "So. Maria. She's back in California...?"

"Yup. Here yesterday, gone tomorrow. She left some things this time." I point at the shrunken bikini bottoms still hanging where they'd dried on the hook next to the hatch. "You can wear her swim trunks if you like."

Jerome laughed, "Maybe I will." And that was that. He slipped on the mask and pulled himself back up the hatch from where he came. Whatever he needed to resolve for himself, about me, about Maria, he just did it, and now it was time to go to work. He was just like that. We were both like that.

Three hard cranks, a flip of the compression release, and the engine was chugging. By the time I got to the bow and started pulling in the anchor chain, I could watch Jerome working five meters deep in the crystal clear water. He had the chain unwrapped from the coral heads and was prying the fisherman anchor away from its nook under the coral. I was wondering how long he could stay down when suddenly he broke the surface, gasping for air. He reached up, grabbed the rail, and pulled himself aboard while I hoisted the anchor over the bow.

We sailed the few miles to the little anchorage on the West End of Tortola to seek out Fred Thomas, a shipwright at the slipway. Fred was an icon in the islands. He had been Charley Morgan's protégé. Morgan, who, at the age of seventeen, built his first sailboat and brought it to a race in Havana, where he was initially denied entry and nearly laughed out of the race due to the lack of an engine on the boat. After managing to appeal the specifications of his unusual craft, Morgan took second in the race. Ten years later, Morgan Yacht Corporation was building some of the most popular and successful racing yachts in the world, and Fred Thomas was there during the thick of it, a young shipwright, perfecting his craft.

Fred lived aboard a classic wooden schooner that was in a perpetual state of restoration. Smugglers and professional sailors journeyed from everywhere under the sun (and from other places, where the sun never shined), to avail themselves of his talents: from building invisible storage compartments, to asking for discrete advice, to plotting illicit strategies.

Fred was probably only forty, but he had a lot of experience, and was a trusted advisor to a lot of "the brothers." And right now, at the helm of my Misty, with Jerome splayed out on the bow, basking in the spray and sun, sailing towards who-the-hell-knows-what, I needed to confer with a trusted advisor.

In the years that Jerome and I had been rock climbing partners, doing risky oddball first ascents throughout the Western States, Jerome had a habit of repeatedly getting us into "tight spots." So, I guess we were going to Fred for a reality check, because I wasn't so sure that Jerome wasn't getting us into yet another "tight spot."

We anchored up and zipped into port on the inflatable Zodiac[2]. Jerome tied us up to the marine railway and we walked up the ways, past the famous Herreshoff designed yacht Royono. It was a well known secret that Royono hosted the tryst between John F. Kennedy and Marilyn Monroe (if hulls could only speak). It just wouldn't do to let Royono, a veritable icon of marine architecture, degrade into obscurity. So her wealthy owner brought her here, to a shipyard with a shipwright he could trust for the project.

My own sailing boat, Misty, was most definitely not an iconic classic yacht like Fred's wooden schooner or Royono, nor was she a modern racing sloop or cruising yacht like those designed by Morgan. She didn't have a shower onboard, not even a head (marine toilet). It was "bucket and chuck it" on Misty. Whoever contracted her construction obviously wanted a sailing vessel that could safely cross oceans, and her 1940s Dutch builders (who are masters of crafting beautifully curved

---

[2] Zodiac: a brand of inflatable boat. Misty's dinghy was a 12-foot Zodiac inflatable boat with a collapsable wooden floor, and a solid wooden transom that mounted a 10 hp outboard motor.

yachts in steel) delivered a lovely package. I had painted her glossy white with glacial ice blue decks. She had low freeboard. You could reach out to touch the sea from her cockpit. Because form follows function in the yachting world, Misty accorded me a status in the sailing community that my experience as a captain didn't buy me. Her beauty played a melancholy chord in the hearts of true sailors that reached into a simpler time when sailing was closer to the sea…lower tech.

Jerome followed me into the dark ramshackle shed that was Fred's current shop. In our momentary blindness we stumbled over open wooden boxes of fastenings, winches, windlasses, and old-school industrial power tools. A craggy, weathered face appeared out of the dust in a dimly lit corner. An American accent boomed, "Well, what brings the elusive Ranen into my humble establishment?"

"Fred, this is my old climbing partner and mate, Jerome."

"We've met."

The two nodded to each other, and Fred gave me a look like he already knew what I would say next.

"Listen Fred, I want your take on a scam we're thinkin' 'bout."

"Okay, it's getting too dark to work anyways, and when Ranen shows up to talk biz, it must be something unusual. You can buy me a rum. Or, if this gets entertaining, you can buy me three."

We found a little table at the only bar that existed back

then in West End and ordered shots of rum with slices of lime. Jerome laid out the situation.

After a few minutes of thoughtful silence, Fred asked, "How're you gonna get paid for this? I mean, is that the intention? It is going to cost you money. Haiti was bad under Pappa Doc, but his kid, Baby Doc, don't let the name fool you. Ain't easy getting candy from this baby. His Army controls everything. He's got a deadly grip on the whole country, and in that country, in Haiti…they shoot to kill."

I immediately asked, "Does Haiti have a navy? Patrol boats?"

Fred chewed on the question, "Navy? I doubt it. I haven't seen anything like a coast guard, or heard about one, but no one I know does any business out of there. That country is so fucking poor there's no reason to go there, unless you need to sell a boatload of old bicycles and plastic bottles. All I know for sure is, they have a serious army. Baby Doc's gotta protect what he's got."

"So?" I asked, "What do you think?"

"Well, it is pretty far from the usual scam. It's for a good cause, and they won't be expecting it, or they would have moved him away from the coast. But, again, how are you gonna get paid?"

"I've been thinking, this doctor might have some Haitian art. Haitian paintings are popular these days. But I don't know how close they're watching him, and I'm not sure if he could

A Smuggler's Guide to Fine Dining

Jerome Sailing Misty

get paintings to the beach, or if we could even get a dinghy in. It would be easier if he could just go for a swim and we could sail by to pick him up. I think Doctors Without Borders won't contribute anyway, even if I was cold enough to ask for money from, arguably, the most righteous nonprofit on this planet. Still, I gotta say, I like the idea of doing this."

"Just curious, Jerome." I turned my gaze on my friend, and gave him a moment to study the whites of my eyes so he could tell how serious I was. "Can you explain, again, how exactly, being half French connected you with some French doctor in trouble in Haiti? Fuck it. Just tell me this is real. Tell me you're sure this is real."

"It is, Ranen. I had a phone call with a few guys in France.

I left California, I flew to the Virgin Islands, I hunted you down and took a swim off the hotel lawn, out to where you were anchored, all to bring this here. To you. It's real."

"All right, all right," I waved the moment away with my shot glass. "I trust you. While we're here, in Tortola, you should have your contact in France pass a message that someone's coming for him. We won't have to take him far, he can get a flight out of Nassau."

Fred pushed his chair back and stuck a finger in each of our nine shot glasses to collect them from the table, "Good luck in Haiti, you guys. Keep her off the reefs."

***

A Smuggler's Guide to Fine Dining

The next morning we visited the little stand next to the marine railway and bought bread, green bananas, oranges, cabbage, and carrots, then sailed away from Tortola.

Like most of the Antilles, Tortola is very dry and rocky, not much agriculture. However, I always carried six months of food onboard. You never know when a long non-stop smuggling job would come up or when you'd lose a mast a thousand miles offshore. Also, whenever I had the luxury of being in an American or European harbor, where a wide variety of non-perishable foods are available, I took the opportunity to stock up. Cases of evaporated milk, canned fish, rounds of cheese, tinned fruit, bags of granola, brown rice, oats–I had an ever-evolving book of provisioning lists. If you don't eat well, you won't have the energy to navigate that seven-day storm that is just past the horizon.

Although Haiti was only five-hundred nautical miles away, the voyage required serious diligence. We had to thread through a lot of small Islands and rocks leaving the Virgin Islands, dodge a lot of small ship traffic passing by Puerto Rico, and over a full day of avoiding the big ship traffic crossing the Mona Passage.

This portion of the Atlantic hosted numerous offshore coral reefs and ship graveyards–great for treasure hunters, but not great for small sailing boats that weren't equipped with electronic positioning equipment. In the mid-1970s the U.S. Navy was putting up satellites for navigation, but actual satellite navigation was still a few years off for non-military vessels. At

(Top) Ranen and Maria's First Misty Voyage
(Bottom) Ranen's First Misty Voyage

that point it was just a well-founded rumor. I was still getting questionable celestial fixes using a sextant, and the latest Timex electronic timepiece, an early digital watch. Look, I should point out that it was a damn good thing Misty was a steel boat, because she was my first boat, and even though I had already made three non-stop voyages from the U.S. to Columbia, my first voyage as captain had only been two years prior, and I hit every reef there was on that journey, teaching myself how to navigate.

During that first voyage as captain, while preparing to depart Georgetown, Exuma Island in the Bahamas, a good friend, George Bond, sat me down aboard his Alden ketch, Restless, and instructed me on how to get to the Virgin Islands.

His instructions: "Just go east for five days and turn right."

That advice didn't turn out very well.

***

At the time, my first mate, Maria, was also my longtime girlfriend. A couple years prior, she and I had sailed on a long voyage to Columbia, but neither of us had been captain and neither of us had done the navigating.

We followed George's advice, turned right on day five, and on day nine, when we should have made landfall in Puerto Rico, there were only endless waves as far as the eye could see.

We had a problem. To the east of Hispaniola, Puerto Rico,

and the Virgin Islands, there are offshore reefs you can hit before you see them. My dead reckoning was telling me that we should be seeing islands, and I was starting to worry. In mere hours we would be sailing in the dark, the trade winds[3] were blowing a steady fifteen to eighteen knots, and we would be hauling ass into the darkness when we hit one of those reefs, many miles offshore, with no one to call for help.

I had three possible positions on the chart, my chart that was littered with lines of possible positions, and I was second-guessing my shaky celestial navigation. The thing is, on long passages, if your navigation is off, the error becomes greater the further you sail. So, yes, I was worried, and for a good reason.

I didn't let on to Maria how worried I was about not making landfall, but Maria was keeping the log on her watches and must have been worried as well. We both just worried about it by ourselves, in our own way. Lost, in the open ocean, miles away from anywhere, from who-knows-where, and we just didn't talk about it. We both knew that we needed to remain in the moment and calmly wait for events to unfold.

My plan was to sail hard westerly, during the daylight hours, then climb the mast and look for land just before dark. If no land was in sight, we'd put up a small foresail and a reduced mainsail and continue to sail very slowly. Just creeping along, watching the depth sounder for any changes. After three hours

---

[3] Trade winds: a wind blowing steadily towards the equator from the northeast in the northern hemisphere or the southeast in the southern hemisphere, especially at sea. Two belts of trade winds encircle the earth, blowing from the tropical high-pressure belts to the low-pressure zone at the equator.

of that, I would take down all the sails and wait for daylight.

On our second night of being lost at sea, I climbed up to my mast perch on the spreaders, and, for only a moment, I saw a reflection on the clouds. The glow of Puerto Rico. Bingo. I had a bearing on San Juan.

Like seeing an oasis in the desert, I agonized over whether or not I really saw it. It did fit one of my possible positions, but I still wasn't sure. Was it real or a mirage? I decided, I had to believe what I saw was real, because what other choice did I have?

We were pretty far off course, something like one-hundred miles east of my positions. Too far for a radio bearing on the airport in San Juan and too far off the approach patterns to see aircraft. Following airplanes to an island was the modern incarnation of the ancient Tahitian navigation techniques.

Within a day, to our absolute relief, we spotted our first airliner. Two days later we made landfall at San Juan.

* * *

During those two days one thing we spent a lot of time not thinking about was what else might be lurking out there, besides the reefs, as we sailed on, full sails up, into the dark night. On only our third morning heading east from the Bahamas, we came close to losing our lives to things that lurk, left forgotten on the open seas.

I had come on watch just before dawn. Big genoa[4] and a full mainsail up with a light steady breeze, the self-steering was keeping a perfect course. Being on watch means looking out for ships and any other thing you'd rather not hit, like an island. Being on watch also means maintaining speed by changing or adjusting sails. Furthermore, being on watch means sailing the boat, which includes keeping the boat on course, either by sitting at the tiller or tweaking the self-steering.

Misty had an Aries wind vane self-steering system that worked by adjusting a paddle to stand straight up when the boat was on course, but the wind would tip the paddle over when the boat went off course, thereby pulling a line attached to the tiller and putting the boat back on course. If you have trouble getting your head around the principle, just know that it meant you could walk around and do other things instead of sitting or standing by the tiller, steering, hour after hour, day after day. So, steering was mostly about watching the compass, and tugging at one of two cords which told the Aries to steer a bit more to port or starboard.

On that particular morning watch, as the sky was showing a blush of color on the horizon, I leaned out to look around the big genoa. I had scanned for ship running-lights ten or fifteen minutes before and had seen nothing but black, so when I saw a big grey shape, vague and giant, there was doubt in my mind and a sick fear in my stomach. I grabbed the binoculars and

---

4 Genoa: a large foresail that overlaps the mainsail offering tremendous power.

double-checked. Sure enough, there was a huge, black wall, directly in our path, about a mile ahead. No lights. No particular shape. Just a wall!

I called out, "M, get up here FAST! There's something out there!"

In a moment, Maria was up in the cockpit, in short cutoff jeans, a tank top and her curly hair plastered to one side of her head, looking around and ready to move. "What the hell...is that??"

"Don't know for sure. Go dump the genoa. I want to slow down and sail up to it."

As Maria started pulling down the sail, I looked behind us while we were still at top speed to see the wake unreeling in a straight line. Then I looked ahead. The sail was down, and I could clearly see a black barge floating all by itself directly in our course. It was HUGE. A giant barge, longer than a couple of football fields, forty feet high, with no lights, and no sign of a human onboard, dead in the water. If we had been here an hour earlier in the pitch-black moonless night, I would have sailed right into that steel wall. The bow would have split open and we would have sunk in minutes. Even if we had survived the impact, we had no life raft, and even if we had a life raft, I think we would have been as dead as the barge before us.

Who knows why the tug captain left his tow out there? Maybe the tow line broke in a bad storm and conditions were too bad to get another tow cable connected...but leaving an unlit, hazardous obstruction floating out there?! Over the years, I'd encountered irresponsible commercial shipping officers, but the captain of that tug, willing to leave his tow out there without a single navigation light? I cannot imagine what could have caused him to sail away. In those days, I listened religiously to "Notice to Mariners" on the shortwave receiver for weather reports and alerts of just this kind of hazard, but we hadn't heard any mention of an unattended six-hundred-foot barge.

It's hard not to find yourself haunted by what lurks in the night, by hazards that almost took your life, especially as you venture forth on a new voyage. But, as helpful as hindsight can be, I had to shake the memories. I wasn't sailing Misty as a first-time captain for an adventure. Jerome and I had a job to do. I couldn't ruminate on every near death incident in my sailing life. I had to keep my eyes ahead, looking for new and different hazards lurking just past the horizon.

* * *

The night before we left Tortola I worked out a course for the voyage to Georgetown, Exuma with a stop in Haiti. When I actually studied the course lines drawn onto the big chart of the North Atlantic Western Part chart (INT 130), I realized that on my sail south from Exuma, when Maria was with me, we stayed offshore to avoid reefs and other dangers by simply going around them. This time, going north, we would be sailing right through them. My usual shipmate, Maria, was much more cautious than

Jerome. I would have to be careful not to let Jerome get me into trouble, which had me laughing at the thought. How could the guy, who flew halfway across the world to locate me based on a handful of lucky hunches in order to present a highly dangerous and illegal rescue mission...How could a guy like that ever not lead me into trouble?!

I couldn't see us getting any money for this job, so we took our time. After all, the doctor wasn't going anywhere. We tucked in behind reefs where we would be protected from the waves, and we speared fish, cooked meals, smoked weed and talked while we enjoyed the cuisine.

Dangerous as they were, those reefs meant that fish were always on the menu. We ate grouper, snapper, mahi, kingfish, all the members of the tuna family, and my absolute favorite, wahoo. Those were the days before global warming was a thing, before carbon started killing the coral. I loved cooking fish, and I was good at it. Jerome and I had some great lime-soaked raw fish ceviche cocktails to cure our marijuanna munchies.

Misty was beautiful but old-fashioned. Even fast sailboats are slow, and a fast sailboat Misty was not. In the most optimal conditions, I was pleased if she did one hundred miles in a day. Yet, even at our slow pace, we cleared the Mona Passage after a week.

The island of Hispaniola is divided into two nations, the eastern two-thirds is the Dominican Republic with Haiti being the western third. We were passing "La Republica," and still we had no good plan. Like all covert endeavors, this needed to happen smoothly, and quickly, and before our doctor's police guards had time to suspect that we were there to pick him up.

I sure as hell didn't want to sail in circles, in plain sight of God and everyone, off the beachfront of the doctor's house. I racked my brain to think of a clean way to arrange the pickup. I assumed that, even as disorganized as Haiti was, the army surely had the sense to monitor all his phone calls.

I was staring at the chart, blankly, almost day-dreaming, when the plan hit me.

I reached for the U.S. Navy publication that listed the official ports of entry for Haiti. We needed a port somewhere not too far from Cap-Haitien, one that was not a port of entry, which meant no customs officials. And, there one was! Just past the Dominican Republic border, fifteen or twenty miles from the doctor's house. Fort Liberte was a big open harbor with plenty of depth for Misty, but the entrance was too narrow and shallow for a big motor patrol boat, even if Haiti had any. I had sailed by different coasts of Haiti over the past few years and never saw a patrol boat or any sign of a navy, and Fred hadn't heard of any either.

I was feeling okay about going into Fort Liberte. Thirty-one is an age when we believe we are fireproof, so of course I was feeling confident about blindly jumping into the affairs of some fascist banana republic. However, even as a child, I had a very reliable intuition when it came to real danger. You might find it hard to believe, but I've always been able to feel when I'm in danger, when something is going to go wrong. Many years before, in San Francisco, I was arrested on a marijuana charge. The charges were later dropped, but there was an important take-away from my experience in the San Francisco County Jail. Every guy in the lockup that night was saying that he had had a feeling something was about to go wrong. We had all failed to listen to the little voice screaming inside of us. I had always listened to my intuition up until that point in my life, but in that moment I resolved to always pay heed to that voice. Not just listen, but listen.

As Misty approached our chosen port of entry, I was feeling lighthearted and hyper-focused. None of the feeling of heavy dread that told me something was wrong.

We motored into the narrow entrance to the Bay of Fort Liberte and dropped the anchor close to the exit. It was just past dawn, and the inflatable was trailing behind with the motor ready to go. I scanned the harbor with the binoculars. It was a dusty little village of shacks and a cinderblock building with a short wooden jetty on the waterfront. Not a car in sight, but there was an army light-transport truck with a canvas covered bed parked by the building. The plan was for Jerome to find a way to the doctor's house and make arrangements for the doctor to go for a swim the next day when we would be able to sail by and scoop him up.

We jumped into the dinghy and motored up to the jetty. The very black, very African-looking soldier leaning against the truck barely gave us a glance when Jerome climbed up to the dock. At that moment five more soldiers, with rifles, casually walked out of the building, heading to the truck. Jerome's French and a lot of gesticulating seemed to be an effective substitute for Haitian Patois, because he got in the back of the truck with four of the soldiers and the truck drove away. So far, so good, I thought, and motored back out to the boat.

I checked my watch. It would be at least 45 minutes each way if the soldiers dropped Jerome close and if he found the house quickly and if he caught a ride back in good time. A lot of "ifs." A cell phone would have been a game-changer, but that technology was years off. I motored back to the boat to wait. After two hours I became a bit nervous. Misty's engine was chugging away and the anchor was on a very short rope, ready to pull right up. I watched the dock through the binoculars, watched and waited.

Finally, the same army truck pulled up, came to a complete stop at the cinderblock shanty army HQ, and Jerome jumped off the tailgate.

I leaped into the dinghy. One pull on the starter rope and I was speeding to the dock.

Jerome casually jogged across the road and down to the waterfront, straight for me. He was a good climber. The more tense the situation, the calmer he became…and studying his body language right then, he was really calm.

I came alongside the jetty. Jerome sprung onboard, and

the dinghy leaped away from the dock.

"We need to get out of here fast. I got away, but they can't be far behind."

"What happened?"

"I found the house fifteen minutes after the army dudes dropped me. His servant met me at the gate, told me the police knew we were coming, they were watching the house. He said, 'RUN!' I took off. Ran all through these shacks back to the road.

"Just when I hit the highway, that same truck I took out of here, those same local boys came by. I waved, and they picked me back up. There are people everywhere. I'm sure a lot of them saw me get in and out of that truck.

"Ranen, if they hadn't been there, I don't know, man. No stopping at checkpoints, just cruising right through. Thank the fuck these local dudes have no idea what's going on."

"Maybe not," I agreed, "not in this village. But they knew we were coming. I bet your French connection, I bet he warned the doc over the phone, I bet you anything he gave it all away. Nevermind the doctor, I just hope we get out of here!"

I cut the outboard and got ready to leap aboard Misty. "Get the dinghy tied long to the stern and outboard up, then man the tiller. We are so gone." I ran to the anchor. While pulling the chain up, hand over hand, I watched another army truck arrive and a bunch of armed soldiers pour out, running and pointing at Misty.

I remember thinking, Wow, I picked the perfect harbor for a failed rescue mission. Soldiers everywhere, but out of the two motorboats in town, we own both of them.

Jerome kicked the motor into gear, and all the soldiers crowded onto a wasted, twenty-foot fishing skiff. I took the helm from Jerome, and he took the binoculars. I'll never forget him shouting out the play by play:

"Four soldiers are standing up, standing in the boat and yelling at the one rowing! They're raising their rifles and…hold on, they've dropped their rifles and the boat is really rocking. Oh God, I think one is going overboard! One fell down, knocked another one down!"

I couldn't help but glance over my shoulder and watch the show, they all bumped into each other and yelled at each other with barely suppressed tension, picture-perfect like a 1920's comedy. We were still laughing hysterically as we passed through the narrow bay exit and they started shooting.

Our laughter faded when we heard the bullets whizz by on the water. Were we nervous? Yes. Were we afraid? Not really. It was all just too ludicrous.

We turned to port into open waters and CLANG, a 7.62 mm bullet ricocheted off the stern rail. A moment of shocked silence, then Jerome and I looked at each other, and we were laughing again, like a couple of maniacs.

We were a couple of fools. That's how it always was with Jerome and me.

CHAPTER 2

JEROME, COLORADO 1970

I met Jerome in 1970 when we both worked at the Buttonbush Mexican restaurant and bar in Steamboat Springs, Colorado. Steamboat was just expanding into the tacky resort it is today, and the Buttonbush was the first and only decent bar on the "mountain." I opened a couple of hours early one morning, and Jerome walked in soon after. No one else was there yet. We hadn't been paid in two weeks and were both hoping to catch one of the three owners, all of whom were functioning, unrepentant alcoholics.

One of whom was my brother-in-law, Mickey Thompson, a legendary wildman hipster from the early acid days in Palo Alto. I met him when he showed up for Thanksgiving dinner at my family home in Atlanta, hand in hand with my sister, to announce they were getting married.

He wasn't just my boss in Steamboat, by then Mickey had become my life mentor.

When I met him, I was in my first (and last) quarter at the University of Georgia, and while most of my peers were busy deciding majors, I was busy trying to reconcile my youthful insecurities amidst the stark and surreal culture of Bible-belt academia.

I was harboring a lot of anxiety about the prospect that the most logical possibility for my inability to cope was simply that I was mentally ill.

Shortly before I met Mickey, I had read an article in Psychology Today by a Harvard researcher, Timothy Leary, about LSD. The article made LSD sound like a good idea for sorting out my head, and when I learned where Mickey was from, I asked him, "Do you know about LSD?"

"Sure," he answered, "I've dropped acid."

"Is it anything like I've read about?"

"Probably more than can be described. It's different for everybody, but it cuts right through the bullshit."

"Well, I want to try it."

I think he could tell that I wasn't just some kid who wanted to get wasted, that the pressure was crushing me, and I sincerely needed some clarity in my life. I think he decided, right then and there in our first introduction, that I was his family and he was going to be my guide. He made me a promise: "Come out to California this summer, and we'll take an acid trip together."

Six months later Mickey and I were watching the walls melt.

We basked in San Jose sunbeams and felt the universe wash through us. In one of those rare moments, when you get yourself back for a fleeting glimpse and can witness yourself from within and without, I asked, "Why can't we be like this all the time?"

Mickey answered, "Because no one in this country will fill your begging bowl."

True to his word, that acid trip cut right through all the bullshit. I got a cold, hard look at my insecurities and where they were taking me. I saw that my quick temper, jealous behavior, and dismissive disregard for my fellow human beings were all layers of ego protection that I didn't need. For all my insecurities, I realized that I was not crazy, but American culture really was fucked up. I actually got to that place in my mind where all that crap was hiding, had a good look, then let it go, and set myself free to live out my fantasies in the real world.

***

When Jerome and I both showed up at the Buttonbush hours ahead of schedule to find no sign of Mickey or anyone else who could cut us a paycheck, it was mid-winter and one of the harshest in Colorado memory.

Jerome had been cooking for a couple months, but I hadn't bothered to get to know him. I was twenty-four, full of self-centered, wild ideas about life typical of young guys in those times, and my girlfriend had just left me. Self-absorbed and depressed about losing a girl (who I realized was smart to leave me), I took solace in every available opportunity to go climbing and mountaineering with Michael Covington, a local "rock star."

I muttered to Jerome that it was a waste to be here

when I could be rock climbing. Jerome had become a really graceful backcountry skier, and when we got to talking about mountaineering he confided that he always wanted to learn to climb.

His confession struck me. "I've got two climbing ropes. Full rack of hardware. Everything we need to climb big walls."

Jerome put his hand on my shoulder. "Listen man, I gotta show you something." He led me out back where his bakery van was parked.

I glanced at him askew. "I don't get it."

He unlocked the back doors, opened them wide, and let me have a good look at his work. "Built it into a camper."

I was surprised at what I saw. He'd fitted the late model delivery van into a very organized home: sink and 2 burner propane stove, a loft bunk, and plenty of room for a second sleeping pad at night on the floor. A perfect, rolling, alpine-climbing hut. I shouldn't have been that surprised. Although he was a long-haired stoner, he was always well groomed with clean clothes and hair neatly tied into a ponytail. When he was on the job, the kitchen was organized and the food came out consistently on time and well-prepared. My funky looking 1948 Chevy Suburban was parked right next to his van, and his van put it to shame.

Jerome and I both knew exactly what we had to do next, but he also knew Mickey was my family, so out of respect he waited for me to be the one to say it. "I think it's time to get paid. You know how much you're owed?"

Jerome nodded, "Oh yeah."

And just like that, we decided to stock up his van and hit the road. There are a lot of mountains in the western United States, and we were raring to get started.

There were plenty of useful provisions in the stockroom and walk-in cooler. Big cans of refried beans, chilis, cooking oil, bags of popping corn, hams, a huge roast beef, a big bag of rice, various spices, a big pot, and a really nice commercial frying pan. We staggered out with armloads of loot. We weren't interested in taking any alcohol, although we did take a few cases of Cokes and all the bar snacks. We were purists. Purist stoners.

As we stowed the loot we laughed at how pissed off my brother-in-law would be when his main cook and dishwasher/busboy/prep guy never showed up that night. Resentful about not having been paid, we pretended to show no mercy, but really we both knew it was the bar that made the money. There were ten construction worker hippies for every woman in Steamboat, and those guys could drink a river. They would hardly notice there was no food as long as there was plenty of tequila and beer.

After loading everything we surveyed our provisions, and Jerome asked what we were going to do for gas money.

"I'm on it," I answered. "You got anything else you need to deal with? Loose ends?"

Jerome shook his head, "Ready to roll."

I talked over my shoulder as I plodded through the snow towards my Chevy. "Meet me at the Cameo."

"The bar?"

"Yeah, bartender is a friend of mine. Peter Szymanski. Gonna find out what an old panel truck and a Shedule is worth to the man." I was living in a coal shed I had turned into a cabin. The "Shedule" had a tiny yet very fancy potbelly stove and a picture window with a stunning view of the Sleeping Giant. Put together, the Chevy and the Shedule were worth five crisp one-hundred dollar bills and a farewell toke to my friend the Poz.

All that was left to do was hit the Shedule and pick up my gear. Conveniently, I had made a recent life decision to reduce my possessions down to only what I needed to be a mountaineer and no more. Everything I owned fit into three backpacks, except my skis and poles, all of which we quickly stowed into Jerome's van.

In the span of those furious few hours, and as we pulled away from my old home, I had been watching Jerome, watching how he moved and how he drove. He was tall, strong, and moved like water. This guy's going to be a great climber, I thought to myself. If he had been born in Russia, he would've been a ballet dancer.

A few minutes later we were barreling west on U.S. 40.

For six months straight we kept our expenses down to peanut butter, brown rice, and gasoline, our packs ready to go for any mountain or rock or ice wall that presented itself.

We climbed almost every day that winter. A month in Canyonlands alone. Spring found us in Yosemite Valley, and, unbeknownst to me at the time, that valley would prove instrumental in my smuggling life.

Jerome and I hooked up with a few solo climbers in "The Valley," some of whom (like Dean and Smitty) became fellow sailor-smugglers a couple years later. We were the oddball crew that didn't live in Camp 4, the now-famous birthplace of modern big wall climbing. Although we shared a lot of meals and tokes at Camp 4, we just needed some distance from the wildly intense social scene over at the base of "El Cap." Maybe we were all a little intimidated by the non-stop climbing electricity. I certainly was. I never climbed at the level of the "rock stars" like Bridwell or Mark Clemens, although some of our ragtag crew were getting there, like Jerome, Dean, and John Mochrie. We often climbed with that very small and extreme community of climbers, and even more often we got stoned with them. Either in pre-climb meditation or post-climb celebration or just because...we definitely all got stoned a lot.

Jerome, myself, and our growing crew of mountain misfits kept following spring into higher altitudes and bigger mountains until Summer finally caught up to us and Jerome fell in love with her...Summer Snyder.

We met Summer, and her identical twin Spring, in a Tuolumne campground. Two very blonde, very thin, elf-like young women, who embodied everything good that came out of the hippie movement. They were both enchanting and spectacular. Summer was the very personification of Galadriel, the elven queen, and none of us questioned it when Jerome deserted us for her.

I never have been much for farewells. However, I made sure that Jerome had a few addresses and phone numbers of people I checked in with or that I visited when I was on the road. Keeping in touch was difficult before cell phones and the internet.

Anyway, I still had a little bit of cash in my pocket, and I had it in my mind to head for the new ski area just going up outside a little town on the Western Slope called Telluride.

A Smuggler's Guide to Fine Dining

Rarin Climbing Bridal Veil Falls, Telluride, 1971.

CHAPTER 3

STEAMBOAT SPRINGS 1970

Perhaps inspired by Jerome and Summer, and with time to kill before ski season opened, I grabbed Dean and we headed down to Berkeley to get laid. He had an old Chevy sedan that looked like hell but still ran okay. We had remarkable success chasing beautiful Berkeley college girls. After all, it was the '70s.

After a few weeks we got burned out on city life and headed back for Steamboat Springs. I planned to meet up with my sister Nancy and her big Ford pickup and leave for Telluride. By the time I got there, Nancy's boyfriend, Roly, had been locked up, and she was hanging around the Western Slope waiting on the outcome of his court case. I was surprised to find that not just Roly but most of the young mountain hippies had been locked up.

* * *

LTV Recreation Development (a subsidiary of Ling-Temco-Vought, a Texas titan in mergers, acquisitions, and hostile takeovers) had purchased not only the Steamboat Springs Ski Resort but 1500 acres of surrounding primetime slopes. James

A Smuggler's Guide to Fine Dining

Ling and his LTV were their own breed of pirates. He had his fingers in the pension funds of every corporation he raided, and LTV had their fingers in the pie of the Vietnam War, producing aircraft for the conflict.

The LTV executives were right-wing Texans, devotees to the thriving cult of American Imperialism in the 1970 heyday, and the one thing they hated more than anything else was a hippie. They were saying the same things about our generation that people today say about millennials: lazy, entitled, spoiled, self-centered, and worthless.

When LTV bought the resort and all the rest of the land, in their self-interested corporate arrogance they figured they now owned the whole town and it was going to get cleaned up. The old cowboys were good for local color, but the young mountain kids needed to be gone. LTV used their clout in Colorado to bring in an undercover agent from the Colorado Bureau of Investigation to get to the bottom of the hippie presence in Steamboat Springs and eradicate it. Mostly on trumped-up weed charges.

This kind of thing was happening all over the Western States. It was the beginning of the "hippy-cowboy wars," made possible by a country torn in two over the war in a foriegn land. Much like our country today.

The weather was below zero and snowing, but things in little Steamboat Springs were heating up. A lot of the old cowboys, and all of the young people, were furious that some big Texas company was pushing an agenda to turn their home into a tourist nightmare. And they all became more and more furious as more and more young people continued to fill up the jail. These weren't your laid-back, nacho-cheese stoners. These were hardened, back-country skiers and mountaineers who were living off the grid, surviving on very strong principals and focus.

One of those young men was my sister's boyfriend, Roly, who tried to burn down the LTV ski corp trailer and ended up in Route County Jail. Nancy told me the story after I found her place in Fairview. She and Roly had been drinking at the Cameo where everyone was buzzing with anger. Alcohol doesn't mix well with anger so he stepped out on his own to do something about it.

When Dean and I rolled into Steamboat Springs, I was done with it practically before we got there. The town was a drag from the first day to the last.

The best thing I got out of my return to Steamboat Springs (little did I know at the time) was the chance to meet George Bond. He and I were introduced over drinks at the Cameo, the first night Dean and I got back to town. He had also been drinking with Nancy and Roly, at the Cameo, the very night Roly got put behind bars.

* * *

Bond migrated to Steamboat from Aspen (by way of the University of Colorado in Boulder), where he became a member of a radical motorcycle racing club of genius anarchists, called the Fuchs. He was tall, well over six feet, and movie-star handsome. He and his running mates were part of the Aspen elite who rubbed elbows with the likes of Hunter S. Thompson.

George had inherited a small fortune from his family back East with which he purchased a house in Steamboat Springs and later on a sailing boat.

It was on that sailboat, years later, when I happened to run into George Bond in Nassau Harbor and we spent some months sharing anchorages around the Bahamas. He was the mentor who famously instructed me on how to get to the Virgin Islands: "Just go east for five days and turn right."

But that wasn't all the instruction (good or bad) I got from George Bond, during those months we anchored alongside one another. He also shared with me the part he played all those years earlier, the winter the ski corp declared war, when we first drank together in the Cameo, long before sailing was even a thought in my head.

As the evening tide lapped against the stern of his ketch, Bond and I shared thimbles of rum in the lamplight, and he regaled me of everything that went through his head that night he had been drinking in the Cameo Bar with Nancy when they heard Roly had been locked up.

He was living in his cabin out in Strawberry Park, and the more he thought about Roly,and his drunken attempt at payback, the more he thought about the dynamite out in his barn. Eventually he said goodnight to Nancy, drove himself home, made himself a cup of coffee, put on a dark coat, and went out to the barn to have himself a look to see if the dynamite was still stable.

He opened the box and inspected it. "Three sticks of this Du Pont Red Cross 40%. Not crystallized yet so I won't blow myself up looking at it. Better use it all, and every inch of this detcord. No reason to leave any evidence lying around." He folded the excess cord up between the three sticks and duct-taped it all into a neat bundle with a short fuse.

Bond collected his bundle, his Camels, a roll of duct tape, started up his old four-wheel drive Ford pickup, and for once in his life he drove the speed limit as he headed up the mountain to the ski resort.

He parked near the restaurant with the rest of the cars, just across from the parking lot where the Colorado Bureau of Investigation was parked: two state patrol cars along either side of a pickup and camper, the CBI command center.

Perfect, he thought. If these guys will just go in for an early dinner, I'll be all set.

He patiently waited and watched from his side mirror.

After only half an hour, two state patrol and two plainclothes CBI officers emerged from the camper, lit up four cigarettes, and headed for the restaurant.

Bond didn't wait.

He jumped out, casually walked over between one of the patrol cars and the pickup, quickly taped the bundle under the truck's frame, lit a "Hump," then carefully inserted the detcord into the cigarette timer, and made sure all was secure with a couple more strips of tape.

Satisfied, Bond sauntered back to his truck and headed home.

It wasn't until he pulled over at the top of the hill to Strawberry Park, maybe twenty minutes later, when it occurred to him that his little surprise hadn't gone off.

"Oh shit! Do I go back?" He asked himself. "No. I don't want to go anywhere near that truck, not now."

He was five miles away from the bomb, as the crow flies, pondering what he should do next, when it went off.

The explosion was loud even miles away.

As he told the story to me years later over spliffs and rum, he jumped and planted his feet hard on the cabin sole of Restless and swore his truck jumped just like that.

No one was injured in the blast, but I don't think he really cared either way. The United States was in two wars: one in Vietnam and the other with its own young generation.

* * *

Who knows how long it would have taken me to sew myself into the elite society of world-class sailor-smugglers if I hadn't just happened to run into an old friend in the Bahamas, an old friend from years ago when we both happened to be mountain hippie outlaws living up and down the Rocky Mountains?

I had already been crew on two major smuggling

expeditions, but I hadn't been introduced into the closed society of world-class sailors who were smuggling to pay for their lifestyle until 1976 when I owned my own boat and ran into Bond in the Bahamas.

I remember the day I ran into him like it was yesterday. Misty was anchored in her spot by the Paradise Island Lighthouse. Maria and I went to town in the Zodiac and tied up at the fuel quay. As usual, I surveyed all the sailing boats moored there. One of them, Restless, was from Key Largo, and I thought to myself, Huh. Last I heard, that maniac Bond bought himself a boat in Key Largo.

A man and a woman were lounging under an awning on Restless, and before I could get a good look at them I hollered a greeting, "Ahoy there! You're from Key Largo? Any chance you know George Bond?"

Bond's girlfriend, Julie, looked from me to Bond, then back to me with a mischievous smile, and answered, "Yes. Intimately."

Bond taught me many things, like how to anchor under sail, to never go ashore without a long-sleeve shirt and your own dinghy, and how to find the Virgin Islands (okay, some of his lessons were more helpful than others).

The Bahamas in the '70s was the epicenter of American marijuana smuggling (much like it was for booze during Prohibition in the '30s), and fate put me right in the middle of it, right when it started.

It was a magical time, and I fit right in.

CHAPTER 4

RANEN'S FIRST VOYAGE 1971

The relationship between serious climbing partners is intimate and very intense.

During this period of mountaineering history, pitons[5] were the main form of protection, the belay was done without a belay device, and big wall climbers didn't wear harnesses like they do today. Instead they fashioned the climbing rope itself into a rope harness.

Your life depended on your climbing partner's attention. The climbing rope was a direct line of communication. It told your partner on belay when to stop giving slack and wrap the rope around his body to stop your fall. When my climbing partners and I became smugglers years later, our intimate knowledge of each other, and our unspoken forms of communication often made the crucial difference in a whole world of life-threatening situations. In a severe storm, when the sea is too loud and chaotic for words at any volume, or in a tense exchange with armed foreigners over piles of drugs and cash, our survival depended

---

5 A steel spike driven into rock with a hammer that serves as an anchor for the climbing rope.

on our ability to just know what each other was thinking.

In fact, it was my climbing partner Dean who got me to crew for my first sailor-smuggler voyage. I was staying with my sister Carole, her husband Mickey, and their two young sons Adam and Timmy. They were living for the summer in a teepee at 11,000 feet on Lowey Gertz's ranch at the base of Wilson Mountain outside Telluride. This was the land where True Grit was filmed and was part of what Ralph Lauren gobbled up when he purchased his 17,000 acres of cowboy paradise in the '80s.

One afternoon I was playing hide and seek with the kids when Mickey pulled his '67 Chevy Suburban up to the teepee and informed me that Dean had left a message for me at the Roma Bar. Dean had requested that I call him back where he was staying in Florida.

So Mickey and I saddled into his ride and headed down the mountain. It was the first time we had been alone together since Jerome and I took our final pay out of his restaurant provisions the prior year, so I figured I better clear the air.

"Listen, Mickey, about what Jerome and I did last year..."

"Don't." Mickey cut me off with an absent wave of his hand. "You know I've done a lot worse than rob somebody who owed me money. Forget it." And that was that.

We pulled up to the bar. I dialed the number that Dean left me, and he asked, "What are you doing this fall?"

"I guess I'm gonna do some climbing with Smitty in

Canyonlands. Why? You want to come with us?"

"Actually, I've been working with this French guy down in Tortola. He has a diving school, but now he's going to do a smuggling trip out of Columbia. On a sailboat. We need another crew member. You interested?"

"I don't know, Dean..." I had never been on a sailing boat nor had I ever had any sailing fantasy. "Smitty and I kind of have plans."

"There's money in it," Dean insisted.

"Can I think about it?"

"Well yeah, but...we need to know right away."

"Lemme call you back in two hours. Can you give me that?"

"Okay. Two hours."

"Be at this number," and I hung up the phone.

Mickey was on his second vodka tonic at the bar. "What's Dean up to?"

I sat down next to him with a sigh, feeling a little exasperated by the whole thing. "He wants me to go on a smuggling trip. On a sailboat. To Columbia. It's cool of him to ask me, but I don't know, I'm not really into it. Smitty and I are going down to Canyonlands."

Mickey was shocked to see me so apathetic about it. "Listen, how many times have you been down to Canyonlands already? A dozen? And how many times have you been to Columbia on a sailboat on a smuggling expedition?! You're gonna regret this 'til the day you die if you don't go. You need to go on this trip! If you don't go, I'll go. If I don't go, Carole will go! Someone from this family is going on that boat!"

Mickey was right. Even though I'd never thought twice about sailboats and never associated sailing with anything but stuffy yacht clubs and canvas Top-Siders, Mickey was right. I had to go.

The next day I was standing at the Braniff Airlines ticket counter in Montrose Regional Airport, Colorado, buying a ticket to Fort Lauderdale, Florida. Dean and Paul picked me up at the airport, and we drove to the Pier 66 Marina.

Paul was a short, well-built Frenchman in his early thirties with dark skin and curly black hair. Born in Morocco but raised in France with a degree from the Sorbonne, Paul spoke English with a very thick French accent. He hadn't learned to speak English from conversations; he learned it in school studying books. His English was good, but his accent was almost comical. During the years we worked with Paul, Dean and I never tired of making fun of his delightfully "froggy" English.

But nobody made fun of anybody as much as Dean and Paul made fun of me, because I was clueless. I'm embarrassed to remember, the first thing I did when we walked down the dock was step onto some big yacht and start looking around. They totally freaked, and Dean ushered me off. "You can't just walk onto any boat. It's just like walking into some stranger's house." I knew absolutely nothing about yacht etiquette, or, for that matter, anything else about yachts.

When we boarded Paul's forty-four-foot boat, Djinn, it

looked small to me. I had no understanding that most of the boat was below the deck. It was a two-masted, steel-hull Calypso Ketch (they said) with teak decks and cockpit and a steering wheel protected by a partial wheelhouse. Hand-built in the '50s by Dutch master shipbuilders, and made for sailing the North Sea, Paul insisted Djinn was very seaworthy.

He opened the varnished louvered doors, disappeared down the ladder, and I followed with no idea of what to expect.

The warm orderly world revealed below decks was astonishing. Here was a beautifully appointed little home with all the creature comforts: a complete kitchen, two bedrooms, a bathroom with a shower, even a little coal stove decorated with ceramic tiles that featured windmills and old-fashioned sailing boats.

Over a coffee onboard, Paul laid out the plan. We were sailing to Colombia for a ton of weed. My old friend Noel had gone there looking to buy emeralds and told tales of weed that put "Acapulco Gold" to shame. I had never seen or heard of any Columbian weed for sale in the states, and Paul was sure that no one stateside was using Columbia as a source. No police awareness, at least in South America.

Paul had just bought Djinn in Fort Lauderdale, and there was a lot of refitting to do. Since I knew a lot more about engines than I did about boats, I volunteered to do all the updating and maintenance on the ancient gasoline engine, a four-cylinder, twenty-five horsepower Gray Marine. The Gray Marine was the standard pleasure boat engine for forty years until the 1960s.

Paul was anxious to get out of Lauderdale. So, I spent ten hours a day squished inside the tiny engine space, covered in grease, replacing, rebuilding, and lubricating everything in sight. What I knew about mechanics came from being friends with hot-rod obsessed teenagers in high school. The rest I learned from the people from whom I bought parts in Lauderdale.

I was the only one of us who did any cooking, and neither Paul nor Dean considered what we might eat or how we would prepare our food at sea, so I also volunteered to provision the galley. I spent a little time each day making a shopping list for groceries, but it was difficult considering Paul was a bit vague about how long this voyage might take, and I sure as hell had no idea.

Dean and I both loved living on a boat in a marina right on the Fort Lauderdale harbor entrance, always fascinated by the ships and yachts entering and leaving this giant international port.

Pier 66 was a fancy marina with two great restaurants. A couple of climbers like us, used to living on peanut butter and honey sandwiches, were delighted to eat a fancy breakfast or an occasional dinner with the rich yachties.

But mostly, after long hot showers in the locker room, we had drinks and dinners at the local yachtie watering holes. The Southport Oyster Bar was our favorite. Yacht crews, yacht owners, and sail bums all showed up after work for beers and fresh seafood. I had done some smuggling by land, enough to know about keeping a low profile, but this was my introduction to the world of boats, a world I never knew existed. Lauderdale was actually a rough seaport under its slick tourist exterior, and we certainly weren't the only smugglers in town. I didn't make any friends besides the sources I developed for marine parts, but I observed and soaked it all in.

We spent all of the daylight hours refitting Djinn. Whenever someone was needed for a parts run, I volunteered. After two weeks of running around, I had just about sourced every existing place for new and used marine parts for an older European sailboat. Getting the yacht-parts-scene wired for the Djinn refit came in handy throughout my twenty-eight year sailing career. Over those three weeks I picked up a lot of valuable industry knowledge and contacts.

One of those contacts was Sailorman. This incredible secondhand marine supply store, where you could also order new gear at a huge discount, grew organically from a small storefront until it took over the entire strip mall just off a canal near the Southport Oyster Bar. Cliff, an old Brit who had sailed into Lauderdale at the end of his ocean-voyaging days, accepted nearly anything that came through the door, all on consignment. The store had been my main source, especially when I needed to find parts that hadn't been available for twenty years. There were rolls and stacks of marine charts piled on top of sails and navigation equipment, all at bargain basement prices. Even Cliff didn't always remember what he had and in which room.

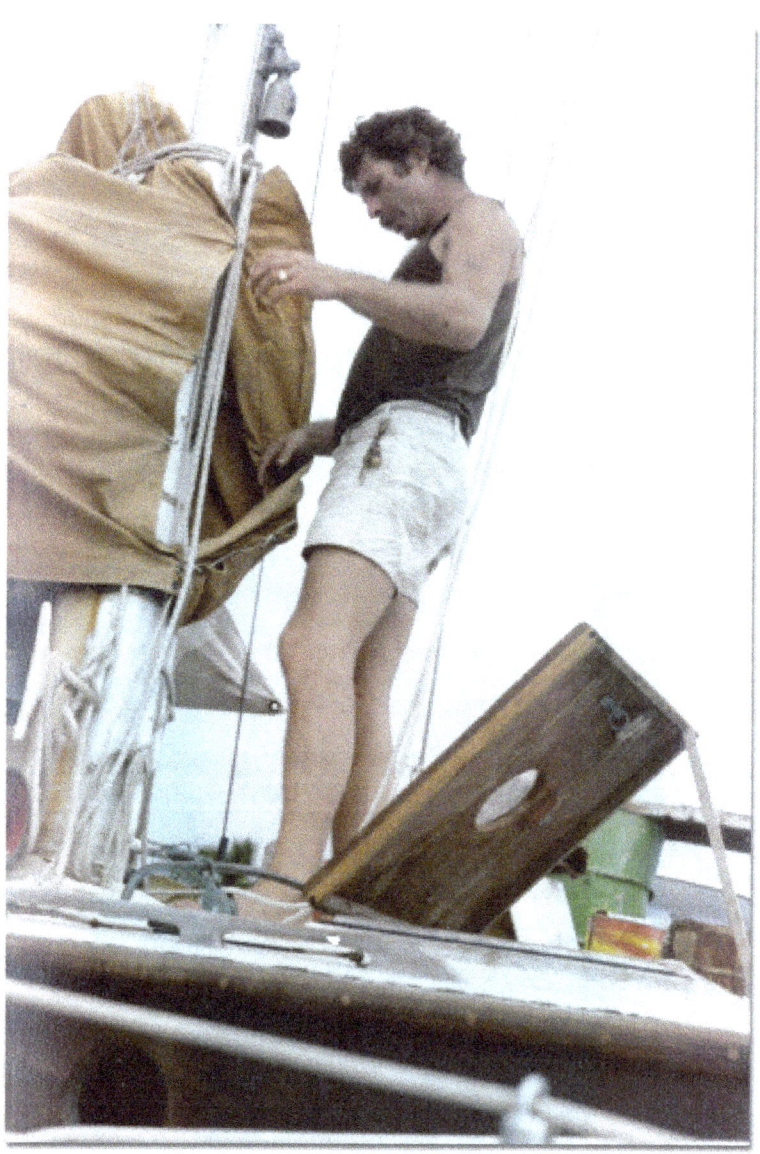

George Bond in Georgetown aboard Restless

A Smuggler's Guide to Fine Dining

Cliff was also a font of information. I constantly asked him about sailing in the Caribbean, and I disguised the questions I desperately needed answered by peppering them in alongside the myriad of other less important questions. Cliff was always glad to talk and talk and talk about voyaging. From my endless questioning, I had determined that we would be at sea for at least a couple of months, there and back. It was a long way. The non-stop voyage back would be a couple weeks, assuming nothing went wrong. I adjusted my food lists to include food for seventy-five days.

At the end of the third week, Paul decided we were ready to fuel up–food, propane, and a few miscellaneous provisions–and we'd be ready to leave.

On our last day in harbor, our first stop was the marina sport-fishing store. It amazed me what forty bucks got us. Not only heavy fishing line, leader wire, hooks, and feathered trolling-lures, but the guy at the store taught me how to put together the trolling rigs I hoped would provide us with fresh fish on the expedition.

After filling up on fuel for the boat, the three of us made our next stop at a big supermarket to fill up on fuel for us.

Paul said he would grab the cart, and I was a little shocked that he grabbed only one. Paul was a truly incredible guy, but sometimes I just couldn't imagine what was going through his head. "Listen man, we are going to need a lot more than what can fit in one cart."

Paul answered, "I'm not going to eat. I'm going to diet."

"Fuck that!" I could barely contain myself. Paul clearly had no idea he was jeopardizing the whole expedition before we even set sail.

So I reasoned with him. "Dean and I eat a lot. We don't need to lose weight. I know exactly how much we eat from our climbing trips. We're going to need seventy-five breakfasts, lunches, and dinners. Right here in this American supermarket is the best and cheapest place to buy food, and we have plenty of space to stow it all. Listen, I don't smoke, but in addition to the food, I figure we need to buy a bunch of rolling tobacco and papers for you two and lighters as well."

Paul answered in his best broken English, "I am quit smoking as well."

I was done trying to reason with him and turned to go get two more carts as Dean spoke up. "Well, I am not going to quit smoking and in case you can't quit, let's buy enough for you."

Because Paul was being difficult, I bought a lot of peanut butter and oatmeal, flour, cornmeal, and baking powder and soda to make bread to eat it on. I filled one cart to the brim with evaporated milk and canned tuna. Another cart we filled with pasta and the fixings for sauces.

Dean and I knew what it was like to run out of food in a snow cave, during a blizzard, with nothing to do but smoke weed, melt snow for drinks, and wait on the weather. We were going to have a ton of weed with us at sea and lots of time to have the munchies. That thought reminded me to buy thirty chocolate bars and lots of cookies.

Even though Paul lacked the foresight to know how much better it was to be over-prepared, rather than under-prepared and weak from hunger, in the end he accepted everything Dean and I shoveled into the shopping carts. Even the chocolate and cookies. I didn't realize it at the time, but our ability to work together, even when we disagreed (especially when we disagreed), would end up being the difference between life and death in our years smuggling together.

Paul and Dean were both into spearfishing, so after groceries we hit a dive shop and bought masks, snorkels, fins, and various slings and spears. Paul was not cheap about diving gear.

Djinn was finally fueled up, provisioned, and ready to go. Paul said we had just one thing left to do: dinner and drinks.

He took us out to a steakhouse for our last meal. We all had drinks, a big dinner, then more drinks at various bars around town.

At three a.m. Paul was flying in our rental Mustang on deserted streets through all the red lights back to Pier 66.

Dean was yelling, "Paul! You can't just ignore the traffic lights. We'll all end up in jail for drunk driving."

Paul answered in his thick French accent, "I am not a monkey. You cannot flash a light and make me do some thing. This is not some Pavlov experiment!" Classic Paul, the Frenchman.

A few days, and a few hundred miles later, I got my first

introduction to Nassau. The small capital city of the Bahamas, a nation of some seven-hundred islands, cays, and islets, bordered by the Atlantic to the east and the Caribbean Sea to the west, stretching more than five-hundred miles down to the Turks and Caicos Islands. This would be my home base for quite a few years.

In the early '70s, Nassau Harbor was magical. The Straw Market Docks, just past the western harbor entrance, were crowded with sailing fishing smacks: sloop-rigged, wooden boats, thirty to forty-five feet long, built by Leroy, a famous boat builder from Andros Island. I don't know anything else about Leroy, even his last name, but all the sailors talked of him.

These fishermen hailed from all over the Bahamas and were consummate sailors, traveling thousands of miles every year with only a compass. Descendents of landlocked African slaves, now evolved into creatures of the sea who carried the tide tables in their heads. They fished treacherous, reef-infested waters, navigating by charts in their head–not parchment charts they possessed, but mental charts passed down from fathers to sons. These guys could smell a hurricane days before the leading high cirrus clouds streamed in.

The scene down at the Straw Market was wonderful chaos. The women sat by tables full of brightly decorated straw hats and baskets, weaving straw, gossiping, laughing, and calling down to the fishermen in their singsong island patois. The men on the boats drank rum and repaired traps and nets, maybe waiting out a storm, maybe just returned from unloading their fish or conchs down by the Paradise Island Bridge.

The three of us sailed Djinn across the Great Bahama Banks, anchoring often to dive the virgin coral reefs for food and wonder. I had never seen a coral reef or even knew such a fabulous world of color and life existed on this planet. That first moment I dropped out of the Zodiac into that brilliant, liquid world is in the top five of a lifetime of memories. Untouched reefs like those barely exist anymore. I was so blown away that, for the first few times, I was out of air before I made it to the bottom, fifteen feet down!

We didn't stop at any Bahamian villages. Just kept slowly moving toward the Windward Passage and an appointment in Columbia to pick up a ton of prime marijuana. That was really all I knew. I didn't know what the actual exchange would look like, what the plan was to keep it safe, none of it. Now I find it odd that I never even asked about the details of the whole smuggling-by-sailing boat process.

I think it was all I could do to internalize traveling across an ocean. It was just all too much: the very male smell of bodies and cooked fish in the cabin below deck, sharply juxtaposed with the pure bright sunlight and clean wind when I came on deck. The clatter of blocks and gear during a tack followed by the sharp crack of sails catching the wind. Picking up flying fish that had hit the genoa and been knocked to the deck, flopping their way back to the ocean or into my frying pan for breakfast.

All this unfamiliar sensory input...

Overwhelming.

Fortunately, I was young enough that my total ignorance of nearly all things nautical didn't intimidate me. If young men don't have arrogance to overcome their ignorance, they would never have the courage to accomplish anything. I definitely had my share of both.

After a couple of weeks we popped out of the islands into the Caribbean Sea. Although I knew better, I was maintaining the incorrect notion that the Caribbean was a gentle sun-drenched sea. I put that idea to rest within an hour of passing Haiti. It was January in the Caribbean, and the trade winds were blowing a steady twenty knots and gusting higher.

Dean and I didn't even have foul weather gear. Having just come from the Rocky Mountains we didn't think it was at all cold. Cold? Really? Compared to ice climbing frozen waterfalls in Provo Canyon, Utah? When we had to work on deck (and it was always really wet), we just went naked. The Frenchman didn't blink an eye at our nonchalance while working on deck under the constant deluge of cold seawater. He was quite a hard-case mariner himself, although he did have rain gear. Our captain and boss was a Scorpio who loved creature comforts.

Paul was a walking contradiction: a Moroccan, raised and educated in Paris, a man of two cultures. We were teaching him spoken English, and he read aloud to us in English from French authors. He translated Henri de Monfreid's classic nonfiction narrative, Adventures of a Red Sea Smuggler. Another was Sailing to the Reefs by Bernard Moitessier whose concept of storm management saved my ass on more than a few voyages.

A Smuggler's Guide to Fine Dining

Books have always been an inspiration in my life, and these two were high on the list. More importantly, everything in de Monfreid and Moitessier's stories applied directly to our daily lives during the voyage on Djinn.

Henri de Monfreid was born in France in the late 1880's. At the age of twenty de Monfreid went to the Persian Gulf and built a native sailing dhow and then spent the next twenty or so years living the sailing vagabond life, financed by gunrunning and smuggling hashish and whatever else would turn a profit in and out of the port of Djibouti. De Monfreid was a contemporary and friend of Ernest Hemingway when they were both part of the famous art scene in Paris.

Paul taught us the rudiments of navigation and how to sail the boat. Unfortunately, we learned all the names of the gear in French. I am astonished at the depth of our ignorance. However, Paul was that captain, the one who had both knowledge and experience. All we had to do was follow orders. Both Dean and I had the sense to listen and the native intelligence to put it all together.

During the voyage I was plagued with sea sickness, which, thank the gods, slowly went away. At the end of the voyage I felt fine even in the heavy seas. Mostly I became seasick when reading down below or if I had to cook for more than ten minutes. Watching the horizon or steering the boat in the fresh air helped to steady my inner ear sensors. Also, eating meals and getting good rest helped as well.

Motion sickness is torture, but fortunately, it is only

chronic for some people. For the rest of us, it usually goes away when our bodies realize we aren't going to quit. However, throughout my twenty-eight years of sailing, motion sickness reared its ugly head the first couple of days of a new voyage, especially if there was a lot of partying and drinking before leaving. For that reason, on the day of departure I almost always sailed down the coast a few miles to a quiet anchorage to sleep off the goodbye party.

Five days of sailing with strong trade winds at our backs found us approaching the coast of Columbia. Paul took us into the Barranquilla, a dirty commercial port midway between the resort town of Santa Marta and the ancient city of Cartagena, the departure port of the Spanish gold fleets.

Paul found a crude third-world marina which was really just made up of some floating docks with no fresh water or electricity. The only other boat was a Colombian police boat. It was a fiberglass Bertram 25 sport fishing boat with an M60 machine gun mounted on the forward deck. I had seen Bertrams in the Lauderdale marinas. They were the first practical and seaworthy production sportfishing boat, and I could immediately see why governments would purchase these boats with a reinforced deck to support a big gun. I looked over at Paul as he parked our vessel just a stone's throw away from the armed police boat. That guy was fly...didn't blink.

Paul said, "I need to make some call to arrange our loading. Take ze night. I will watch that boat."

That was all Dean and I needed to hear. We grabbed

our passports, some money, then headed to town. We found a taxi just outside the gates to the port. I could count to twenty in Spanish and had a few other words. Dean spoke no Spanish at all, but mimicking drinking a shot of whiskey got us delivered to a bar called Casa Verde. At ten in the morning, aside from the bartender, we were the only males there, and at first we didn't even notice this particular oddity.

"Let's see if we can get some food," I said to Dean. "Food food," we said, while pantomiming eating. "And cerveza," I used one of my few words.

Then came a major revelation. Two striking teenage girls walked in from a back room. They were both dark complected with long shiny curly hair. The bartender brought out two ham and cheese sandwiches on local loaves and two bottles of beer. He set the food down on the bar and asked in passable English if we wanted the girls as well.

Dean nodded his head. "Well, wha'd you know! This is a whorehouse."

I answered, "But those girls are great looking. They don't look like whores."

They came over and sat down at the bar. One on either side. Just like typical girls, they chose. Carlita chose me and Anna chose Dean. Anna and Carlita had just come to the big city from some far away village. They actually spoke a little English, I suppose from watching American movies with Spanish subtitles. We ordered them food as well, and by the end of the meal we were all laughing about nothing. Anna reached into her bag, pulled out a neatly rolled joint, lit it, took a long pull and said, "Venga" as she blew a cloud of fragrant smoke for me to inhale. We all shared the joint and the girls led us out into the streets where there was some kind of festival going on. We danced in the street to a band that featured an accordian. The music was a kind of salsa they called vallenato.

We were all young, naive, and maybe a little foolish. Carlita and Anna were just a year or so younger than we were and took the opportunity to have fun with a couple of young, good looking, rich guys. At some point, night came and they took us to their rooms. Carlita had a young woman's thin body with small breasts and all that long curly hair. She was not very professional yet, and I sure as hell wasn't very experienced either. We shared a long night of innocent sex, kind of an extension of our street dancing. Lots of laughing and kissing.

I awoke to Dean shaking me and bright sunlight flooding through the dirty window. "Man we've gotta get back to the boat. Paul's going to be furious."

"Shit. Let's go. What time is it anyway? It's so late…Fuck it. Let's go face the music." I left Carlita a hundred dollar bill.

We stepped over the lifelines at eleven. Paul snapped, "What ze fuck? We were supposed to leave here six hours ago. Now it is too late to make the pick up! What happen?"

"We went to a whorehouse, the Casa Verde, and overslept. Sorry Paul. Just call 'em and say we'll be there tomorrow," I said, like it was no big thing.

"You don't get eet. Now is too late to call. They are already

A Smuggler's Guide to Fine Dining

bringing the weed to zee coast. There is no way to contact them. Thees is not ze first-world. They have no telephone. I have to call and leave a message."

It wasn't until years later, when I actually visited that part of Colombia where the weed came from, that I learned what our missing that appointment meant. The weed had to come from the finca (ranch) where it was grown and packaged. They loaded it into trucks up in the mountains then drove down to the sea off the La Guajira peninsula. This was an area of Colombia that was so ungovernable that the government put up a border to isolate the entire peninsula. So our contact had to fight their way to the sea with armed guards only to find that we didn't show. They then had to return to their safe territory in the mountains. We ended up waiting two days before we could arrange a rendezvous that worked for them.

Suffice to say, Dean and I stayed onboard until we departed. The Colombian police boat left the harbor one of the days we were there, much to my relief, but then it motored back in before evening and tied up even closer to us this time. That boat worried me. But I had an idea about how to protect us.

I went to the market and bought a kilo brick of panela, unrefined cane sugar. The night before we were due to leave, I dissolved the entire kilo in a jar of diesel fuel. After the police boat crew left for the day, I walked down the dock, opened the fuel tank filler cap, then poured the jar of diesel panela into the tank. If they followed us out, they wouldn't get far before the brown sugar caramelized in the injection pump.

We left at first light the next day for the pickup. Sailing up to Riohacha took all day. We arrived just as the sun was setting, and we needed the darkness to get a bearing on the lights of Riohacha and some other lighthouse to find the meeting position a half mile offshore.

I am amazed, in retrospect, that we didn't even have a walkie talkie to facilitate the illicit exchange. There were no other boats in sight. The Colombian weed connection had not happened yet. We were among the first Americans coming here for weed. But that didn't mean we were safe. Piracy was common on this lawless coast. There were all kinds of illegal activities going on. Marijuana wasn't the only contraband. Colombia was in a constant state of civil war. The government had never been stable in the entire nation, and there was no government at all on the Guajira peninsula. Paul was our mentor, and in his informational lectures he told us that gunrunners used these waters as well as all the smugglers in the illegal trade of luxury goods and pharmaceuticals. Where there is illegal trade, there is cash changing hands. Where there is cash, there are pirates.

Paul didn't have a gun. The only weapons onboard the Djinn were a couple of machetes I bought in Florida. It's ironic that the machete is really just a cheap cutlass, the classic defense against pirates. In close quarters fighting, edged weapons are quite effective and less likely to accidentally get a friend killed, so the cutlass is still king when it comes to defense from pirates, even if your "cutlass" is just a five-dollar machete from the Sailorman's bargain bin.

A Smuggler's Guide to Fine Dining

But, as luck would have it, we didn't get to use the machetes. The only boat that approached was carrying Louis, our Colombian rancher contact, and a ton of what would become known as "Santa Marta Gold." The delivery craft was an enormous canoe with the biggest outboard engine Johnson produced back then. They came alongside and we all scrambled to get fenders placed and their lines made fast to keep them tightly rafted alongside.

I had never seen a ton of weed. A ton of weed, tightly hand-packed in burlap bags, takes an impressively large amount of space. I quickly jumped below and cleared out anything we might need to access on the return voyage before everything was buried under all the weed. We never used the head at sea on Djinn, so I planned to fill the head with weed. I got everyone's washup bags out of the way, but sadly I forgot my toothbrush... not to be seen again for a couple weeks.

The bags of weed filled the boat. The only spaces we didn't fill were the galley and the access to the engine. We just laid our sleeping bags on top of the weed. Nothing was concealed. If we were stopped, we were caught. In 1971 the U.S. Government wasn't allocating a lot of funds for boat interdiction. We were headed for the Florida west coast, Fort Myers. We had favorable winds and the bags of weed made a comfortable mattress.

The three of us got along well, and Dean and I were becoming better sailors. We sailed through the Straits of Yucatán, then headed for Florida. Around the time we passed the Yucatán, we ran out of all the interesting cans of local cuisine that were within Paul's budget. Good thing I bought all that oatmeal and tins of evaporated milk. We were down to eating hot cereal with corn bread. There were days that I caught a tuna or a wahoo and we feasted on fresh fish. Being guys with big egos, they never thanked me but continuously complained about the food. I, of course, never failed to point out my role in keeping them fed. It gave us a subject to safely argue over. And Paul…no American is going to win an argument with a French citizen over cuisine.

After a couple of weeks we approached the coast of Florida and zeroed in on Ft. Myers. When we were one hundred miles off, Paul had us doing Zodiac drills. We practiced inflating both the fifteen-foot boats and mounting the forty-hp outboards. Each boat had two-foot pumps, so we kind of ran in place on the pumps to inflate the Zodiacs as quickly as possible.

Once we had the inflatable drills perfected, Paul closed on the coast of Florida, looking for the lighted buoys marking the Charlotte Harbor entrance north of Sanibel Island. As soon as we could see the navigational lights, we headed back out a few miles to a distance where we couldn't be seen from the coast and got the Zodiacs inflated, rigged, and trailing behind the boat. We then headed back in until we were close enough to once again see the lights. We stopped. I pulled a Zodiac alongside while Dean and Paul passed the burlap bags of weed down. Paul jumped down to the first inflatable as Dean threw the last bag. The last of the weed was on deck and so far we hadn't seen even a fishing boat. There was a lot of tension being ignored as I passed bags down to Dean in the second Zodiac. He had the engine running before the last burlap bag hit the deck, and the moment it landed they were gone.

I headed back out to sea to wait. They were unloading in a swamp on Pine Island. The plan was for them to unload then, on the way back out to Djinn, to stop at a channel marker and spray paint the post with black paint as a signal. The people waiting to pick up the weed were checking twice a day for that signal. The round trip by Zodiac was ten miles plus the time it took them to unload.

Our plan was for me to motor slowly out into the Gulf of Mexico in the meantime. Even hanging around as long as we did to load the Zodiacs could look suspicious on a Coast Guard radar screen. I don't really know how long it took, but it seemed like forever before I heard the Zodiacs pull alongside. It took an hour to get the engines and boats winched onboard and stowed. Finally it was done, we raised sails and assumed a course to round Key West, staying outside the United States twelve mile limit[6].

I was on watch in the early afternoon of the next day. Steering and watching the very white clouds fly by overhead in a bright blue sky. The only sound was the hissing of the Djinn moving through the water. I was totally at peace when my entire field of vision was captured by a menacing, red and blue arc against a massive white wall. This is one of those potentially

---
6 Legally 12 nautical miles off the coast is the limit of U. S. territorial waters.

life-altering adrenaline-fueled moments that I can call up as if it occured five minutes ago.

I called down to Paul and Dean, "Get up here NOW. We have a visitor." I knew we were close to the twelve mile limit somewhere off to our port, and we were hard on the wind, and the 150-foot Coast Guard cutter was forcing us toward the line. Djinn was flying a Panama flag, but I doubted that our foreign registration would be a factor in their decision about stopping and searching us. However, they were blocking our path to move away from American waters. Paul was visibly nervous, "Leesen, I think we become too close to ze twelve mile limit."

I answered, "If these guys really think we are up to something they will stop us. I think they're just curious and will only stop us if they can force us into American waters. I'm going to tack right at them. We have the right of way and I think they won't allow a collision."

"Okay, Lezz do eet."

"Ready about hard a lee!" I shouted and spun the wheel to the right. Dean and Paul pulled and winched in the sheet lines. Djinn started gaining way directly toward the long port side of the big cutter. Our move totally got their attention. Horns started blowing on their ship as they turned sharply to starboard. The cutter completed its turn until it could maintain a close parallel course. Three people on their bridge had binoculars trained on us. After half an hour of causing Paul a lot of anguish, they turned away and soon were out of sight. Probably they called in and found we weren't on any list, or maybe they had somewhere else to go.

    Personally, I wasn't really worried. After the original shock of seeing that warship so close, I realized that they didn't know anything. If they had anything on us they would have stopped us immediately. America's Monroe Doctrine of 1823 has been used successfully countless times to condone search and seizures throughout the Caribbean and Gulf of Mexico. If they had stopped us, they would have found a small amount of weed. Not really enough to hang any kind of smuggling charges on. Paul, a foreign national, might have had to pay some stiff fines.

    As it was, I was thrilled to head back to Nassau to babysit the boat while Paul went to the States to see about getting us paid. I am sure he had partners, and I respected that he didn't discuss any of that part of this project with Dean and me. I learned a lot from Paul's sailing/smuggling mentoring, both from what he explained in his lessons and from what he didn't talk about.

    I had done quite a bit of smuggling before. Nevertheless, this voyage on Djinn opened my eyes to an entire lifestyle of travel and adventure on the sea that paid for itself with a decent profit to boot. I never expected the Djinn voyage to become something more than any of my other smuggling adventures, but the moment we set foot on dry land, at the end of our expedition, I started hatching a plan to return to the smuggling lifestyle at sea. The genie was out of the bottle. I learned I had a surprising affinity for a mariner's life.

CHAPTER 5

TURKS AND CAICOS ISLANDS 1977

The adrenaline wore off an hour or so after sailing away from Haiti, leaving Jerome and I feeling exhausted and more than a bit guilty about leaving the doctor even though we knew it wasn't our fault that the police were expecting us. I was pretty sure that Jerome's French contact had used the telephone to tell the doctor someone was coming by boat to pick him up. They should have known better. We were reckless, but we weren't stupid. They knew we were there, and I was not about to volunteer for a rematch. Sadly, it was time to leave the doctor to his fate.

Early winter brought strong winds from the west and the north, all opposed to everywhere we wanted to go. I was hoping to persuade Jerome to stay with me until at least summer when my girlfriend and partner, Maria, was due back from California. We had to go somewhere to think about what to do with ourselves. One moment I had been reading a novel in a Virgin Island anchorage with not a care in the world, then

Jerome showed up and now we were sailing with no idea of what (or even where) was next.

I studied the chart, looking for a safe course to anywhere with an anchorage. There was no simple or safe course to anywhere. Misty was sailing in a stiff breeze and there were coral reefs everywhere, some closer than others. The Turks and Caicos Islands were something like one hundred nautical miles away, and I figured if we could get there without grounding on a coral reef it would be a perfect spot for us to hang out and re-group.

Since the mid-nineteenth century this little archipelago had been a British colony, but England let go of its empire. What to do with these islands? In 1976 the Brits, who had been supporting the Turks and Caicos, built an airport on Providenciales, the biggest and most appropriate island for tourism, as a kind of "parting gift." They also set them up a government and cut the little island nation loose. Fortunately for the Turks Islanders, their country was in the perfect geographical position to support the drug trade. Smugglers paid huge amounts of money to quietly refuel boats and planes. We were headed there just to hang out, but first I had to get us there.

The trade winds were blowing hard, and we were hauling ass parallel to a few miles of coral reef. For a change, I was certain of our position. We were on course according to the chart, but it was nerve wracking. The coral off to port was flying by so close and so shallow that even in the big waves I could see the colorful reef fish. Out of nowhere, we were sailing in the middle of a big school of mackerel, then there were dolphins speeding along

CARIBBEAN BOUILLABAISSE

This is an elegant dish made with ingredients from a few hours diving.

Ingredients
2 large conchs
2 fresh shot medium snappers or grouper
3 Florida lobsters
1 onion
4 cloves garlic
   rosemary, oregano, pepper
1 small ghost pepper
1 tin butter or 1 cup olive oil
2 cups dry white wine

Remove conch from shell and peel the skin (keep feelers). Beat peeled conch with hammer until lacey then cut into pieces.

Skin and fillet fish. Keep the throats. Set aside the heads and tails. Wring tails off the lobsters. Save the heads with the fish heads. Place ends of onions and garlic with fish heads. Dice the rest. Put fish heads and tails, lobster heads, and onion/garlic bits in big pot with 2 liters of water with some oregano and rosemary. Pressure cook for 45 minutes, then strain. Throw stock solids overboard.

Sauté the fish fillets and throats with lobster tails (shell on), and conch with one cup of wine, garlic, onions, and ghost pepper in olive oil and or butter until just cooked then add all to the stock. Season and simmer and drink wine until it tastes done.

with us, weaving back and forth, gorging on fish. Then came the sharks. It was the big time ocean scarf scene. Hammerheads, tiger sharks, and dolphins, all aggressively eating everything in sight. A reminder: life in the ocean can be scary...and violent!

Slowly, very slowly, the dolphins squeezed the sharks out. As the sun set we continued sailing north by a little east. According to my dead reckoning[7], we had a clear course toward Providenciales at least until morning, when we would start having to sail around the reefs that surround the Caicos Islands.

Jerome woke me at midnight. Misty was still speeding into the night, and it appeared that Jerome had been paying attention and noting any course changes in the ship's log. Looking at the chart, I figured we were where my position on the chart said we were and felt safe on the present course.

An hour later the dolphins were back. This time they weren't hunting. There were eight of them swimming fast in a line alongside Misty. As the dolphins passed the cockpit where I was standing, each dolphin made eye contact, then turned to starboard and swam on. After half an hour of the dolphin choreography, I became uneasy and woke Jerome. These dolphins had been with us for a couple of days, all the way from Haiti, and maybe before. Jerome and I both thought they were warning us, but still it was hard to accept.

Forty years later it all seems obvious, but that night I

---

[7] In navigation, "dead reckoning" is the term for plotting your position by advancing from a known point on the chart. Each subsequent position is calculated by speed, time, and course.

wasn't so sure whether they were being playful and naughty or if they were warning us. Six months before, I was offshore in my Zodiac when a pod of dolphins showed up. I was by myself and foolishly put on mask, snorkel, fins, and dived overboard to swim with them. They playfully tricked me into following them down deeper than I had ever dived. It was so exciting that I was captivated and not paying attention until I looked up and the surface seemed like a small circle above. Rising slower than my bubbles[8] wasn't going to be okay. When I got to twenty feet, my air was gone and I raced for the surface but passed out at some point. Suddenly, I found myself awake, bumping into the dinghy. The dolphins were swimming around, laughing at me. Maybe they pushed me the rest of the way up and saved my life, maybe they just swam around and laughed at me as my momentum carried me the rest of the way to the surface. Either way, after that experience I never totally trusted them.

I did believe they were telling us to turn, and really, when sailing in dangerous waters, it's always better to err on the side of caution, so we took down the sails. When dawn arrived, I climbed up the mast with a pair of binoculars. Sitting up on the spreaders, I could see the reefs extending from Ambergris Cay dead ahead. There are a lot of unknown currents running from the Caribbean through the islands into the Atlantic, and without GPS there was no way to figure that in. We were way

---

[8] Slowly ascending from a dive prevents nitrogen that is saturated in the tissues from forming bubbles that cause painful and even deadly decompression illness. The "bubbles rule" is an oversimplification of the proper decompression technique.

north of where we should have been. The Spanish treasure fleets had found out the hard way about those currents, but those dolphins were not going to let us hit those reefs.

Since we were there, we found a little reef anchorage on the south side of Little Ambergris Cay. These little low islands were miles from any other islands and uninhabited then, and probably still are, considering the recent record of category five hurricanes. The reefs around the Ambergris Cays were absolutely alive. We were spending our days snorkeling and spearfishing in clouds of colorful fish. We feasted on bouillabaisse cooked with conch, lobster, and snapper. Every once in a while when the weather was settled, Freddy Forbes, a spear fisherman from South Caicos, would tie up his "speed boat" to smoke a spliff and regale us with his wisdom. Freddy was probably forty-five, a proud father of two young children and a master diver who regularly speared twenty-kilo grouper at one-hundred feet, free diving (no scuba).

Of course, he supplemented his income by providing Colombian smugglers with fuel, water, and food when the opportunity arose. Probably they helped him acquire his boat. It was a kind of V-hull ski boat with a one-hundred-plus horsepower outboard engine. Not very sophisticated, but it was a strongly built twenty-two-foot open boat that was fast and had a lot of room for fish or fuel and water containers.

After smoking half a giant spliff of quality weed, Freddy would say in his stentorian voice, "I...me, one Freddy Forbes, got my little boat, got my family, spear some fish to eat, grow some peppers, I Sat-is-FY... I satisfy."

    Years later in 2001, my partner Elizabeth and I anchored by Ambergris Cay on the way back to the States from Europe. There was a fisherman there who stopped to greet us. I asked if he knew Freddy Forbes. He said, "Freddy? He die a few years back. Got a cough and die. No doctor, no clinic in Caicos, you know."

    The flip side of paradise, I guess.

    Jerome was slowly opening up about what he was up to in California, and it sounded pretty sketchy. He was involved with a very slippery guy known as College Jay. Jay had been showing up in all the new ski resorts springing up around Colorado. When the ski corp wanted to bust every stoner ski bum to clean up Steamboat in 1970, Jay somehow didn't get touched, and the defense lawyers were convinced he was the main rat. Then, a few years later in Telluride, Jay just happened to find my friend Kent's body. Somehow it was a suicide, even though when Jay found the body, Kent had just put on a pot of chili. However, the San Miguel County Sheriff couldn't care less about some dead hippy, so suicide was what it was. Telluride in 1971 was still the wild west–no smoking gun, no arrest.

    So I asked Jerome, "Are you really doing something with College Jay? Because I truly think he is downright evil. In fact, I'm sure he killed this guy, Kent, in Telluride. Kent was a regular good guy who didn't need to die. I don't know why Jay did it, just like I don't know why he ratted all of us out to the ski corp, but sure as shit Jay did. He's a fucking sociopath.

"Listen Ranen, Charlie has a degree in chemistry from Berkeley. He has some new way to refine cocaine. Jay is in on it. We're sharing a house and all my stuff is there in my van. I've got money invested in this."

"Look Jerome, leave it all there and stay here on Misty. We can bring some weed up to New England from Jamaica. Just walk away from it all. We all know now that cocaine is bad shit. Stay, and we'll dive all the way to Jamaica. We'll make enough to buy you all new stuff. Just walk away with your health and your sanity. I don't like Jay, and I don't trust anything he's got his fingers in."

I guess he wasn't listening because when we sailed over to Providenciales, Jerome immediately went out to the little airport and hitched a ride to Miami on some guy's Cessna 180. I was still a little annoyed that Jerome was putting all his trust in his California cocaine crew, and not heeding my warnings, so when he took off to the airport I didn't even offer him a goodbye. I hung around for a few weeks just eating fish and smoking weed. I guess that paradise has an expiration date, because I left by myself for Nassau directly.

Six months later, I heard College Jay had found Jerome dead of an overdose. I'm sure Jay killed him. Forty years later, I still regret not pushing Jerome harder to stay with me on Misty, and I still regret that I couldn't push past my own ego enough to say goodbye to him while I still had the chance.

CHAPTER 6

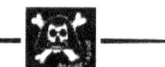

MARIA, NASSAU HARBOUR 1977

It was a brilliant day in Nassau Harbour. My serene sailing vessel Misty had the perfect private mooring fifty meters from Paradise Island, right under the old lighthouse. You could clearly see ten meters through turquoise water to the sandy bottom. Misty was moored there with one-inch, stud-link chain to an ancient ship anchor that I had found after a hurricane had scoured the harbour bottom a few years back.

    On sunny days I would jump in my inflatable speed boat with my laundry, three big buckets, and my water jerry-cans, then motor over to the little landing to avail myself of the amenities offered by the abandoned lighthouse. Those amenities were the long forgotten rainwater catchment tanks. I was the only sailor I knew of that had noticed that British-built lighthouses, from the 1750s on, all had rainwater catchment systems. Once I figured that out, my boats always had a source of safe drinking water. Even on the African desert coasts, I had full fresh water tanks, thanks to the famous Scottish lighthouse architect, Robert Stevenson, and his sons.

After filling Misty's water tanks and washing and hanging my laundry, I would go to West Paradise Island beach and collect seashells until the clothes were dry.

There were all kinds of wonderful reasons for living in my corner of the Paradise Island side of Nassau Harbour (and I always enjoyed the spelling of "Harbour," a quaint reminder that until very recently the Bahamas were part of the British Empire). One of those wonderful reasons was that Misty was anchored just off the seaplane "runway" for the Chalks Airline Miami-Nassau flight. I got so friendly with those hot-rod Caribbean Sea pilots that my Zodiac became a semi-permanent fixture on the Chalk's ramp.

Once, on a flight to Miami when I was the only passenger, and as we were descending over the city, the pilot pulled the curtain aside and asked, "Hey Ranen, do you mind if I do some real flying?"

"Okay with me," I answered.

"Crank up your seat belt!" he replied, and immediately dropped down to the street between the buildings, about four stories up.

He flew right through downtown Miami, just clearing the masts in Miamarina as he swooped into the harbor. Pretty tense, white knuckles gripping my arm rests, major sigh when the floats hit the water of Biscayne Bay.

This living situation was a perfect fit for a smuggler. A hundred miles from Florida but still outside the United States.

Fresh fish, fresh water, pristine beaches, a bounty of Carribean cuisine, an international community that respected and admired the ideal of sailing boat living, and as much weed as I could smoke: all the ingredients of the greatest lifestyle the world has ever seen.

It's strange to think about how the foundation of that spectacular lifestyle was the ancient, rust-encrusted ship anchor, long buried in the sand in a corner of Nassau Harbour.

* * *

One of those days in paradise found me waiting for my partner, Maria, who was flying in from Miami on the afternoon Chalk's flight. She and I had been together through three smuggling expeditions over the past five years. A couple days beforehand I had called her up in Santa Cruz where she was staying with my friend Beach Rat and stole her away from him.

After Maria agreed to pack up and join me, Beach got back on the phone to ask, "You're not going to keep her all the time? Are you?"

My answer was, "Absolutely not, no way."

Maria lived with Beach when we weren't doing business, and honestly, I was glad for it, she was too much as a year-round companion–too demanding and fiery for any one guy to live with all the time.

But the thing was, Maria was the perfect sailing partner.

That woman was brave and bold as hell, and even though

she was a force of nature in her own right, she always kept her cool when the situation demanded it. Whether we were lost at sea, being bashed about by storms, or under attack by pirates who had no qualms about taking our lives, whatever we faced Maria had it handled. Whenever we were confronted by some government official she would assume her demure southern belle persona, flutter her eyes, and ask, "Well, officah, can ah make you a cup of sweet tea?" Pretty hokey, but somehow it worked every time.

Maria was a diminutive brunette with huge brown eyes in a tiny oval face. In her high school days every teenage guy in North Atlanta would have given a month's allowance to get close to her. By the time she was twenty-five, Maria had become finely tuned from long-distance sailing and mountaineering, and she was irresistible. She mostly wore her hair in two braids that hung to her shoulders, which made her look young and innocent. However, Maria was not an innocent little southern belle. She was a fearless long-distance sailor who loved a shot of whiskey and a lot of sex. Maria had a restless soul that drove her from one place to the next, one man to the next, and one experience to the next.

Dean, Jerome, Smitty, and myself began as a group of climbers. Then Dean and I went sailing for weed. Climbing and sailing are not just sports but more like lifestyles, so naturally we brought our climbing partners–and then our girlfriends–into the sailing/smuggling life.

Most of the girls who became part of our group were

skiers and mountain hikers. Maria was a city girl from Atlanta. I met her at a party when I was back visiting the city and found myself high on acid and twenty-feet up a tree. I remember seeing her step under the foliage below, a magical, sparkling, beautiful being, gazing up at me with a giggle, "Why hello up there! Aren't you Noel's friend? Are you Ranen?"

Maria might have been from the city, but she took to outdoor adventure like she was born to it.

Through the years our group maintained a less intense version of our original climbing lifestyle. We would often get together in one of our various Colorado hideouts: Jerome, Summer, Dean, Wendy, Smitty, Maria, and I, taking turns leading "hikes." Whenever Jerome took lead I always ended up with cottonmouth, because he loved to take us places where we should have had ropes, and make us face some dicey moves. Someone would bitch, "What the fuck, Jerome?" He would laugh, "Come on. Really? Are you going to let go?"

We were smugglers. We played together like we worked together. We took risks, but we tried to keep them down to calculated risks. It was understood why I invited Maria to come on a job. When making a lifestyle out of breaking the law, image and profile became the key to staying out of trouble. When the Marine Patrol or Coast Guard saw Maria and me, they saw an innocent couple on a romantic cruise. On the other hand, when they saw Jerome and me, they wondered, What are these two guys up to?

I practiced the "pocket method" of accounting: When my pockets were empty, it was time to go to work. However, like all gamblers, I always banked enough to buy into the next game. As much as I loved hanging out in Nassau where life was easy, my secret stash of cash was nearly empty.

On the afternoon that Maria was due on the Chalk's flight, I must admit that cash flow was not foremost in my mind. Yes, she was enlisting as my partner in a covert operation, but the dominant theme in my head on that day was having her back in my bunk again.

Maria's connection flight from Bimini wasn't due for an hour, so I zipped over to the Nassau Commercial Fisherman Quai under the Paradise Island Bridge to visit Charles, who had a livewell[9] barge full of grouper that supplied the local restaurants in Nassau.

"Hey white rasta!" Charles greeted me, "Come on aboard for a conch salad! You goin' down ta Georgetown for de Regatta[10]? I could use a ride down deah."

"Listen Charles, I am heading down to Great Exuma, but I'm going to leave for Jamaica from there, so I couldn't bring you back here."

"Dat's cool mon, I can sleep on one a de racing boats and catch a ride on de mail boat baaack here. I bring a bag a dry

---

9 Tank used to keep fish alive on a fishing boat.

10 Native sailing boat racing event.

(Top) Misty from the Stern
(Bottom) Maria in Virginia

conch for your sail down islands. But, maybe I catch a ride with another boat. Jus' checkin'."

Just then the Grumman Goose and the roar of its two Pratt & Whitney radial engines announced the arrival of the afternoon Chalk's flight. "I gotta go man, Maria's on that plane!" I scarfed down my conch salad, jumped off the quai into my dinghy, and sped down the harbor to meet her at the Chalk's ramp.

The seaplane and I both approached the ramp together, and the pilot threw me a salute through the spray around the cockpit windshield. While I pulled the dinghy up out of the water, I could see a suntanned, elfin, hippy sailor in sun-bleached braids, faded bell bottom jeans, and a tank top, walking my way across the tarmac.

My heart thumped with anticipation as soon as I saw her. The shirt revealed smallish breasts on a lithe, ropy-muscled body. God! I was so hooked on that sexy woman, even after all these years.

As she neared our eyes locked, she flashed me a smile that sunk us into our own world, and we both broke out into a run. All I wanted was to have her out of those clothes.

We collided on the seaplane ramp in an explosive embrace. Our welcome back kiss ended with applause and whistles from the crew and passengers who I noticed (for the first time) were waiting for us to clear the ramp for the return flight to Miami. Maria and I did what anybody would naturally do in our situation, we turned to face our admirers and took a bow, then I threw her bag in the dinghy and we headed back to Misty.

We spent the next few days making love. Maria enjoyed her orgasms, and she didn't impose any limits on where to find them. When I rebuilt Misty I cut out the cockpit footwell, so the cockpit was just a deck with little walls--just a bed with closed-cell foam cushions--a wonderful venue for unrestricted love under the stars. Maria didn't wear underwear, just in case an opportunity arose for sex anytime, anywhere, no matter who might be spying on us from a nearby boat. Washing day at the lighthouse was a popular outing for us.

Our lifestyle could only last as long as my wallet could, however, so as the days went on we started talking about going to work. We'd been talking about what kind of cargo would pay the bills and decided to soon head for Jamaica, an island with an entire culture based around marijuana. Misty wasn't known in Jamaica. Load up in Jamaica with good Rasta weed and sail away. That was the plan.

We were sitting in the cockpit, having a coffee and toast, talking about going to Jamaica and thinking about places to unload weed along the Carolina coast. Maria was nervous about this detail. "I don't know, Ranen. That coast was hot two years ago…do you think it's simmered down by now?"

"Well, I guess I really don't know, but I don't want to think about going to work today, anyways."

Maria batted her eyes, and walked over to where I was lounging in the cockpit. "Well, we should probably give it one more day. To cool down."

She bent over like she was about to sit in my lap, but instead she leaned out over the cockpit and nearly shouted, "What the fuck?! Isn't that Serious? Is that Jeffrey?" I turned around to look out into the horizon and sure enough, there was his boat.

My third smuggling trip to Columbia (twice for weed, and one time to break Noel out of prison–a tale for the next book) was a scam dreamed up by Jerome, Maria, and me. An "Old Friends" voyage from Fort Lauderdale to the Carolinas with one off-the-books stop in Columbia. Jerome brought in an old prep-school friend from Boston to be captain, Jeffrey Richardson, an experienced and knowledgeable sailor. Also, an arrogant snob and a bully. The boat we purchased for the trip, Serious, a Cal 40, was included in his payment. We survived the voyage, he got his boat, and my plan for my money was to get my own boat. I wanted a boat that had a clean history and something smaller than Serious. Jeffrey had a yacht broker friend who found Misty in Riviera Beach, Florida, and Jeffrey did the survey when I bought her.

The morning we saw his boat entering Nassau Harbour, he didn't notice Misty in the lighthouse corner and motored right by on his way to the big marina past the Paradise Island Bridge.

I knew he had connections in Jamaica. I also knew his giant ego insisted that he live a rich trust-funder lifestyle, and he enjoyed an expensive apartment in Boston and all the expenses that go with it. By now, I figured, he had to be out of money. If he was headed south, he was headed to take a cargo from Jamaica where he knew people. Jeffrey wasn't brave enough to organize business in Columbia.

I dumped the remains of my toast overboard, to be carried out to sea by the tide, and Maria scarfed down her leftovers while I carried the cups and dishes down below.

She called out, "If we're going to talk to Jeffrey, let's get it over with. Looks like he's got a girl onboard. Good. He won't be hitting on me."

"I think it'll be fun to see him again. For some reason," I replied. In some weird way, Jeffrey was strangely entertaining. His arrogance was fascinating.

We took the Zodiac over to the marina and found Serious tied alongside the fuel dock. Jeffrey and a tall thin young woman were fitting a cover on the mainsail.

"Ahoy, Captain Richardson," I bellowed. "Permission to come aboard?"

Jeffrey looked up from his work, studied Maria and me in a moment of confusion, and then I watched as annoyed recognition washed over his face. He didn't seem to relish the idea of running into "old friends," and he didn't seem to care enough to hide it. Pretty typical East Coast social pecking order bullshit, classic Jeffrey.

"Tie up and come aboard," he begrudgingly responded. "We're getting fuel then moving to the anchorage. Kenny and Maria, this is Kerena Copely."

We climbed over the lifelines and shook hands with Kerena, an attractive, dark-haired woman in her late twenties. Kerena greeted us with a slightly nasal New England prep-school accent.

After some curt introductions, I decided to get out of his hair.

"Okay," I said, "We'll leave you guys to it. By the way, you should set anchors fore and aft. The tidal current rips through the anchorage both in and out. Let's meet up around sunset for a beer at the Pirate Marina Bar, just over there. It's a local bar. No tourist could find it if they wanted to. Serves the best cracked conch in Nassau."

That evening Maria and I were already into our second rum and sour-orange when Jeffrey and Kerena showed up at the bar. We talked sailing and anchorages through three more rounds of rum and a huge platter of cracked conch, beaten to lace then fried to crispy perfection. When we were tipsy and picking at the crumbs, I broached the subject we had been avoiding all night. "So! Are you and Kerena on your honeymoon cruise or...are you sailing to Jamaica for a load of weed?"

Jeffrey threw his napkin on the table. "You never were one for beating around the bush, Ranen. And yes, Serious is headed for Jamaica. I don't even want to know how you know these things."

"Look man, I wouldn't have brought it up, but Maria and I are headed that way, and I'm thinking that if we share a contact we can both get a better deal."

Jeffrey thoughtfully sipped his rum. At least, it seemed like he was sipping it thoughtfully, but after a while of nobody saying anything about the alligator at the table, I realized he was just waiting for someone to change the subject.

Finally, I broke the silence, "Listen, you guys, forget I mentioned it. Frankly, I'm not even sure if you would be an asset or a liability. Since we saw you enter the harbor I've been on the fence about whether or not to just avoid you. You motored right by us without noticing. Low awareness is a bad trait for a smuggler." Maria and I both stood up at the same time, "I've got the bill. Nice to meet you, Kerena."

We managed to walk out and jump in the Zodiac without a single look back. I shook my head, "Let's head south. Just talking to Jeffrey annoys the shit out of me. He feels the same, but at least I try to suppress it. Fucking arrogant preppy!"

The next morning we picked up whatever fresh fruit and greens were available in Nassau, topped off the water and fuel tanks, and filled the spare containers of fuel and water lashed on deck and stowed in various corners below deck. By nine a.m. we were feeling our way across the forty miles of shallow, turquoise sandy bottom of the Great Bahama Bank toward the chain of the Exuma Islands.

We were on course, but we still weren't in a hurry to get to Jamaica and start the four (or more) months of intense and stressful action that is a smuggling trip. It started with finding someone who could load us with a hundred or so pounds of good quality weed and who wouldn't cheat us or kill us for the money, then sail the gauntlet of Coast Guard and police to get somewhere to unload without being seen and caught, and finally the work of getting it all sold, hopefully at a profit. The whole process looks like a "fool's errand" from this end, but we were not looking at the big picture. I just knew we were going to need money soon.

After my misadventures in Columbia, I made a point of never doing the same project twice and to change venues each time to stay off the law enforcement radar. "One and done." My policy was to do a voyage, hang around the minimum time it takes to get paid, then sail away. Far away. Even far, far away–best to a different country. Barring an unlucky, chance encounter with trouble, I was gone before law enforcement was aware that something had gone down.

It is more profitable to repeat a trip. The second trip would have fewer surprises, mistakes could be better avoided, and you usually wouldn't have to establish new contacts. However, when you hang around, people start to notice you. They remember you. That's when the police start to notice, and they ask questions. Some smugglers get filthy rich by milking the same trip for all it's worth, but some get caught trying, so I never hung around for any of that.

Maria and I had never been to Jamaica. I was thinking that by the time we loaded and left Jamaica, we would arrive in New England in the early summer and be able to disappear among the hundreds of sailing boats cruising in and out of the little ports and anchorages from Maine to Long Island. Misty was small, thirty-feet long, and wouldn't look like a boat that had just sailed a couple thousand miles against the wind from the foreign, golden sands of far-away Jamaica.

CHAPTER 7

SOUTH TO JAMAICA

Success at smuggling hangs on profile. When you and your vessel appear on the radar of some random government official, your freedom hinges on controlling what that person perceives in that first instant of her or his awareness. In that instant the observer's mind sees everything presented. Most people think they are capable of shaping an objective perception as they continue to interact and get to know you, but the truth is everybody abides by their first impression.

We needed to actually be living the image we were presenting. Any incongruity in Misty's, Maria's or my appearance, especially the subtleties of our body language, could and would raise red flags. Once an impression is made it will not be changed. If we can be seen as a clean-cut cruising couple at the outset, that will be our jacket.

We cultivated our image. I had wild, curly hair down to my shoulders with a short-hair undercut beneath my long locks. When I needed an image change, all that unruly hair could be tucked up into a clean baseball cap, and all of a sudden I had a neat, short haircut. Amazing how someone who knew you as a long-haired hippy wouldn't recognize the short-haired version. I had a whole bag of tricks to control the narrative.

The boat was the major piece of our image. Misty was a perfect little sailing yacht. All of her thirty feet was flawlessly spray painted white. Her sail covers, sail bags, and awnings were matching blue canvas. I kept the chrome rigging shiny and the sails snowy white. If you knew your boats, you could see that all the equipment was the highest quality and well maintained. Below decks the paint and varnish were immaculate and the brass polished. In short, Misty was a "proper yacht."

In the end it all worked because we were, in fact, just what we were trying to project…except for the small detail where we were smuggling weed to pay for it all. Sailing down the Exuma Islands, stopping in deserted anchorages to dive and spearfish for dinner and beachcombing for seashells, was what we enjoyed doing. I cannot deny that the "buzz" derived from long distance non-stop sailing was a powerful attraction as well. The whole lifestyle had it all: idyllic cruising under sail, exploring the world's hidden ocean environments, and the adrenaline-fueled sailing/smuggling lifestyle to pay for it. The whole aesthetic worked in our favor. People tend to give you the benefit of the doubt when you are living out their fantasies.

We anchored off the then-deserted Halls Pond Cay Club during a period of settled weather. The anchorage wasn't really protected, but there was a rickety dock to tie up the Zodiac when we went ashore. The club was a large, one-story building

(Top) Misty Anchored at Halls Pond Cay
(Bottom) Maria Getting Ready to Do Laundry at the Club.

on a high hill (for the Bahamas) with a huge concrete veranda overlooking the turquoise waters of the Bahama Banks. There was a workshop with a solid bench and large vice as well as a generator that was powered by the same Lister engine that Misty had. It was handy to have a shop to make repairs and rebuild things like pumps and winches from Misty. A typical day would involve a diving trip to the reef on the ocean side of the island for lobster and/or a grouper. Then we would stop by the boat to pick up a bag of tools and a winch that needed a rebuild as well as some odds and ends of barbeque tools. The rest of the day we spent grilling fish and lobster over the club's fire pit and getting some maintenance done in the shop using that big bench.

    We also shared a lot of intense love-making on that veranda, hours of it. Maria had no inhibitions. She was a dedicated teacher of that art, and I was a willing and passionate student.

    Eventually we had to pull up the anchor and move on to a protected anchorage a few islands down when a "norther" came through. For weather reports Misty had a multi-band radio receiver, and I tuned into NOAA Notice to Mariners radio broadcasts twice a day. It provided a great service for ships at sea, including updated weather forecasts for the North Atlantic and other pertinent notices. Nassau radio also gave good island by island weather reports throughout the day. Additionally, Misty had an accurate barometer. I was getting better and better at sifting through weather reports and mapping the isobar lines to get a picture of what was going on.

A Smuggler's Guide to Fine Dining

We were headed south and west, and south and west we went. I was meditating on the calendar when I began to realize that there was a timeline for this project. On the list of my natural gifts you won't find "organizational skills," so I tried to make up for that by being exceptionally diligent, because there were very serious penalties attached to mistiming this voyage. Each year we had to sail further to outflank the Coast Guard, which meant we had to leave earlier to avoid the likelihood of encountering a hurricane. Sailing further north also meant that we were going to end up in the land of winter storms, where staying too long could mean sailing through snow storms when we finally sailed south again.

Having said all of that about timing, I always was the last to leave. It's difficult to sail away from paradise once you've got it all organized. Misty, however beautiful and seaworthy, was designed and custom built in the late 1940s, and she did not have the design features that enable modern boats to go upwind, making fast passages for Misty unlikely. We needed to keep moving. Stopping to anchor and go diving before the end of the day was okay. But alas, hanging around for days on end in a hidden diving paradise was not on the menu.

At this point, I need to talk about the situation in the Southern Bahamas during the '70s. The direct route from Columbia to the Atlantic Ocean through the Windward Passage was established by the sixteenth century Spanish fleet who needed a safe route to transport their stolen gold to Spain. Of course the pirates soon established their base of operation in Jamaica, an easy shot to intercept the gold fleets at sea or plunder the gold shipments that wrecked on the reefs in the southern Bahamas. During the '70s the route was the same from Columbia to the Atlantic. What had changed was the cargo...from gold to weed. And now cocaine. The hazards had also changed from pirates to the U.S. Coast Guard (actually the pirates were sailing under "letters of marque" from Queen Victoria, official vessels of war for the British empire, which makes the U.S. Coast Guard pirates by the same definition). Now there are lighthouses to guide the way, but the passages are still littered with dangerous coral reefs. Good fishing, but navigation was always uncertain in those pre-satellite navigation times. Every navigator had antacid tablets on the nav table for nervous night watches.

In the beginning, the North American and European smugglers were picking up their dope on the coast of La Guajira, a lawless Columbian peninsula adjacent to Venezuela. I can clearly remember climbing to the mast spreaders as we approached that coast at sundown in 1971. As far as the eye could see, there were boats of every description, awaiting darkness, rolling in the swell at the twelve mile line. It was insanity, waiting at the rail of a lurching sailing boat, trying to figure out whether the approaching fishing skiff was carrying your weed or someone else's load, or if they were bandits with shotguns looking to rob you of the cash they knew you were holding.

By the mid '70s the Colombians were running their own loads of contraband to the deserted islands and rocks in the southern Bahamas to avoid the confusion of that offshore loading scene. They would arrive in some lonely anchorage in a rusty trawler or coastal freighter to hook up with fast motor vessels from Miami or wherever. When these guys arrived in your anchorage, it was time to go below and wait for them to leave, keeping guns handy. It just wasn't smart to volunteer to be a witness. Generally they were just fishermen trying to make a living, but the Columbian culture has a long history of violence.

We sailed past the rest of the Exuma chain heading for the Windward Passage. Maria was staring at the chart, looking for a safe course to the Castle Rock Light. She looked up. "Let's find an anchorage near the tip of Acklins Island. No one lives on that island. I'll bet there's great seashells there. Probably good diving as well. We should be there tomorrow morning. We can sail by to have a look. If it's not good, we can still make Castle Island well before dark."

"Okay," I replied. "I've always wondered about that island."

The weather was settled with a steady barometer and a light easterly breeze, and in the morning we sailed into the bight at the southern end of Acklins Island. We had the mainsail up but no foresail in anticipation of anchoring. Maria was at the tiller, edging us closer to the shore. The 12-gauge pump riot gun was in its place inches from Maria's right hand.

We had practiced a defensive dance in case of an attack from an approaching small boat. It was based on the Columbian loading madness. Meeting a stranger at the rail in a lonely spot in a foreign country is always dicey. Carrying a gun seems to be the safest bet, but the thing is, guns make everyone nervous. Even if your visitor has no intention of violence, the sight of a gun starts the ball rolling. I had a Smith & Wesson Airweight. The Airweight is a very small 5-shot .38 caliber pistol with no external hammer to get hung up when you pull it out of your pants. Carried in the front pocket of a pair of cutoff jean shorts, it was invisible. Still, pulling something out of your shorts could ignite a situation. The dance we practiced started with me dropping flat to the deck. At that moment Maria would pick up the shotgun, aim just over the rails, and pull the trigger.

    Misty was close enough to see details of the island and to see a man pushing a ratty wooden skiff off the shore. My brain shifted gears. "Maria, grab the gun and take off the safety. Looks like some guy is stranded here. He's definitely not a Bahamian and there is no water on this island. He looks pretty rough, but we can leave him some water and food. The Columbians probably left him here to guard a load of something and nobody showed up for the pickup. No way any fast boats were crossing the Gulfstream from Florida in that last northeaster that came through. Let's see what he has to say."

    "I don't know, Ranen, maybe we should just leave."

    "I can't see leaving someone here to die of thirst."

    He was sculling with a single ore from the stern of the skiff. I let him come closer, but we were still sailing slowly. He had to sweat to catch us. I shouted in Spanish, "Necesitas ayuda or algunas... Agua? Comidas?"

    He came closer, and I didn't like the look on his face.

Things started happening fast. As his boat bumped alongside, he dropped the oar and grabbed a machete. I dropped flat to the deck at the very moment he raised his weapon and started to come over the rail. Even tucked behind the steel cabin I could see him, and hear the deafening roar of the riot gun. Our "visitor" flew backward from Misty, over his skiff, and into the sea. I shouted, "Hard to starboard, I'm getting that genoa up. We're getting out of here!"

Fueled by adrenaline hysterics, Maria asked in a husky, shaky voice, "Did I hit him? Is he alive?"

I was wired and shaky from my own adrenaline rush, but I instantly knew what I had to say. "He's alive but he isn't happy," I blurted. "It happened fast. I think you hit the machete. Maybe he caught a few pellets in his hand. What fucking idiots these Columbian dopers are."

I'm sure she had her eyes closed when she pulled the trigger, so she didn't see the gaping hole in his chest. She definitely killed him, but there was no way I was going to load his death on her shoulders after she had just saved my life. The turn to starboard turned her back to the island, and we were picking up speed now that the big genoa was going up. "Let's head for the Castle Island lighthouse."

During our many years together, and our many adventures that followed, I never told Maria that she had killed another human. You might disagree, you might feel I owed it to her to tell her the truth, but in that split-second, after she had just saved me from a cruel death, I decided I'd rather be the one who had to ask myself, for the rest of my life, Did I do the right thing?

Looking back, I think the Columbian was sitting on a load of cocaine and probably using the drug to stave off hunger. Cocaine is well known to generate paranoia and violence.

We needed plenty of high-carb comfort-food to compensate for the energy expended from that adrenaline-charged shooting scenario. I dove up crawfish on the reef under the Castle Island Light, and that night we ate bowls of creamy lobster bisque, and every twelve seconds the beam from the big lighthouse momentarily illuminated our dinner party.

We never talked about the shotgun episode. Maria was a remarkable partner. Strong, smart, brave, always had my back, and never revisited her past decisions. Anybody who thinks women are unfit for battle has never faced a woman in combat or fought alongside one. As I put it in my first book: "Women will pull the trigger. Men will take that crucial moment to think about it."

A Smuggler's Guide to Fine Dining

BAHAMAS LOBSTER BISQUE

This recipe is made with Florida lobster, which are really salt water crawfish. We kept the boat well supplied with spices and canned goods, especially milk and tomatoes to flavor our diet of fish and brown rice.

Ingredients
- 4 medium crawfish
- 1 medium grouper or snapper
- 1 can of evaporated milk
- 1 small can of crushed tomatoes
- 1 onion
- 2 cloves garlic
- 1 bay leaf
- Salt and Pepper
- 1 pinch of Zatarain® shrimp boil
- 1 pinch of saffron
- 1 hand full of flour
- ¼ cup olive oil
- 6 cups water

Wring the crawfish, crush the heads and set aside the tails. Clean and skin the grouper. Chop half the onion and set aside. Boil the crawfish heads, grouper, onion chunks, bay leaf, 1 garlic clove, and shrimp. Boil until only 4 cups of drained stock are left.

Saute chopped onion, garlic with the saffron and cubed tail meat until onions are translucent then remove from pan and set aside. Throw the flour into the pan with the oil and whisk until smooth then slowly add the fish stock and tomatoes. Combine remaining ingredients in the pan and stir in the milk. Add salt and pepper to taste. Simmer until crawfish is tender.

CHAPTER 8

SCORING IN JAMAICA

Jamaica lies over a hundred miles south of Cuba in the southern part of the Windward Passage, one of the busiest shipping lanes for ships coming from the Panama Canal into the Atlantic. The passage to Jamaica seemed to take forever. Ships were all over the place even though there were north and south lanes clearly marked on the chart. After a sleepless night of dodging ships, our approach to Jamaica had that waking dream quality. Compared to the dry, rocky Bahamas, Jamaica seemed like a glistening emerald in the distance. As we drew closer, everything above the sea was a study in green. Green was just not a color we had seen in a long time. Bright, verdant, glorious greens.

It's always exciting to sail into a new port. But this was Jamaica, the home of Reggae music, the home of Bob Marley, the home of Rastafari! We never thought of starting the engine, the moment was way too magical for that noise. We set the Aries to steer us in, and Maria and I furled the mainsail. Misty sailed slowly past Navy Island, once owned by Errol Flynn, the Hollywood pirate from when dinosaurs roamed the Earth.

As our first port of entry in Jamaica, we were required to

fly the yellow quarantine flag and check in with customs and immigration for the time-honored clearing-in formalities. Just ahead was the only solid-looking dock around. This was a small port, and the building by the quai was flying a Jamaican flag, marking it definitely as the port official's office. Maria dropped the genoa, and we drifted up to the quai. I jumped ashore and got the stern line on a post, and Maria flung a big mooring line that nearly knocked me over. That girl could throw a line!

As one might expect, the Jamaican official was barely interested in the clearing-in ceremony. He hardly gave our papers a glance as he stamped a visa in our passports. We walked out of the office into the blinding sunlight and steaming heat of the day.

There were little homemade hibachi-style grills along the edge of the street. The air was filled with wood smoke and the enticing scent of jerked chicken. Neither of us had ever heard of that Jamaican delicacy, but I am sure that I ate at least an entire chicken. I was instantly addicted to the spicy, slightly dry but crispy meat from chickens that had nothing in common with the first-world, fatty chicken sold in the States. Reggae music blared from boom boxes everywhere in the neighborhood.

"Okay, I guess it's time to leave this wharf. Let's drop the hook by Navy Island. We should be out of the way over there."

When the anchor was good and buried, we inflated the Zodiac, winched the outboard up and out of Misty's forward hatch, and secured it onto the transom of the inflatable. Now that we had transport, it was time to start making friends. This was Jamaica for Christ's sake. We just bought some jerk chicken on the street that came with a spliff appetizer. How hard could it be to buy a couple hundred pounds of ganja?

There was a good place to park the Zodiac at the little dock in front of a bar restaurant called the Port Antonio Yacht Club. It wasn't a tourist destination. No big hotels. Just guesthouses. The only foreigners were the odd sailors and world travelers looking for non-tourist spots. I thought, this little club just might be the hangout where we might connect with someone who knows the players in "the game." It's a bit pricey for street people.

I had heard that the Rastafarians who grew all the weed were living in the mountainous interior that was traditionally their own province. I had heard that it was the place they had developed their culture as runaway slaves. I had no real information–just what I had heard. What I did have was a lot of misinformation based on urban legends and Caribbean stoner-sailor bar talk.

We were confined to the coast, and that was looking like a problem. Jamaica was a poor island where marijuana was the main export, and I was surprised that we hadn't been approached by some ambitious dealer looking to move up. I was feeling impatient and thinking we were in the wrong place to score a load. Jamaica is a big island, and the clock was running.

A few mornings later, while Misty swung on her anchor and Maria was still asleep, I was making coffee when I spotted Serious lying alongside the customs wharf.

I thought Jeffrey might be useful yet.

Later that day they were anchored fifty meters off the yacht club bar, so we zipped in on the Zodiac to say hello and have a cold drink.

Jeffrey and Kerena were sitting in a corner of the bar with an awkward preppy-looking guy. Jeffrey pretended he was surprised to see us even though we had the only two sailing boats in Port Antonio, and Kerena introduced us to her friend, Timmy. I pegged him immediately for what he was…an East Coast weed dealer. So this is Jeffrey's backer, I thought.

I ordered a round of rum and coconut water. I could see clearly that Maria was skeptical of Jeffery. She didn't say a thing, but she was watching it all play out. Maria wasn't interested in the business end of things. She was in it for the adventure and mostly let me take care of the money part. Even though she didn't talk much, Maria let her discernment be known. Women have the faculty to emit disapproval without the slightest movement. I really should have listened to what she wasn't saying. I knew better than to cut corners by inserting myself into the business of someone I didn't trust instead of developing my own contacts. Looking back, I can see I wasn't paying attention to the signals.

"So Timmy," I asked, "are you here to pick out your weed? Because I know that Jeffrey isn't connected down here. He's just too much of a tight-assed white boy to know any Jamaicans. I'm looking to get loaded with a hundred or so kilos, and I'm sure whoever you're buying from would appreciate you turning him onto someone who will pay cash for good weed. You could offer my name as a way to get yourself a better price, I don't mind. Otherwise we're going to sail to Negril."

Timmy replied, "I'm meeting up with him tonight. I'll let you know."

"Okay, that's done. Let's have dinner. I'm buyin'."

Throughout dinner, I observed Timmy and Jeffrey. Timmy was almost embarrassingly naive, totally out of his element in Jamaica, and, for that matter, so was Jeffrey. I think Timmy's naiveté was what threw me off guard. He was a marijuana dealer who was married with an infant. He wasn't a slick dealer. I felt that I wouldn't have to worry about him ripping me off. He seemed to be an honest businessman, a solid member of his community.

We spent time with the three of them doing tourist things, like going swimming at the waterfalls near Ocho Rios. Spending time with Jeffrey, Timmy and Karena should have created a rapport with them, but we just didn't like them and I am certain they didn't like us. They were just snobby eastern city people and they looked at us like we came from another planet, and a dirty one at that.

Meanwhile, Timmy made a deal with a Jamaican dealer named Johnny. He was taking some cash and fronting the rest of the load that Jeffrey was transporting. Johnny was happy to load me as well. I told him that I expected better weed because I would pay upfront when they delivered offshore. I was foolish to trust any contact of Timmy's, but in this situation there was no way to insure getting what was promised. The only way to avoid a "bait and switch" was to trust my instincts and hope that Johnny would appreciate the value of not having to risk his own money and appreciate me as an asset who would return again with cash up front for more quality weed.

I had a lot of anxiety about what I might be transporting. My business model of not doing the same project twice meant that I frequently had this anxiety of working with a stranger. However, I was looking for a reliable and honest grower to load me. This was the one leg of my projects that might be safe to repeat. There were a lot of routes from Jamaica. Columbia had become too dangerous. In the end, I left the western hemisphere altogether, but I digress…

At this point, Maria and I were committed to receiving, in six days, 200 pounds of (hopefully) excellent Jamaican buds off the coast between Montego Bay and Negril. While we were waiting for Johnny to put together a couple of loads, we were eating a lot of Jamaican street food, jerk chicken, fish patees, and coconut water. The patees were a puff pastry stuffed with fish, kind of like the Jamaican fisherman's version of a savory croissant. Maria and I were enjoying our visit to Jamaica as much as we could with this uncertain scoring and loading scene looming.

Jeffrey was starting to worry about sailing all the way to New England with just Karena whose sailing experience was limited to this one trip, a single leisurely sailing cruise from the States. The voyage back would be nothing like that. Sailing back by the direct route through the Windward Passage was dangerous, because the U.S. Coast Guard was closely monitoring the traffic through the "Passage," stopping and searching every vessel possible. Jeffrey intended to outflank the CG by detouring through the Anegada Passage west of Tortola. This put an extra couple of thousand miles or more onto the voyage. All of these extra miles were directly against the trade winds–that meant slamming into big, powerful waves, with the boat uncomfortably heeled over, lots of frantic sail changes, and reefing[11] at all hours. He was right to be worried.

Jeffrey asked if I knew any experienced hardcore sailors who would fly down here to make the voyage–fixed wage, ten-thousand dollars, no bonus.

"I know a guy who has more deep sea experience than you and is a better sailor. He and his wife sailed offshore from Maine to Key Largo in an open Block Island Cowhorn sloop, in the month of January. In an open boat, man!

"I'll contact him," I continued, "but first I want to clear up an issue. Lightning Florida John is well known, and well respected, in the world of old school, world-class sailors. So, in your cheap ass, arrogant manner, you told me there will be no bonus (or thanks) for a long, dangerous voyage, but you understand that you have to pay the full agreed wage, even if you don't make a profit?"

Jeffrey just nodded, with a nasty look on his beefy face. I

---

[11] Reefing or reef: to reduce the area or size of a sail exposed to the wind, usually to prevent damage or increase sailing efficiency. The phrases used are: 'put in a reef' or 'take a reef.'

was reluctant to call John, but a long, upwind sailing voyage on a seaworthy sailing boat was something he would want to do. I thought, John's a big boy, let him decide. So, I left a message at the boatyard in Key Largo for him to call me at the Yacht Club bar in Port Antonio.

John got right back to me.

"Listen John, Maria and I are getting ready to sail up to New England. There's a guy here with a really nice fiberglass sloop who is doing the same non-stop upwind voyage. He's with his girlfriend, who is tough enough but has no idea what's coming. He needs another strong sailor. This guy is a bully, but, like all bullies, he's a coward, so he won't lay that shit on you. He won't because you're better and tougher than he is, and he needs you. He's paying ten grand plus expenses. Give it some thought and if it's a go, leave a message here and get a flight out of Miami. There'll be a ticket at the Bahamasair counter."

Three days later, Maria and I tied up to the Serious, and Lightning Florida John's grinning face appeared. Maria and I weren't just envious, we were down right jealous that Jeffrey had Lightning Florida John.

Misty was first on Johnny's loading schedule. We were due to meet a boat offshore, half way between Ocho Rios and Montego Bay, just after midnight. At noon we went to the Port Captain's office with passports and the ship's papers to clear customs. The port captain seemed angry for some reason. He then called in some other official. Now they were really aggressive. Maria was becoming uncharacteristically nervous.

I couldn't see where they could be going with this. Then the second official took over.

"You two are going to pick up drugs! You're not leaving, no way."

"Listen man, if these clearance papers aren't stamped in the next five minutes, I'm going back to the boat and calling the U.S. Navy at Guantanamo. Misty is an American registered vessel. If you don't have a good reason to impound her then you better be prepared for the U.S. Navy to consider this an act of piracy."

I, of course, knew that what I was saying was a load of crap. The Navy couldn't care less about us. I just felt that I could bully these guys. Sure enough, they couldn't handle my threats and unblinking stare. The customs officer broke and without a word stamped the papers and passports, and we walked out. Breathing a sigh of relief, I said to Maria, "That was close. I don't know how we could have contacted Johnny to put the meeting off for another day. Let's get out of here before they change their minds."

CHAPTER 9

LOAD AND LEAVE

Back on Misty we didn't waste a moment. Within the hour the outboard was stowed on the forward cabin sole, the Zodiac folded and lashed on the cabin top, and fuel tank secured on the aft deck. We had bought all the fresh food the afternoon before: a woven basket of fifty eggs packed in straw, six cabbages, green tomatoes, kilos of onions and garlic, now all stowed in straw baskets on the cabin sole just aft and all around the outboard. We wouldn't be needing the dinghy for weeks and weeks. By the time we got to New England we would be down to brown rice, beans, oatmeal, and canned tuna.

In addition to the provisioning, we had cleared the space I figured we would need to stow the two hundred pounds of weed. The Jamaicans didn't press their weed. Johnny said that his boys packed it tightly into burlap bags. Maria had a plan on how to stow the bales. She cleared space along the hull. I had installed a new (varnished and painted) "proper yacht" interior in Misty, with a well appointed galley, nav station, saloon, with a settee that converted to a double bed in port. The whole area forward of the mast was open. Misty was really a cargo vessel pretending to be a yacht.

We motored out of the harbor, with just enough time to make it to the rendezvous. You don't want to be late for a meeting, but being early can be worse. If there is any heat around they will definitely notice a boat loitering. Our plan was to get close then move slowly into the neighborhood.

At midnight Maria's dead reckoning showed us to be at "X marks the spot." I turned on the spreader lights for a moment, briefly illuminating the deck. A few minutes later a thirty-foot, narrow, low-slung fishing boat came alongside. Judging by this boat, the Jamaicans were clearly not seafaring people. It was more like a big canoe with an outboard motor than a seaworthy fishing boat. There were four men in the boat. They were all sitting on the big square bundles that filled the boat to the rails.

Maria went below to receive and stow the weed. I positioned myself to receive the bales. They pulled alongside and I quietly shouted, "Pass me the bales slowly, we need to stow them carefully."

One guy answered, "We need to do this quickly, mon. Big storm commin' now. Look up at the sky, mon!" These guys were clearly not comfortable being this far offshore at night.

The wind was rising as the bales came up the supply chain, across the rail, through me, down into Misty's cabin. The stars were gone and the sky was black. After a nearby bolt of lightning lit the dark scene accompanied by soul shaking thunder, the Jamaicans started slinging the bales faster than I could catch them. "Hey boys, how about one of you coming up here to catch?"

"No mon. We be leavin'. This be some bumbaclot t'ing. Johnny not be payin' us for die out heah."

Now all three were pitching bales and the boat was rolling in the waves. The pile of bales blocked the hatch so Maria couldn't get out on deck to help, and I was leaping around trying to catch bales flying overboard. The useless Jamaicans left as the squall passed. Maria appeared out of the forward hatch just in time to rescue a bale on its way to Haiti. She laughed at me, and in her best Jamaican said, "Boyy, you be in some kine trouble over deah. But doan' worry, I heah now." I was still laughing at that nervous, crazy, and out of control loading scene that she summed up in that comment. We had been lovers and smuggling partners for years, and we had learned to keep our sense of humor in tense situations.

The two of us got busy getting fifteen burlap bags secured on deck. That done, Maria went below to stack and disguise the bales I passed down the companionway.

I had left the mainsail up to keep the boat steady during the loading fiasco, and the genoa was ready to go up. Some serious hand-over-hand pulling, a few turns on the halyard winch, and the big forward sail was flapping in the light breeze. Maria came up on deck long enough to help winch the sheets before going below to continue arranging the bales. I spent another ten minutes adjusting the sails and setting the Aries wind vane self-steering to the course for the west end of Jamaica. It was already light enough to see the mountains of

Jamaica, but we were far enough offshore that the coast wasn't visible. A quick look around for ships and I was ready to grab one of the sandwiches we made on the sail to the pickup.

Down below, Maria had masterfully stacked and positioned the bales along the hull, then placed sails, tarps, and anchor lines over them so that, although you could see some of the burlap, it all looked like benches and storage lockers. And it was all secured with lines to the pad eyes I had welded on during the eight-month refit. We had a rough voyage ahead of us, but there was no way that any of those bales were going to shift. Brilliant work on her part.

I knew that we were sailing along in the light winds of the leeward side of the island, and that on the windward side of the island strong winds and big waves awaited us. My plan was to sail by the Negril lighthouse to get an accurate position before jumping into the fray.

Punching out of the Caribbean against the trade winds is difficult at best. I had sailed a lot of miles on Misty, but nothing like this. We were trying to sail east to the Virgin Islands against strong easterly winds. Jeffrey was worried about doing it in Serious, and Serious was built to go upwind. She had a modified fin keel that made her fast and agile. Misty had a blocky wide keel, not very hydrodynamic for cutting through fast-moving waves head on. However, we did have a lot of food, and we were strong and determined.

A couple nights later I began to see the Negril Light marking the western end of Jamaica and started thinking,

A Smuggler's Guide to Fine Dining

Okay Ranen, time to get to work. As soon as we have this light abeam,[12] the wind's gonna come for us. Let's get the 110% Genny up, take two reefs in this main, and find out how far we can push this boat.

I shouted down to Maria, "Better get up. We're about to turn the corner into the Caribbean, and this vacation will be over."

"I'm up," she answered. "You want some hot chocolate? Is the main reefed? Where are we?"

"Sure. I'll have some hot chocolate and yes, two reefs. When I reset the log at zero, our position was three miles off the Negril Light at 270 degrees."

We were about to embark on a long passage out of sight of land. Without electronic navigation we needed to be very careful to maintain accurate records in the ship's log to maintain a reliable position. Although precise electronic navigation wasn't available, we had lots of traditional navigation tools to aid us. My favorite tool was the Walker Taffrail Log, a mechanical instrument that we tied to Misty's aft rail. It dragged a propeller behind the boat that rotated as we moved through the water and turned a dial on the reading unit that mechanically recorded the mileage we traveled.

Records of times, distance traveled (as taffrail log readings), and compass courses—all Misty's data was religiously recorded in the log book at least every four hours, and whenever

---
12 Abeam: right angle to the side of the boat.

there was a course change. Even a single, small error will become amplified with every following course reading, and that can spell disaster when you're sailing the open sea with carefully calculated provisions and carrying a cargo that will make you think twice about seeking (or accepting) any help in an emergency.

CHAPTER 10

BEATING OUT OF THE CARIBBEAN

Our course to leave the Caribbean while outflanking the U.S. Coast Guard was directly into the wind. Sadly, sailing boats cannot sail directly against the wind. In spite of that, Maria and I still needed to drive Misty as close to the wind as possible. Sailors call this beating, because it involves slamming into the oncoming waves. and the bigger the waves, the harder it is to get close to your course.

The attributes of waves are determined by the laws of physics, and those laws say that the length of fetch (distance traveled) and the strength of the wind dictate the size of the waves. The distance from Tortola, in the Virgin Islands, to our position, off the west coast of Jamaica, was over a thousand miles, and the wind was blowing a force six and seven–plenty of factors for pretty big waves to oppose.

Passing the Negril Lighthouse was pleasant sailing with a light wind abeam. Over the next day we slowly came out of the wind shadow of Jamaica.

Every hour or so we were busy raising smaller sails

and securing gear on deck. Below deck gear was crashing everywhere, showing us what needed to be re-stowed. Although we were expecting strong winds, the reality of those seas was a shock. Maybe we had become lazy, loafing through the Bahamas for the past month.

By evening Misty was hard on the wind. These waves were nothing like long Atlantic swells I had been sailing for the past year or two on Misty. They were generated more by the wind than the fetch and were short and steep. This was a violent headlong beating, against steep wave after steep wave. Still, we had to carry as much sail as we could and still keep the rail above water.

It was tricky sailing. The four-hour watches were exhausting. If we were distracted, the boat would veer off the wind. All the forces at play were to our disadvantage.

There is a small window of efficient sailing upwind. A bit too far off the wind and we were sailing very fast toward South America, Columbia at best. A bit too close into the wind and the boat would heel over and feel as if she were flying, but in reality we were going slower, even stalling and drifting down wind. I'll say it again, "Boats don't want to go into the eye of the wind."

We had to play the waves as well. The architecture of the keel was old school. The forefoot was not cut away like modern boats. Our keel would get knocked sideways if we headed right into those steep walls. In the first days I set the Aries wind vane self-steering to keep us close to the wind. After twenty-four hours, I tacked[13] to port. Twenty hours later we got a bearing on the Negril Light and it became apparent that we weren't getting anywhere. Every wave we hit head on was knocking us sideways.

I cracked it off the wind a bit, hoping that if we gained some speed we would generate lift from the increase of wind rushing past the sails. It works just like the shape of an airplane's wings that produce upward momentum (or lift) once you accelerate fast enough. An airplane generates lift to defy gravity, and a sail generates lift to pull a boat against the wind. "True wind" is the wind speed and direction when you are standing still. "Apparent wind" is the speed and direction of the wind that you actually experience based on the speed and course of the boat. Apparent wind is the wind you feel when you stick your hand out the window of a moving vehicle on a still day. So even when the true wind is pushing you back, you can still harness its energy to create an apparent wind direction that's in your favor. My sailor readers understand I was factoring sail dynamics and wind physics into my thinking, but if you find it confusing don't worry, it won't change the story either way. Just know that we were using everything in our toolbox in this struggle against the wind.

All this slamming into waves was taking its toll. When Misty hit one of these walls of water the mast shuddered and

---

13 Tacking or coming about is a sailing maneuver by which a sailing vessel, whose course is into the wind, turns its bow across the wind so that the direction from which the wind blows changes from one side to the other, allowing the boat to work its way in the desired direction.

the boat lurched. There was a moment when the boat hesitated for an instant before she hit. If whoever was below cooking missed that cue of impending impact, the punishment was to get thrown across the cabin. Cooking was a workout, and so was sleeping. Anyone sleeping behind the restraining net was rudely awakened when Misty rammed a big one. Quality sleep was a distant memory.

In the first days it was a matter of getting accustomed to the motion and the unrelenting pressure of staying focused on keeping Misty moving fast on course. However, we were strong, physically strong. We were on a strict "four hours on, four hours off" watch schedule. We didn't see this as torture. For Maria and I, this was the best part of the lifestyle. Two sailors at the top of their game. We chose to do this.

The depths of the Caribbean water was dark teal, the breaking waves pure white against the bright blue sky, and the very air tinctured with rainbows everywhere a wave created spray.

Maria came on deck for her noon watch, looked up, and yelled in a drill sargent's voice, "What in the fuck are you thinking!? Get down off that boom. You aren't even tied in!"

I jumped down, put my hands up and replied, "Sorry amiga, I was so jazzed by this sunny, windy day. I started thinking I could sail Misty like a windsurfer. Watch." I climbed back up, grabbed the leach of the mainsail with both hands, leaned out and turned the boat upwind. "See!"

Maria remarked, "Look Ranen, it freaks me out to think of

single handing this boat full of weed by myself if you disappear overboard. Look out there. Do you think there's any chance of finding you in that wild sea?"

The last forty-eight hours had gotten us nowhere. My new tactic was to tack way out into the Caribbean toward Columbia instead of short-tacking off the Jamaican coast where we could more easily check our progress. I was hoping that we might get a more favorable wind once we got away from the mountains of Jamaica. I kept us on the port tack toward the west coast of Jamaica, and just before dark when I could see cars on the coast road, we tacked west.

We were both still struggling with the learning curve of sailing upwind, but we were confident that we could come up with a technique that would safely get us out of this ocean. We approached it the way we learned everything else. When you don't know how to do something, just throw more energy at it.

The wind was strong, force six. Averaging twenty-five miles an hour. We were flying; Misty loved strong winds. She was designed and built for North Sea winds. Seven days later we saw the light on la Isla de San Andrés, off the coast of Central America. We had been getting a course that was more south than east. We were trying to go east, somewhat disappointing. Undaunted, we tacked.

It was a lot harder to cook on this tack because the boat was leaning away from the galley, making it harder to hold ourselves in front of the stove. I was in the cockpit when Misty hit a big wave head on. I was drenched by the wave and pitched against a winch in the cockpit. There was a crash of pots down below and I looked down the companionway to see Maria covered in baked beans, cursing and nursing the elbow she had cracked against the chart table.

"Are you okay?" I asked.

"Just bruised, but I'm rigging a safety belt in this fucking galley! Where'd you stow that roll of seat belt webbing?" she answered.

Sailing upwind day after day was physically hard work. Changing sails, cranking winches, even taking a piss, required concentrated effort on a moving, lurching platform, where a moment's inattention could throw you overboard to a certain, slow death. Every chore was accomplished one-handed. "One hand for the ship, one hand for yourself," is an ancient mariner's homily.

Life upwind was stressful, but we had small luxuries that made life better. Maria baked two loaves of bread every four days. Peanut butter and jelly sandwiches were a night watch favorite.

All the physical work of sailing required a lot of calories to maintain. Dishes we would never eat normally were strongly appealing while sailing upwind. One of my signature dishes was eggs poached in a pot of sweet baked beans. Lots of calories and protein. We craved calories and protein. Maria always had a pot of hot chocolate made with lots of evaporated milk on the stove, held securely with the adjustable pot holders.

Misty had a stainless steel, two burner propane stove

with an oven that was gimbaled so, when the boat was inclined, the stove was level. An efficient galley–with foot-pumped fresh and salt water, countertops with rails, and a good stove–was a key ingredient for enduring a difficult voyage. Eating well was a big factor in maintaining a high energy level and a positive attitude.

An important part of watch keeping was checking the fishing line trailing from the lifeline. Fresh fish was a treat. Maria baked the bread. I caught and cooked the fish. Sushi, fish chowder, fried fish, baked fish, and fish jerky (slowly dried in the oven with soy sauce), were on the menu when we landed a fish. Tuna fish salad sandwiches take on a new meaning when made with fresh tuna on fresh baked bread, and especially when your mind and body is pushed to the limit, when every ounce of your being is ravenous for the calories.

Tuna, mahi mahi, wahoo, even a barracuda, yielded no less than five sumptuous meals. I used a big 9/0 stainless hook, covered in strips of yellow and blue spinnaker cloth, with braided stainless rigging wire for a leader, clipped to the thickest monofilament line I could find. Over the past five years I had become pretty damn good at landing a big fish with a handline. Nevertheless, I have to admit that throughout my career at sea, I always hated cutting up a slippery fish with a sharp knife on a pitching deck. You can be as prepared and careful as a person can possibly be, but it requires only a single slip to skewer yourself.

CHAPTER 11

"WE'RE GOING TO HAVE TO TAKE SOME CHANCES"

Maria and I sailed, day after day, through those breaking saltwater waves, in our small boat that was only a foot above the sea. Those were the times before modern, double layer, foul weather suits that keep you dry but allow moisture out of the inner layer. We had the best fishermen suits available: Helly Hanson, rubber-coated jackets and bib overalls that kept the seawater out. The drawback was these suits didn't breathe, so we were soaked in sweat at the end of every watch.

When I bought Misty one of my first projects was to have a spray dodger custom made to cover the main hatch. It had a stainless steel frame strong enough for two people to safely hang on to or lean against. Most cruising boats had dodgers that were generally too large to be sufficiently solid to endure the constant abuse of big waves. Our dodger was covered with heavy blue canvas with isinglass windows so we could duck behind it to look around for ships or see the compass without getting hit by a wave.

That dodger also allowed us to keep the hatch partially

open for some air. After all those days, over two weeks now, things were pretty damp down below. Our Caribbean chart was so soggy that we couldn't use an eraser without making a hole where our position was.

Years ago, Maria introduced into our lives a little ritual that was now an important factor in maintaining our sense of humor while we flung ourselves against a resisting sea. It was a monthly calendar, an alternate ship's log not useful for navigation, filled with notes and pictures of daily events. Maria drew little cartoons of me getting hit by a wave in the face while taking a peek over the dodger. We laughed like fools when she got knocked down to the deck changing a sail, and that became another little cartoon in our calendar. We traded months for who drew the calendar in colored pencils. I still have a few buried in a closet in my house.

We tried like hell to keep up as much sail as possible, never hesitating to quickly change sails when overpowered. I can still clearly remember my fast sail change process. As soon as a sail was down, the boat slowed or even stopped, which meant that we were drifting backward. So, it was essential to think out every move beforehand, get the next sail out of the bag and hanked on ready to go up, get the blocks and lines ready to switch, then once all the steps were in place for the fastest sail change possible, go for it. Maria and I were hardcore sailors. This was true "Kung Fu Sailing."

It must have been brutal, because Maria and I neglected our intensely intimate relationship. Until we left Port Antonio

MISTY'S FISH JERKY

Fish jerky is high protein snack food. On watch, day or night, especially when night boredom strikes or maybe you need a bite to eat to keep you awake. Often I would catch a fish that was too big to eat before it went bad even in a fish stew, heated twice a day. Fish jerky keeps for weeks without refrigeration. Also it tastes wonderful. Crunchy. Salty. Tasty.

Ingredients
Any species fresh fish fillets
Soy sauce
Pepper
Hot sauce (like Tabasco® or Cholula®)

Cut fillets into thin strips. Soak strips in soy sauce with small amount of pepper sauce (depending on how spicy your preference). Place soaked strips on greased cookie sheet and place in the oven on low heat. Occasionally turn strips and brush with soy sauce, pepper sauce mixture. Cook until fish is dried to a consistency of soft leather.

DRY GOODS WET RIDE

we never missed an opportunity to make out or explore under each other's clothes. Yet, we barely shared a touch after passing Negril. After a four-hour watch, we were barely able to get out of our clothes, before falling into our bunk, in a coma-like sleep.

As another week passed we were thinking we should be seeing the island of Hispaniola, hopefully the Dominican Republic on the eastern part of the island. Around midday Maria spotted land. Just before dark we realized that we were looking at the island of Hispaniola, but the western shore of Haiti. This was a serious blow.

"Okay, we need to rethink our strategy," Maria said from behind the binoculars. "We cannot spend another month getting nowhere. We've gone a hundred miles east in two weeks. That's fifty miles a week!" She came right out and said, "We're going to have to take some chances."

I answered, "Okay, but it's gonna get a little tense."

I got out the high frequency receiver and The "Top Secret" Registry of U.S. Government Radio Frequencies. Some anarchist type had published this useful tool that actually listed the U.S. Coast Guard frequencies. I started listening to the USCG transmissions to find out where they were positioned in and around the Windward Passage. This was a very sophisticated radio that could be programmed to scan a list of frequencies, both HF and VHF, and we were listening to them hailing boats and talking to each other. We did not have a VHF transceiver, so we couldn't talk to ships. VHF radios were out there, I just hadn't got around to buying one.

Now that we were tracking our enemy, I felt a lot more confident about heading through the Windward Passage. Just like the patriots before the American Revolution, we were blockade runners on a sailing vessel. Unlike John Hancock's ships, we could intercept government patrol communications.

As we started up through the choke point between Cuba and Haiti, we were closely monitoring a Coast Guard cutter stopping an American fishing trawler off Cuba. Their interdiction took a long time. We listened as they got the trawler's crew list and found that one of the fishermen had an arrest warrant. They went aboard to search the trawler and arrest the fisherman. All this took hours, and now that we were off the wind on our best point of sail, Misty was making her best speed. Our tactic was to hide out on the coast of Haiti if the USCG came our way, but fortunately they were busy elsewhere.

I had to wonder how much it cost the U.S. Government to ferry that fisherman to Guantanamo. The poor guy was probably wanted for failure to pay parking tickets. I really hated the Coast Guard. Enforcing American law far from the U.S. border. Fuck the Monroe Doctrine.

Maria woke me, "I think we have another Coast Guard cutter. Different voice stopping another ship of some kind. It's getting light out so I've headed us closer to Haiti. I don't feel that confident with our position, but the depth sounder puts us past the shelf in deep water, and Haiti is just coming into view."

I was nervous, but Maria was calm as usual. I guess she trusted my luck, or my intuition, or both. She was a natural risk taker. She liked the danger buzz. I couldn't figure out where this other cutter's location from the radio chatter, but they were out there somewhere. We were sneaking into the Bahamas, hoping our radar signature was lost in the busy shoreline, and (more realistically) hoping they weren't nearby.

Another very nervous forty-eight hours went by before we closed on Inagua Island in the Bahamas. We then headed south and west toward Provo in the Turks Islands because of the absence of a government there. Also, heading in a southerly direction gave us a better profile for the Coast Guard choppers that were bound to be lurking. They weren't interested in sailing boats headed down islands, away from the States.

We had spent way more time then planned trying to get across the Caribbean and figured we needed to re-provision once we got to Provo. As for food, there wouldn't be much to choose from. Provo was almost a desert island, but I wanted fuel and water more than anything. Plus, there was another thousand miles or more to New England, and we needed a short break. I actually had a dream that featured a pint glass filled with crackling ice and fizzy Coca Cola.

For the second time that year, Misty crossed the barrier reef into the Providenciales anchorage. Things had seriously changed since Jerome had disembarked from my life here some months back. There were a lot more boats at the dock and at anchor, all large, serious, long-distance vessels, both motor and sail. The smugglers had definitely caught on that the government was open for business here (ripe for bribery).

A Smuggler's Guide to Fine Dining

Immediately after getting the anchor down we put up the full awning that covered the entire boat, and made the name and registration numbers impossible to read from above. We inflated the Zodiac and got the outboard going for a trip to the bar.

I tied up the dinghy and followed Maria to the bar, hungry for a meal we didn't cook and thirsty for drinks with lots of ice. My friends from when I was here with Jerome, Tay and Linda, were there still running the bar and restaurant. They were loving all the new action, and Linda filled us in on what was up in Provo. Although these new smugglers were a bit rougher than the usual yachties that showed up here, they had unlimited expenses and were stupendous tippers. Tay told me that there were planes landing for fuel, but they didn't want the fuel and maintenance crews to see their illegal cargo. So the air crew unloaded at the end of the runway, then taxied in to fuel up, turned right around to pick up their load and the armed guard, then took off...all in fifteen minutes!

Later, while we were eating and drinking on the covered veranda, a U.S. Coast Guard helicopter flew in and hovered over the anchorage. They were so low that I thought the rotor might hit a mast. We could see the crew through the open door taking photos of the boats. Good thing I thought to put up the awning in anticipation of this. I kept my baseball cap low and Maria had a wide brimmed straw hat that covered her face. We were careful to avoid eye contact with the chopper crew. They weren't even being discreet about photographing faces. They clearly wanted everyone to know why they were here.

After the Coast Guard left we moved Misty to the quay to take on fuel and water. Maria organized the available fresh food with Linda: eggs, cabbage, limes, lemons, green tomatoes, and green coconuts.

As soon as the sun set we struck the awning, deflated the dinghy, put it and the outboard away, then went for a last dinner.

At the bar we ran into Tom, a smuggler, off one of the vessels in the harbor. He recognized me from a boatyard in Florida years back. We talked a while, and after swapping a few stories of danger on the high seas, we told him about the unnerving incident we survived at Crooked Island. It was the first time we told anybody about that, and, in fact, the first time we revisited it together since it happened. Living the lifestyle we did, you collect stories of overcoming danger, and many sailor-smugglers become seriously entertaining storytellers in their own right. You end up collecting so many tales to tell…but that story was still unsettling and uncomfortable to talk about. On top of the fact that I had to amend the truth, I had my reasons for why I didn't like to talk about it. I could see, a little to my surprise, that even Maria, the hardcore adrenaline junkie, also didn't enjoy revisiting that particular experience.

Once we had confirmed our bonafides, Tom opened up a bit, "I'm headed down to Columbia. Do you have a pistol you can sell me?"

Maria said to me, "What about the Python you bought from Scott in Atlanta? It's kind of big to hide, and I'm thinking if the law finds it up in the States it wouldn't fit our profile."

"A Colt Python is perfect," Tom said.

"I'm okay with selling it, but it's gonna cost you. Nickel plated, .357, four-inch barrel. Fifteen-hundred bucks."

"That's fair," he answered.

After dinner, Tom came by while we were stowing the food. He gave me fifteen Benjamin Franklins for a pistol that had cost me four-hundred dollars two years before. I thought, All right! I tripled my money!

CHAPTER 12

STOWAWAY

We crossed the reef at first light, heading down islands, hoping to evade surveillance. Once we were far enough away from the heat in the Turks Islands, I planned to head east out into the Atlantic for two days before turning north toward New England. I must have been freaked by those assholes in the chopper, because even though we knew we were running late, we were determined to outflank any possible Coast Guard patrols.

Misty was making good speed up wind on a course I was okay with for the moment. We could expect any and all kinds of weather, including an early hurricane, as we turned north away from the northeast trade winds. We were sailing into summer. Light variable winds with the odd tropical storm thrown in was a breeze compared to the madness just out of Jamaica, but we weren't done yet.

Our high tension break in the Turks Islands had left us energized. We'd spent days and days way too close to the American Coast Guard and made it through untouched. It seemed that our patron saint, King Neptune, favored us, at least for the moment.

Out there, way east of the shipping lanes, we had the Atlantic to ourselves. Our provisions were set for a month or even two. Having plenty of fuel, water, fresh veggies, and eggs boosted our chi. After all, when you're piloting a little space capsule, a little speck of dust afloat in the cosmos, it's all in your head.

The radio provided a touch with reality. In those days Cuban radio stations broadcasted salsa for thousands of miles. We never tired of listening to Celia Cruz and Tito Puente. I also loved listening to Soviet propaganda on Radio Moscow.

Our lives were divided into four-hour segments. We were either on watch or off watch. Romance was back, a clear indication that stress was put on hold. Years later my girlfriend Nancy Freckle would tell me, "Sex is the glue that holds relationships together." So, I suppose it could be said that Maria and I were curing our bond.

The days slipped by without notice. Summer had arrived in North America and we were closing on Cape Hatteras, well, eight-hundred or so miles away.

One bright morning, eight or nine days out of the Turks Islands, I tuned in to the NOAA North Atlantic morning weather report. After plotting the low pressure centers on the big North Atlantic chart, I realized, Crap! It's June. We're into hurricane season. The low pressure systems were moving from the super-heated Sahara Desert to cross the Atlantic Ocean. One of these intense lows was headed in our direction. Still pretty far away, at least 350 miles. Our daily jobs from that point on included plotting low pressure systems and making sure to listen to every weather report.

We kept moving, meandering in a northerly direction, our course determined by the wind, and our waning and waxing focus. The low pressure system kept moving across the Atlantic, feeding on the humid air rising off the summer sea. I saw it coming. Actually, I felt it first. The air got heavy as the isobars[14] began edging onto the navigation worksheet.

In those days, before computer plotters, I drew up navigation worksheets. Putting positions on the big chart, North Atlantic Western Half, was pointless, because the position dots were too close together to make sense of our course. I had been taking sights with my sextant, which added to the mass of lines on the chart. Celestial navigation using a sextant doesn't result in an exact position. What you get is a line of position, or LOP, which becomes more accurate as the day goes by, and eventually it crosses other LOPs along the course to indicate a more refined position. A lot of lines. The art of navigation is only partially science.

The sunny days, with clear sextant shots of the sun, were a big help now that we were two weeks without any land-based aids like lighthouses or sight bearings. We knew that a storm was approaching, so I wasn't surprised when the cirrus clouds began flying by high overhead. I was thankful we were far from the Gulfstream. NOAA weather was calling the approaching weather a strengthening tropical disturbance. The Gulfstream is a serious force of nature and is a nightmare when it crashes into an opposing tropical storm. I was just hoping King Neptune wasn't going to turn this storm into a hurricane.

Misty was mostly immune to storms. Mostly. Constructed of steel, with the mast stepped on deck, meant that even if the mast broke it wouldn't rip a hole in the deck when it fell. She had small, strong hatches, and, literally, bulletproof ports and portlights (windows). There was nowhere above the waterline for sea water to enter and sink her. If we got hit by a huge breaking wave it wouldn't shatter a port or crush a hatch.

I was feeling good about our position. I knew that a storm was coming, and I felt pleased that I had overcome my tendency to be lazy about navigation. We were as prepared as we could be, storm sails on deck, everything below deck well-stowed, and Maria had baked bread and made chili beans in the pressure cooker. The clouds were getting thicker and lower but still moving so fast that it made me dizzy to watch.

The wind was steadily rising and the wind direction was moving counterclockwise on the compass. Misty was moving fast on a northeasterly course, straight for Cape Cod. It looked like this storm was working in our favor and the wind was strong, something like forty knots, but we still had sails up, a small working jib, and three reefs in the mainsail.

Night had come, and in the dark the smell and feel of the sea was more noticeable. The smell most people associate with the sea is really the reek of decaying organic matter washed ashore. The scent of the sea far from shore is cleaner, like a freshly shucked oyster.

Misty's rail was close to the water even at anchor–in these seas waves were washing down the deck across our bare feet. Now and again a big one would break right over me. The bright taste of seawater was not unpleasant. Astringently salty.

Maria was jammed into the corner of the cockpit behind the dodger and had to holler above the din of the storm, "Good thing we listened to all those weather reports. We've got three days of food cooked, but I wonder how long this'll last? It seems we're moving with the storm, the wind is almost behind us and it's not changing direction."

"I think we're just going to have to ride this out," I answered. "The weather service thinks this storm's going to veer toward Bermuda. Hopefully it will spit us out somewhere east of Cape Hatteras. It's pretty uncomfortable rolling in these seas, but we are hauling ass in the right direction for a change."

And just then Misty took a big gust as she sailed over the foamy crest of a twenty-foot wave, and rolled until the starboard deck was right under water. The boom even went under. No big deal, Maria was wedged in and holding on, and I had a solid grip on the tiller. I steered her upwind a bit for some stability, and looked around to check if anything went overboard. I breathed a sigh of relief, nothing was missing, then glanced at the compass that was mounted in the middle of the cockpit...

...It was smashed.

When we took that roll, a winch handle (made of solid bronze and plated in chrome) had flown across the cockpit and shattered the glass dome of the compass.

I was lucky the projectile hadn't shattered the dome of my head, but I wasn't feeling lucky. Out at sea with old school navigation means sailing with minimal tools. Losing one is a big deal. I have never had much use for dogma, but as a sailor I believed in the Boy Scout motto: "Be Prepared." Ironically, I did have a nice Boy Scout compass and a hand-bearing compass. However, the steel of which Misty was constructed really interfered with any compass onboard. Before leaving the States I paid an old sea captain to come onboard and motor around the harbor, taking known bearings and adjusting the compass to compensate for the deviation caused by our steel boat's magnetic field. Hand-held compasses obviously cannot be adjusted.

Fortunately, during the summer months the sun rises and sets close to east and west, respectively. So at sunrise and sunset we had an approximate reading on where north was. I could then approximately figure out how far off the hand-held compass was reading. Celestial navigation in the summer months produces mainly north/south lines of position, which, when combined with a noon sight (for reading your latitude), results in a fairly accurate position. At night we picked a star to steer by that didn't move much, like the North Star.

Having said all of that, I still wasn't comfortable with our position. It was like feeling your way around in a strange, dark house—one hand on the wall next to you and one hand reaching out to grasp at the darkness in front, shuffling forward bit by bit with probing steps. It felt like we were in a horror movie, and the audience we could neither see nor hear was screaming at us, because we had foolishly gone into that room.

***

The chronometer rang four bells. Two a.m. About time to put in our position, I thought. I stepped out of the cockpit to the stern and leaned out over the rail to get a clear view around the sails to check for ship lights. No ship lights. Nothing out there. My little flashlight illuminated the Walker Log dial for distance. Looked like we had sailed ten miles in the last two hours.

I dropped through the hatch to the cabin sole in the nav station. It had been cloudy since the tropical storm arrived, so trying to make sense of where we might be was something that needed to happen. I looked down at the chart and there was a hole where our last position was! Really?

It all started to make sense—holes in the food bags, scratching noises late at night, and now a hole in the chart—we must have picked up a rat in the Turks Islands. Maria and I were sharing our small thirty-foot sailing boat with a rat. "Fuck this. This is the last straw," I muttered and reached for the .38.

I looked over to check if Maria was in the bunk, but she was standing there, glaring at me in a tee-shirt and shorts, with her feet wedged across the cabin, and hands on her hips.

"What are you doing with that pistol?"

"I'm going to kill our stowaway," I answered. "The rat we picked up in Provo. I've got some peanut butter and cheese in the galley, and when he appears I'm gonna shoot him." I could tell from her darkening scowl that Maria wasn't following my train of thought, so, just to make sure she understood, I hastily added, "Because we don't have a rat trap."

"Have you lost your mind? You are not going to shoot anything down here. In case you hadn't noticed," she punched the bulkhead for emphasis, "THIS IS A FUCKING STEEL BOAT! If you miss, it will ricochet... You idiot!"

"Okay. What's your idea? Because apparently graphite is a rodent delicacy. It's taken to eating the pencil marks on the chart, and now there's a hole where our position is. Navigating without a compass is bad enough without holes in the chart."

She answered in that quiet but firm and commanding voice that somehow only women can manage. "If we don't want it eating the chart, then we just have to feed it. Sooner or later, one of us will have a chance to bash it. No guns. Bashing only. Got it? I'm leaving your fish-killing billy club here next to the chart table."

We continued weaving north(ish), slowly. Our steering was certainly off, since we no longer had a big compass in the middle of the cockpit that could be checked from every working position. Now that we didn't have it, we realized how much we relied on being able to get instant feedback on sail changes or windvane steering adjustments. But then, as William Bell said in his 1961 Stax hit, "You don't miss your water 'til your well runs dry."

According to the position on the chart we were a couple

hundred miles southeast of Cape Hatteras, still heading for Cape Cod. The wind was blowing a steady fifteen knots from the north, which meant Misty was heeled over with a jerky motion. The wind had picked up, and I was sleeping crammed against the settee on the cabin sole when our new crewmate ran across my arm on her way to the feeding station in the galley. I lurched violently into the air, slamming my head against the edge of the cabin overhead. "Okay. ENOUGH!" I yelled in horror.

Maria stuck her head in the companionway, "What's enough?"

"That fucking rat just ran across my arm. We're going into Hampton Roads[15] then up to Norfolk to buy a rat trap. God. Rats are so creepy."

Maria, rolling her eyes to the sky, inquired in her best southern accent, "You want to sail into Norfolk, home of the You-nited States Navy? Honey, halve you lost yo mine?"

"Yep. Right into Little Creek. The Cruising Guide to the Chesapeake says there is a small marina that has a few transient slips, right next to the Marine Naval Base. No sane smuggler would come in there loaded. There are lots of young couples on small sailing boats cruising these waters, and a lot of traffic in general...ships, commercial fishing vessels, and loads of pleasure boats. Anyway, I'm dumping our stowaway. Jesus! She has bad hygiene, and won't stand watch, or cook."

---

15 Hampton Roads is a body of water that provides a wide channel for the James, Nansemond, and Elizabeth rivers where the Chesapeake Bay flows into the Atlantic.

A Smuggler's Guide to Fine Dining

Making the decision was easy enough. Getting there was another issue. I did not want to go anywhere near Cape Hatteras, a well-known ship graveyard sticking way out into the Atlantic. I set the course for a waypoint north of the Cape just outside the Gulfstream, which flowed north at four knots right there. When we got near the Gulfstream we should start seeing a lot of ship traffic catching free rides north to ports along the American East Coast.

Two days later we started seeing ships, lots of ships, headed south. I figured they were steaming just outside the northerly current to Southern U.S. ports, which somewhat confirmed my calculation of our position. Another day passed, and now the ships were heading north. My noon sights showed we weren't far enough north to see any vessels headed for Hampton Roads for another couple days. My plan was to sail into the neighborhood then follow the ship traffic into the Chesapeake Bay. Once we got under the big Chesapeake Bridge Tunnel, I was sure I could find my way, by sight, into Little Creek. The Marine Expeditionary Fleet is pretty obvious from a long way off.

Maria called down, "Ranen, come up. Will you?" She pointed to an old-style ship flying a Greek flag motoring slowly in our direction. I could tell the ship was old school–they were trailing a Walker Log. The Greeks are big on tradition. Just the sort of sailors who would go out of their way to lend us a hand. Quickly, I jumped below and pulled out one of the plywood boards that transformed the main cabin into a double bed in port. I had painted it bright white with POSITION? in large letters for just such an occasion. I scurried back above and signaled with the horn for them to slow. As they came closer, Maria turned to parallel their course and closed on their starboard side. A sailor came out on the bridge with a pair of binoculars. He clearly saw the question and the ship slowed. Five or ten minutes later an officer came to the rail holding up a chalkboard with the latitude and longitude written on it. We waved to each other and went along our way. Probably the last time that happened in the North Atlantic Ocean. Satellite navigation came along soon after.

 In a boatyard later that summer, someone saw my sign and everyone in the yard had a good laugh. Still, we all appreciated that it was a great relic of times gone by. Funny, I had learned about it from a Rudyard Kipling novel, Captains Courageous, written in the 1890s. I only had occasion to use it that one time, but it worked. Broken compass, who would have guessed?

 The next day I was pretty sure we were crossing the Gulfstream. Maria spotted it on her morning watch, "There are a lot more ship lights out there. None of them are close, but it looks like they're all headed more or less north. It's not your watch for another half hour, but have a look. I think we should add a couple of knots northerly current into the navigation."

 Sure enough it was there, if you knew what to look for. Not traffic like a freeway, but four vessels headed north, not necessarily close but within sight all around us. Some were barely visible, others close enough to keep a close eye on. We continued to see ships all day. I headed westerly thinking (hoping, really) that we were south of Hampton Roads. So far we were in water too deep for the depth sounder to register anything. My plan was to head north when we crossed the continental shelf. There were no offshore reefs, so we could afford to wander around looking for ships headed into the Chesapeake.

Someone once asked me, "Aren't you afraid out there in the ocean?"

My answer, "Hell, no. There's nothing out there to hit. All the danger is on the edges where all the hard bits are."

So there we were. Not lost, but not found either. My celestial navigation showed us to be south of where the Greek ship's position should have been. In those days I didn't always know where we were. Shipwrecks still happen. So we watched for a change in the color of the sea, from the deep purplish blue of the Gulfstream, to the green water near the continental shelf. The old depth sounder we had was accurate but wouldn't register anything deeper than one hundred fathoms. We were also looking for ships headed in, and, of course, the regular flash of lighthouses on the coast. I wasn't worried, but I was feeling anxious.

All this time we had forgotten that our forward cabin was stuffed with bales of weed, but now, as we approached the American East Coast, a sense of danger began to seep into our awareness. We would be less exposed in a marina than out here, where some bored Coast Guard patrol might stop us for a "safety check."

The first real clue came around noon when we saw the outline of a big naval ship in the distance, headed northwest. It was moving fast and soon out of sight, but we got a bearing on its course and turned to follow, full sail. Still no bottom.

We were looking for the Chesapeake Light, a lighthouse thirteen miles offshore, marking the entrance to the bay. The lighthouse can be seen from nineteen nautical miles. It is mounted on a Texas Towers style platform that in 1965 replaced the famous lightship that had been anchored there since 1930. My dead reckoning told me that we should be able to see the light in another forty-eight hours. The color of the sea had changed from the Gulfstream deep purple/blue to a murky green. We had crossed the continental shelf. The depth sounder should be showing a bottom soon, but so far the only ship we had seen in a while was the naval vessel, now long gone.

That night the old Raytheon depth sounder showed sixty fathoms (360 feet). Around midnight Maria spotted the Chesapeake Light, white flashing, at a fifteen second interval. When she woke me, cup of coffee in hand, at four a.m., Maria said she could see ships showing anchor lights. Maybe they were waiting for morning to enter, or more likely waiting for a pilot.

The wind went light then died at daybreak, so I started the engine and took the tiller. Maria, who was awake to see our first landfall in four weeks, bagged the sails and lashed the mainsail to the boom. The lighthouse is thirteen miles offshore.

A Smuggler's Guide to Fine Dining

I didn't have a closeup chart for the Chesapeake entrance, but I just went with the traffic, being careful to stay out of the fairway. The little two-cylinder five-horsepower diesel only pushed Misty at four knots, so the surrounding ships were flying past us. No problem, the channel was clearly buoyed.

Our slow pace would give us just enough time to tidy up our whole profile. We needed a new compass, a rat trap, and a few other provisions, but, more than anything else, we needed to appear like a fortunate couple on a leisurely sailing vacation. We needed to look like the kind of privileged weekend sailors who don't actually need a damn thing.

This would be the most crucial test of our profile yet. We'd find out soon enough if we really had protected our identities from the USCG chopper back in Provo.

CHAPTER 13

A FEW NERVOUS DAYS IN VIRGINIA

Maria and I took turns steering while one of us scrubbed the decks with a weak solution of oxalic acid to brighten the decks and rinse away any rust stains. Our profile did not include looking like we had sailed many hundreds of miles, nearly nonstop, to get here. Our LPL (latest pack of lies) was that we just sailed up from Charleston on a summer cruise to New England. Just another twenty-something couple on a romantic vacation.

Misty was sparkling both above and below deck. All the hatches were open to dry everything out from all the weeks she was closed up. More importantly, to air out the smell of weed. Maria and I broke out the clean "entering clothes" that we had carefully folded and stashed in sealed plastic bags before we left Jamaica. Her hair was washed, brushed, and braided, and my long hair was tucked up under a crisp Mount Gay Rum baseball cap. Both of us were wearing navy blue yachting shorts, white shirts, and Top-Sider shoes. We were breakfasting on fried canned ham sandwiches as I steered under the Chesapeake Bay Bridge Tunnel toward Little Creek on the Norfolk side of the bay.

We were about to sail into an unknown marina in broad daylight with a barely disguised load of contraband. Yet, Maria and I were comfortable doing it. We knew damn well that if we were caught the boat and everything on it would be gone, and we would both go to jail for a long time. But neither of us was tense or even worried. Our LPL was both real and realistic. We had been sailing with this load of weed for so many weeks that we didn't think about it.

There are different ways to be covert. One of them is hiding in plain sight. We were coming into a marina to buy a new compass and a rat trap. Why would anyone think there was more to us than that?

A good actor delivers a compelling performance by convincing himself that the lies he tells on stage are really the truth. Misty was our stage, and we'd rehearsed this act for years.

As we approached Little Creek I was relieved to see quite a few masts. At this point we really wanted to be tied up to a dock and become invisible. As we chugged past all those naval vessels, I felt as if we were motoring into the shark's mouth. Maria and I were at the top of our game and determined not to let anything break our cool, but there were long moments of suppressed panic as we passed a police boat...and then another... but we were just another uninteresting pair of weekenders playing with our toy sailing boat. We found a little marina just as we came into the harbor, right across the creek from the huge U.S. Navy's Marine Amphibious base.

The marina consisted of a few floating docks. I called out to a guy who was washing down a small fiberglass weekend sailboat. "Hi, do you think there's an open slip for a couple of days?"

He pointed across the dock from his boat and said, "Sure. The folks who have that spot just left for Florida for two months. The marina's using it for a transient slip." He crossed over to catch our lines. I jumped over to the dock and was promptly thrown down. After a few weeks at sea, for a moment, the land seemed to be heaving. I laughed it off with a tug on my Mount Gay Rum cap, and loudly muttered something about needing a hair of the dog. I far preferred this stranger to assume I was just another drunk captain, rather than a sailor who'd been beating the open sea for the last month.

Misty was tucked away in the corner of a little, out of the way marina. The temptation to feel secure was right there with our pride in making it this far, in spite of all the obstacles. We were standing side by side on the cabin top, leaning over the boom, talking and putting on the grey canvas sail cover. Maria quietly pierced our bubble of conceit. "I wonder what the penalty is in Virginia for having a couple-hundred pounds of weed? Would we get possession in Virginia and federal charges for smuggling?"

"I see your point. We need to get out of here quickly. Let's see about getting a good meal, a ride to a grocery store, and a hardware store for the rat trap. I'm pretty sure, with all these ships around, we should be able to find a retired ship officer to replace and swing our compass. I'm going over to talk to the guy across the dock."

Maria followed me over to our neighbor's boat.

Jim was a doctor in his early forties. His wife Megan, a blonde around thirty-five, showed up during the introductions. Jim wandered onto the dock to get a better look at our sailboat while we talked and noticed that our compass was broken. He was observant. That raised a red flag for me. Would he see through our LPL? Would he notice something we had missed? The burlap packages of weed were visible, but only recognizable if there were other clues.

We needed to win them over as fellow sailors. Nothing makes a person less suspicious of you than deciding you are part of their tribe. Plus, I hoped to get information and rides to the store. Here is where Misty being a perfect, unique little cruising boat came in handy. She was a boat that garnered a lot of respect but without being ostentatious. She wasn't modern or fancy enough to create jealousy amongst other sailors.

Maria turned up her southern twang and asked, "Megan, is theya a grocery store neahbai? We picked up a rat in Charleston so we also need a hardware store for a rat trap...actually the trap is the first thing Ah want."

"There's a grocery and a hardware store across the bridge," Megan answered. "I'll give you a ride there. It's on my way home. If you can wait half an hour?"

Jim spoke up, "Kenny, what are you going to do about your compass?"

"Actually, I'm going to try to find a compass adjuster. Usually they sell as well as adjust compasses. You know that you can't just bolt on a new compass on a steel boat?"

Jim nodded, "You can call the old man who installed mine. He's a retired Navy commander. Funny old guy with endless stories, but he knows compasses. I'll get his card.

By evening we had put away our two large backpacks full of food, and by midnight I had thrown our stowaway into the dumpster. The old man was due at twelve the next day to install and adjust the new Danforth compass. And so far…no one had seen through our smoke and mirrors.

Things were falling into place for us. We were going to need a little luck going forward, or at least not bad luck. Being careful and smart wasn't enough. It never is.

The next morning was a Saturday, and Jim showed up at dawn to get his boat ready for a race day. We were having a coffee in the cockpit, and he invited himself onboard. He was plainly curious about us. I made him an espresso in our little moka pot. Coffee in hand, he confessed that he envied our ability to go cruising. He described how his life was programmed from high school to put him where he was.

I could see Jim wanted to know how we managed to be so free. He and Megan had everything, except freedom. This was always a problem when we, as outlaws, got too close to middle class sailors. Freedom must have a smell.

Maria gave me a look that said, We need to leave here. And soon. She was right. We'd seen this kind of thing so many times before. Whatever reason we gave him, whatever story, no matter how simple or elaborate, it didn't matter what we said. He would start looking for a reason to resent us. It was predictable. It was dangerous.

I much preferred the company of really wealthy yachtsmen. They had the freedom that their wealth afforded them and had no reason to feel threatened by our freedom. Actually, the wealthy always appreciated my eccentric style and lifestyle. They never bothered me with questions, just added me to their collection of interesting characters to show off over drinks at the club.

But Jim, who was still good with us for the time being, drank his espresso. Even though he looked directly at a bale of weed disguised with some ropes draped over it, he never saw anything amiss. It was a good test.

Precisely at noon, a dapper old man in his late seventies, wearing a proper naval officer's cap, came walking down the dock with a canvas toolbag in one hand and a box under his other arm.

"Ah, Commander Johnson. Welcome aboard," I said.

The commander stepped aboard and immediately looked down at the broken compass. "How far did you sail without a compass?" he asked.

I chose not to bullshit this guy with an LPL. I suspected he was way too canny. "Oh, I don't know. Probably a thousand miles. Since that tropical storm a couple of weeks back."

"Well done, young man. I have to ask, how far off was

your DR position at the end of that thousand miles?"

I answered, "About 120 miles."

"Yes, well done indeed. Well, let's get your new compass installed, and hopefully adjusted without any deviation. I swing all the fleet compasses for the Navy, so I have the bearings for all the compass points memorized. Saves time, don't you know."

He removed the old Danforth compass and installed the new one. Then we motored in circles around the harbor pointing to Misty's bow at all the bearings around the compass. He glued little magnets around the compass's base to compensate for the boat's magnetic field, until the compass read the correct magnetic bearing on every point around the compass. This guy really had it down. No wonder the United States Navy trusted him.

The commander never noticed that we had a cargo, because he wasn't interested. We paid our marina bill that afternoon and were gone at first light the next morning.

CHAPTER 14

ONWARD TO CAPE COD

The fragrance of Maria baking bread had the seagulls circling as we passed the Chesapeake Light Tower. There was a fresh breeze blowing from the west so I put the first reef in the mainsail and set the working genoa. The wind was just forward of the beam on our course of fifty-five degrees, northeast toward Martha's Vineyard, an island off Cape Cod. I had never been there. Nevertheless, I was becoming better at picking out places to anchor where we wouldn't stand out in the "what's wrong with this picture" game in the Coast Guard mind.

We had to sail to a place somewhere near Boston where we could take a few days to contact Timmy and arrange for him to pick up the weed. I knew almost nothing about the coast of New England. A few years before, Jerome and I delivered a load of weed up to our old contact Jimmy in Boston. However, visiting a place by land doesn't even come close to understanding the coast and coastal subculture.

Coastal subculture is a thing. At this point I had lived nearly all of the past six years on boats. Each of those succeeding years my perspective changed…more and more I began to view life on the land as an observer, an outsider. Think about life without a car, how being with or without a car not only defines where you can and can't go, but it also defines your relationship to the land around you and your relationship to the people you encounter. Unconsciously, I restricted my movements to fifteen minute walks from wherever I tied up my dinghy. So fifteen minute walks from the water defined my habitat. However, I always had a fast inflatable boat with the most powerful outboard engine manageable, so I couldn't go far by foot, but I could tear across a coast at hell bent speeds.

Believe it or don't, life is different beyond a block from the water. My interaction with the people who lived in the coastal subculture took less effort. Our presence was less suspicious, more understandable to that subculture of people who live and work on or near the water. Fishermen, marina workers, beachcombers, tugboat crews, ferry drivers, writers, and all the rest of us semi-amphibious folk share an affinity with those who arrive by water.

I prefered to tie up to commercial vessels. People who actually go to sea for their livelihood always had respect for our lifestyle and were more helpful than others living on the waterfront.

Collating all the factors involved in finding a place to stage the unloading near Boston was complicated. When I looked at the chart, I wasn't even sure what ports and towns were in which state. We needed to get into the area, anchor off, dinghy in to make phone calls, and, above all, keep a low profile. I chose Martha's Vineyard because it was not accessible by land. Everyone there was coastal. There was a better chance of slipping in, not unnoticed perhaps, but at least not suspect.

I was in my twenties. I was smart and careful. Going to jail was something that happened to other smugglers, the gold chain crowd who didn't have a leash on their egos or profile. Or so I thought. Not consciously, but I thought it.

Still, I wasn't reckless enough to tie up in some unknown marina without a good reason where a local policeman might get a sniff of marijuana or be tipped off by a brief flash of intuition. Or where we might stumble into some other situation that had nothing to do with us…some other smuggler being less careful than we were. This was an island where a lot of wealthy, very cool people lived, weed smokers all. The local police would avoid causing trouble for the local gentry. However, busting a dealer who brought his weed delivery here by boat, to avoid using the supervised ferry, that was another matter.

All of these details were running through my head as we continued north with light favorable winds. Misty was sailing along with very few course corrections. It seemed so easy now that we had a compass again. The small awning I rigged from the spray dodger to the boom offered some relief from the blinding summer sun. We were stripped to nearly nothing, showcasing our lean, fit bodies and sun-bleached hair. Maria was looking good and flaunting it. We were flirting and teasing at every opportunity. Both of us knew we needed a distraction from the tension embedded in this voyage, and the tension made our lovemaking more urgent. Hotter. It was all very sweaty, which only drove us higher. Our scent was driving us. We made love everywhere on the boat, everytime we passed. All alone out there. No reason not to explore our obsession with each other.

The dolphins were picking up on our pheromones. They swam alongside the cockpit on Maria's watches. One night when I came out on deck, Maria was hanging overboard with her feet on a dolphin's back. Sexual energy is compelling, and animals always pick up on it.

Misty sailed northeast and the Walker Log rotator spun the indicator, mile after mile, as we closed on Cape Cod.

A day came that we started seeing ships, a lot of ships, all kinds of ships. It made sense. My navigation put us in the "approaches to New York" lanes on the chart. Maria and I were sailing across the lanes, dodging fast-moving ship traffic. VHF transceivers had become within our budget, but I hadn't bought one yet. I think, looking back, that I didn't like the idea of being connected at sea. One of the main attractions of living on a boat was the inherent privacy. I loved the isolation and resisted and resented the interruption that a transceiver would bring. However, now that we were winding our way between ships, I wondered whether or not I was crazy. It would be so easy to call these monsters to make sure they saw us, and agree on how to safely pass them. Ships in the night and all...

After two days of ship stress, our mood had shifted to a more serious level. We were mentally prepared to get to work. I was looking at the Georges Bank to Nantucket Shoals chart for an anchorage outside of a town on Martha's Vineyard. There were only two choices: just off Edgartown and the bay at Vineyard Haven. Vineyard Haven, the ferry port, seemed too busy. We headed for Edgartown, but since we had to pass Vineyard Haven on the way we could check it out to be sure. However good I was at extrapolating information from a chart, nothing beats the information gained from being there, and soon we would be there in person, for better or for worse.

I had a lot of confidence in my ability to sense danger. Call it intuition, but throughout my life I was always able to spot a threat. Years before, I was in a dealer's kitchen with my old partner in climbing and crime, Dean, at a table with three other men going over a plan to deliver a load. I leaned over and said quietly to Dean, "Let's get out of here, man. I've got a bad feeling about this deal." When we stood up to leave, Dean answered the unspoken question on their faces, "I've learned to listen to Ranen's feelings. You guys should listen, too."

The point is, I switched my head into extra sensory perception mode as we approached Martha's Vineyard. Maria spotted the lights quite a few hours before dawn, a perfect landfall. She didn't wake me, just reduced sail until Misty was barely moving toward the brightest lights. The chart showed us on the opposite side of the island from the two prospective anchorages. New England coastal waters are fraught with wicked currents, many days of dense fog, and lots of offshore rocks and reefs. Consequently, all of these waters, including the entrance to Vineyard Sound, were clearly marked with lighted sound buoys.

    The wind was blowing a steady fifteen knots from the northwest. Easy sailing with no waves. We were flying up Vineyard Sound close to the beach, just checking out the island on a sunny weekday. I was at the tiller sailing through the anchorage at Vineyard Haven. I didn't feel that it was the spot for us…too much ferry traffic, too busy. We headed for the next anchorage at Edgartown. Turned out to be the perfect anchorage for our needs. Not much action but just enough that we didn't stick out.

    We dropped the anchor in fifteen feet of water over white sand. Misty was parked off Chappaquiddick, well away from the entrance to the Edgartown Harbor. We got busy inflating the dinghy. Within the hour Maria was standing in the bow directing us to a dinghy dock in Edgartown. We were ready for a shot of tequila, with a beer, and I was fantasizing about a splendid meal we didn't cook. The prospects were good for a great restaurant; this was Martha's Vineyard. James Taylor and Carly Simon lived here. Rock stars like to eat out, right?

    It took five trips to town, but we finally got through to Timmy. We were a little more than three weeks behind Jeffrey, so he was prepared to pick up our weed during the coming weekend. So there we were, sitting on a couple hundred pounds of weed, for another five days.

    Edgartown wasn't a bad place to wait. Waiting is an integral part of illegal business. Okay, probably any business, but with illegal business, waiting is more stressful, more tense.

A Smuggler's Guide to Fine Dining

Fortunately Maria was an excellent partner for waiting. Although she had quite an explosive temper, stressful situations put her into lighthearted focus. Pressure just pressed her "let's have fun" button.

We went to town for lunch each day. There were some pretty chill little restaurants right there on the waterfront. Maria and Ranen were an unusual couple walking out of the marina where we tied up our fast Zodiac. No classic rowing dinghy for us stylish sailboat hippies. This whole island was part of the "coastal culture," and most of the wealthy homeowners were sailors or at least had adopted the culture. We were noticed and respected as people of the sea.

Actually, we were part of the local color, with our dark suntans, and sun-bleached hair and eyebrows. Hair in two braids, Maria wore strappy, silver-glitter-infused, midnight-blue jellies with elevated heels, and a pair of cutoff overalls with a bikini top underneath. I was sporting canvas shorts, a Mount Gay Rum tee-shirt, red hightop All Stars, and a faded blue North Sails cap restraining out of control, shoulder length, curly hair.

On the way back from lunch on Wednesday, a tall, lanky guy stopped, pointed to Misty and asked if we were the couple living on that boat. I answered, "Yep. That's our home."

"Where'd you come from?"

"The Caribbean," Maria blurted out. We walked on. Maria exhaled, "That was James Taylor! I was so blown away that I completely forgot our LPL!"

"I wouldn't worry. I'm sure he's not on close speaking

terms with any cops. Definitely a stoner."

We weren't spending much time off the boat, and we sauteed a lot of garlic to cover the smell of marijuana. Good thing, because on Thursday afternoon we had a visit from a Coast Guard patrol. Kind of unusual. They usually didn't bother anchored boats. Maybe the local cops asked them to check us out. I guess our profile wasn't as good as I thought.

There were two uniformed guys in a twenty-foot, semi-rigid, center console inflatable, with a couple of high-horsepower outboards. They came alongside and the chief petty officer asked for our registration. Misty was registered in Georgia and the registration was up to date. Maria and I both had Georgia driving licenses. We sure as hell didn't want to present our passports, which had enough stamps to put us in the Smuggler's Hall of Fame.

I took my time finding the papers. Didn't want to seem like I was trying to hurry them away. One of the guys looked really young, like twenty. The older uniform snapped out an order, "Stark, make a line fast on that cleat while I check their registration."

"We're secured, Chief," the younger seaman answered.

I handed the chief petty officer the registration card. He stepped back to check the numbers painted on the bow against the card and handed it back. Maria looked the Chief in the eye and in her sweetest southern drawl asked, "Would y'all like to come aboard for a cup of coffee?"

The chief answered, "No thank you, Ma'am. Whatever

A Smuggler's Guide to Fine Dining

you're fixin' for dinner sure smells good though. We have to be movin' on. You all enjoy your cruise."

It seems that garlic repels more than vampires!

CHAPTER 15

THE OTHER DANGEROUS MOMENT

Friday arrived.

Oh shit, it's on!

There are two definite dangerous moments in any smuggling voyage, when the cargo is out in the open for anyone watching to see: The loading…and the unloading.

Five a.m., mug of coffee and bar of chocolate in hand, I was standing in the cockpit in fog so thick I couldn't see the Aries wind vane twelve feet away. Our appointment, off a beach in Buzzards Bay, was thirty-three hours from now.

We spent all of Thursday, and the evening before, studying the tide tables and tidal charts for the Woods Hole area. There are islets and hidden rocky shoals all over the place. Sometimes, at that time of year, the fog lasted for days.

Okay, the thought of doing this whole thing blind worried me. Maybe I was afraid, but I sure as hell wasn't allowing my mind to go there. One thing that mountaineering taught me: once you let fear run loose in your head, panic is not far behind.

Who were the bad guys here? Tidal currents faster than

we could even motorsail, rocks, narrow passages, heavy fog, my inexperience, and fear. Who were the good guys? Good charts showing the currents at all stages of tide, a reliable depth sounder, and buoys with fog horns everywhere, all charted.

Running blind through these passages was a challenge. This was my first time close quarters navigating in fog. I'd memorized the charts showing the set and drift[16] of the current during this moon phase at these places. Still, finding my way through the rocky shoals to each buoy required me to constantly reconcile (in my head) our true speed and direction with the drift and set of the tide.

It took every bit of energy and focus that Maria and I could muster to do this blind.

Visibility was down to fifty feet at the best of moments, and there were times when a vale of fog would drift across Misty so that we couldn't see each other three feet away. Maria was at the helm, staring intently at the compass, except for when her eyes flicked over to call out the depth from the sounder's repeater. I had the detailed chart of the Woods Hole passage at hand to check distances and whether the tone of each buoy was a bell, horn or whistle.

A light wind was blowing from ENE, the mainsail and working jib were up, and the engine was running. Still, we were making only two knots against the current, and we were thirty minutes before slack tide. We were looking good for getting through the Woods Hole passage into Buzzards Bay during slack tide, before the tide would start sweeping us out of control to crash against who-knows-what rocks. I had a place picked out to anchor near the nighttime rendezvous, nearby the entrance to the Cape Cod Canal.

It was good that Timmy would easily recognize Misty, having spent time with us in Jamaica. We made it to the rendezvous just before dark. I didn't really want to anchor. We just kind of sailed around the area, looking like a couple of weekend sailors.

Soon after dark, a fast twenty-five-foot Formula pulled alongside. Timmy was there with two friends. They had lines ready and fenders already hanging over the side. This was way smoother than the chaotic loading scene in Jamaica. Within ten minutes everything was stowed out of sight in the Formula's lockers, within fifteen minutes they were long gone, and we breathed a huge sigh of relief.

We headed for an anchorage just a few miles from Falmouth, off the shore near Mashnee Road, just needing a place to sleep until dawn. Our plan was to head through the Cape Cod Canal, then up to one of the small towns north of Boston. Marblehead was somewhere I had heard of. Hood Sails was there which made the little town an East Coast "Mecca" for sailors.

Now that our mission was over, and our pockets soon to be full of cash, we could go anywhere we wanted, and heading into Marblehead on a whim seemed as good as going anywhere else. Maybe not just a whim. It was a sailing and coastal community where I would be accepted as a long-distance sailor.

Also it was close (but not too close) to Timmy, who now owed me a lot of money.

After completing a smuggling trip, I usually liked to get as far away as possible as quickly as possible, so by the time the goods hit the streets, and the local law enforcement started digging around, I was long gone. But this was my first time sailing this coast, and I wanted to soak it in, get to know it better, and I didn't figure Timmy was dumb enough to start selling dime bags in his backyard. Besides, we were a needle in a haystack. Even if the local authorities caught wind that somebody had just unloaded a few hundred pounds of weed in the huge urban (and suburban) area that is greater Boston, they would have to search a lot of sailboats that looked like cruising sailboats just like us.

For the first time in a long time we could just enjoy ourselves, without managing any underlying fears, without worrying about profile, or sticking fast to our LPLs.

Now I could get back to doing whatever the hell I wanted to do.

CHAPTER 16

A SOUJOURN IN BOSTON

The next day found us sleeping until nine. I awoke in the middle of a sexual dream that turned out not to be a dream. Just like Maria to take advantage of her sleeping lover, bless her hormones!

We cooked a luxurious breakfast of canned corned beef hash, eggs (not canned), and a stack of toast. Misty had a really crude stovetop toaster that worked a treat if you watched it closely.

While we cooked and ate, we spent some time looking at the NOAA East Coast Pilot for the rules on passing through the Cape Cod Canal. It is a real time saver for going from Buzzards Bay to Boston, and it looked like fun, sailing across land. What a change from the kind of sailing we had been doing. Around fifteen miles long, all the bridges were tall enough for our mast to pass under. There was a wicked current and the tide chart showed that. If we got sailing before noon, Misty would make her best speed ever with the current behind us. Not only that, but there was a light breeze blowing WNW. It was a perfect wind for motor sailing.

A Smuggler's Guide to Fine Dining

By eleven that morning the summer sun burned off the fog to find us sailing into the Canal with the full mainsail and a working jib up with a five-knot current behind us. Jimi Hendrix was blasting from the Alpine cassette deck down in the cabin, and we broke into our rum collection to have a shot of Cruzan in our coffees. I was making coffee in a two-shot, stovetop espresso maker with Café Bustelo. Jamaican Johnny had made us a small packet of special weed for smoking on the voyage...a little gift, I suppose. The coffee and rum, with a spliff of "Johnny's Reserve," made the day even brighter.

Even if we hadn't just unloaded our contraband, and even if we weren't comfortably enjoying a nice buzz, it would still be surreal sailing the Canal, alongside a road, waving at people on bicycles and kids fishing from the shore. Maria pulled the fuel shut off and, after a few knocks from the little engine, the loud engine din was replaced by the soft hiss of Misty's hull passing through the calm water at the other end of the Canal.

She said, "Let's stop in Boston. I can catch a flight to San Francisco from there. I am ready for a few not dangerous months with Beach Rat in Santa Cruz."

Both of us knew from the four or so years we had been together that we did not get along when we weren't at sea. We fought. Maria had a really bad temper, especially when she had a few drinks. To be honest, I also had a pretty short fuse, and when she pushed my buttons I couldn't back off. Six months seemed to be the limit of our patience with each other. I had mixed feelings about her leaving. I was looking forward to a break from her, but I was always attracted to her, and more strongly now that she was leaving.

"Okay," I answered. "But, I'm thinking about what you have under that skirt." And there we were, applying glue to our relationship, right out there in broad daylight.

We worked our way through all the shoals into Boston Harbor. I headed for the big ocean-going Moran tugs that looked like science fiction, battle ready, dull black space cruisers. There were four of them rafted two abreast, and I motored alongside. One-hundred feet long, three stories high in the bow, and low to the water in the stern, these powerful monsters were moored alongside a commercial wharf. Maria was coiling a stiff three-quarter inch, three-strand mooring line, separating it into coils in each hand, getting ready to throw. Two guys on one of the tugs were having a cigarette on the low aft deck outside a huge winch.

She called to them in her sweet southern drawl, "Are ya'll going out tonight? We've been at sea for weeks and need a safe place to tie up for a few nights."

One answered in a Boston "Southie" accent, "Toss that line down heah by our fendahs, dahlin.' We can all go for some beeahs and steamas across the whaaf."

And, once again, Maria won over these very tough deckhands by overhand flinging twenty pounds of stiff dock line, fifteen feet straight into that sailor's chest.

The two sailors explained that they were crew on one of the other tugs. The two rafted tugs, alongside which we were moored, were out of commission for a week of repairs and maintenance. These weren't harbor tugs. They were deep-ocean vessels, used for worldwide towing and salvage.

Bobby and John were on watch because their tug was on standby and might need to leave for a tow on a thirty-minute notice. They escorted us across the road for a beer and steamed clams at a waterfront bar. "We ain't got much time and really can't do much drinkin' t'day, bein' on watch and all," John said. "I got the radio in case we get a call. But you two are good wheah ya ah for at least a week. Our skippah's gonna love you two."

We finished our beers and a huge platter of steamed clams, then headed back to the boat with Bobby and John in tow. They came aboard Misty and we smoked a big joint. John went below for a look around. He filled the cabin. No way these two huge tugboat deckhands could fit below at the same time. The four of us traded sea stories for hours until their captain and the rest of the crew showed up.

The skipper, Stan, came aboard for a look around and graciously said, "The chief is stahtin' up our engines. We've got to pick up a containah ship dead in the water five hundred miles offshore. But you two are welcome to stay alongside as long as you want or until someone from the hahbormasta's office notices you. But I wouldn't worry. Those lazy bastahds never come around heah. I'll let the other skippers know you all are heah. When we move any vessels the crews will move y'ah little boat to keep heah safe. I gotta say Ranen, this is a tidy vessel an you two got a lotta guts sailing this little boat the way you do. I always think about gettin' myself a blow boat when I retiyah."

* * *

Maria caught a flight from Logan to San Francisco the next day. I wouldn't see her again until I was ready to sail south in the late fall…I was always the last boat to leave…here I was hanging out there in Boston.

 Captain Stan was good for his word–the other tug crews were beyond helpful and would stop over for a toke of weed. Ahhh, the days before drug testing.

 One of the perks of being friends with the officers of ships was having the use of their well-appointed machine shops. These deep-ocean tugs had an extensive equipment list to effect salvage of wrecked ships. They had huge generators and pumps that could be placed onboard sinking or damaged ships in all conditions and climes. The crew needed to be able to float a grounded cargo ship in the Arctic. For these types of salvage, the chief engineer might have to repair a hole in a steel hull then pump the ship dry, so it could be towed a few thousand miles to a shipyard. Every day I was alongside the tugs, I spent a few hours in one of their shops, using the bench, vice, and tools as well. I repaired and rebuilt all of Misty's pumps and winches using their parts. They had everything–emery paper, industrial grade lubricants, even lathes for making parts from scratch–and I had carte blanche.

 Maria wasn't the only one who needed to blow off some

steam. I went out every afternoon around 5:30 for drinks at the bars in Faneuil Hall, an upmarket restoration of the huge 1700s indoor marketplace. I was looking and feeling good, so picking up girls was easy. The tug crews loved watching me escort the young women, in their big-city footwear and stylish dresses, across their decks for a drink or a smoke on Misty. They especially loved seeing them the morning after, hungover and unsteady on delicate heels, clumsily picking their way around the cranes, winches, and coils of five-inch braided line, scrambling to get back to the wharf. My lifestyle and freebooting image always attracted women way above my "paygrade." And I never failed to take advantage of it.

I knew that the port officials would eventually notice Misty's presence, and also I was getting tired of big city nightlife. I think I spent well over a week there before I left for Marblehead. More importantly, it was time to get some money from Timmy… or at least hear how the sales were going.

There was one thing I knew I was going to miss: the Two Sister's Italian Restaurant, where I went every night for dinner, with or without a date. I never knew the restaurant's real name; there was no sign. I happened by one night just wandering around the waterfront area. The rich aroma of garlic tomato sauce drew me in. It was a little hole in the wall place with four small tables, run by two Italian sisters in their thirties. They didn't have a menu. You ate whatever they made that day. Good but cheap red wine, served in small thick glasses, some kind of fresh fish dinner, and fresh baguettes served with a wine bottle of olive oil. The place was always full, but I never had to wait. The raucous sisters loved to talk about the food they were making and serving, and they loved to embarrass me by comparing my "skinny" date to the "skinny" girl I brought in the night before. "Always the skinny girls, Ranen?"

Maybe life in the Boston "coastal subculture" was getting too comfortable, and time was slipping away. Misty was in need of a boatyard to antifoul her bottom and (if I made some money) she needed a new mainsail. Early one morning before sunup, after having an espresso with Captain Stan at a fisherman restaurant bar with an ancient espresso machine, I cast off to sail up to Marblehead.

CHAPTER 17

MARBLEHEAD

Although the voyage from Boston to Marblehead is only around twenty miles, it is a bitch if you're alone. There are lots of shoals and rocks and rocky shoals to avoid. I got started out of Boston with mild anxiety. I was fresh from a good night's rest, with espresso as a boost, and the ship channel was well marked. After I got away from Boston, there was a light fog, the visibility wasn't great, and I didn't have Maria to steer while I followed the buoys on the chart. That was a long twenty miles, with a lot of sweating and swearing, but, finally, I made it around the neck of land and isthmus that encloses the Marblehead Harbor.

Surprise! There were boats moored everywhere.

Aside from the open middle of the mile-long harbor, the anchorage was stuffed full of moored boats, mostly sailing boats. It was a forest of masts. There was barely room to motor around the harbor to look for a spot to drop an anchor. Finally I found a clear spot. It was a bit tight but still a spot. As soon as I put down the anchor, along came a navy blue motor launch with a discreet red stripe, a yacht club flag on the bow, driven by a young guy in a dark blue blazer, sporting a captain's hat with the same insignia as the little yacht club flag.

"There's no anchoring allowed in Marblehead Harbor. You have to have a mooring."

"Okay," I answered. "Point me to a mooring. Because I just sailed over two-thousand miles from the Turks and Caicos Islands, most of the way without a compass, and I need a mooring, a shot of rum, and a shower, and...in that order."

He was impressed by the boat, nothing like what he was accustomed to seeing, and by the fact that I had sailed in here from who knows where. I am sure he never heard of the Turks and Caicos Islands. He asked, "You know that this is a yacht club, right? Are you a member of a yacht club that might give you privileges here?"

I looked up at the huge, ancient, imposing clubhouse, standing guard on the point of the island, with its turrets and impeccable dock, and thought, People are watching this with binoculars from one of those huge mullioned windows. Taking his tip, I answered, "I am a member of the Savannah Yacht Club." I figured I could get through this with bravado, charm, and seafaring tales.

He pointed to a floating ball. "Pull up your anchor and take that mooring. Just blow your horn twice and I'll be back to take you to the club. My name is Stephen."

Things went well at the club. They didn't bother to check my references in Savannah. In the days before GPS the old school sailors respected real mariners, and this club was a bastion of old school mariners. I was given a guest membership to one of the most prestigious yacht clubs on the East Coast!

Maybe I was lucky the old commodore happened to be having a drink in the bar overlooking the harbor when I sailed in. It was probably why things went so well. The commodore was a U.S. Navy Admiral who retired just before WWII. He just liked my style and was old enough not to care what other people thought. This was his turf. Without asking he bought me a shot of Mount Gay Rum. That was the start of a friendship that made my summer in Marblehead.

The club was perfect. There was an organized locker room with the thing all sailors value most: hot showers! The bartenders knew how to make a decent drink from an extensive rum selection, and there was a big veranda overlooking the harbor for watching the races, drink in hand.

Marblehead was a dual community: the yachties and the townies (my terms not theirs). The quaint town was (and I suppose still is) a bedroom community of Boston. However, it had a prestigious maritime history. An early colonial fishing village, Marblehead was active during the American Revolution, and its sailors are considered to be the forerunners of the United States Navy. Most of the businesses in Marblehead were centered around sailing and boating, so many of the townies were connected to the marine industry.

The "yachties," most of whom were residents of Boston or the wealthy Boston suburbs, were there for the sailing club scene, which revolved around the very sophisticated racing programs hosted by the exclusive yacht clubs. During my stay there, the strongest America's Cup team effort was headed by Ted Hood and based in Marblehead. Hood Sailmakers was across the harbor, a big part of the reason I chose this port. A visit to Hood was an immediate priority, right behind a visit with Timmy for cash.

Misty and Ranen were curiosities that had wandered in from another universe. I truly think I was the first "Kung Fu" yachtsman that had been blown into their world, and the coastal subculture dictated that I be treated with a modicum of respect. I believe they enjoyed my crazy personality and found my style refreshing. I was a sailor, as was almost everyone else along the harbor, but aside from that I might have been from another planet.

I contacted Jeffrey to see if he'd gotten paid yet, and he sounded less than happy with Timmy the dealer. Jeffrey wanted to come down to Marblehead to talk about using someone else for sales. I wasn't worried that Timmy was holding my cargo. Mainly I was pissed off that we might have to physically move it to another dealer, involving yet another exposure of the entire load.

Misty needed cleaning and I just didn't have the energy for hours of drudgery down below. Stephen, the launch driver, told me his sister was looking for work. Fiona was an upbeat eighteen year old on her way to Boston College in the fall. I started her cleaning the forward cabin. Meanwhile, I got the Zodiac up and running. I left her to it and went to town to meet with Jeffrey for a beer at a local bar and grill on the waterfront.

Jeffrey was pissed off, because Timmy hadn't sold anything. He had a newborn at home and just wasn't up to the task.

"Look," I said, "Let's take our weed to Jimmy. He's living in Maine. You can let Timmy keep enough to pay the Jamaicans. We're gonna need a pickup with a cap."

"Okay," he agreed. "I can organize the truck next week. You talk to Jimmy today and call me. I just hope he's up for this."

Jeffrey and I parted, and he clearly expected me to get on that phone call immediately, but I already had another stop planned, one that was long overdue: the Hood sail loft.

The door opened into a colossal room, with a raised wooden floor the size of a basketball court, lined with commercial sewing machines along the edges. Sailmakers were seated below their machines, sewing sails spread out on the wooden floor. A sailor in his mid-thirties came walking off the loft floor and slipped on his Top-Siders. He reached out a hand, "I'm Jess."

"Hi Jess, I'm Ranen. I've got a thirty-foot boat moored across the harbor that needs a new mainsail. Actually, I need a new mainsail that will allow me to punch out of the Caribbean... against the north-east trades."

"Oh, we all know who you are. We wondered when you were going to come by. I had a look at Misty when I was out measuring that Swan moored near you. I think you need more than a new mainsail. The word is you've come in from a long voyage. I guess you're needing a haul out? We don't normally haul boats that aren't Hoods, but since you're buying a mainsail, we'll haul you here so we can really assess your boat."

I wasn't expecting them to allow me into their shipyard, but I had it in my mind the minute I noticed they had a small yard capable of hauling out big boats. Over the years the sailing industry supported me. I always paid for equipment and services, but almost always was given commercial rates and great deals. As the yachting industry became more and more geared to weekend yachting, I became one of the last vestiges of sailors actually living "The Dream." And the dream was what drove the sailing world. Odds are Jess dreamed of living my lifestyle.

You don't lie to your doctor, your lawyer...and you don't lie to your sailmaker. "Honestly, Jess, I was hoping a haul out would be possible, but I didn't expect it. We almost got nailed, because Misty wouldn't make the upwind voyage across the Caribbean. We ended up dodging the Coast Guard through the Windward Passage and into the Atlantic. We just need a few more degrees up wind. I know my main isn't drawing that well."

Jess answered, "Let's take her for a sail before we pull her out. I'd like to bring along our lead layout guy, and maybe we can get Robbie to come. Misty's design predates a lot of modern sailing technology. She's what? Like forty or fifty years old?"

My heart thumped. Robbie Doyle was the up-and-coming, boy-genius in the yacht racing world!

I nodded, "Well, she was built in Holland just after World War II, but the men who built her were probably old master boat builders. Holland in those days was not exactly at the forefront of yacht design. So yeah, I see I haven't been looking at the larger, more modern view, and frankly, all my sailing experience has been on older, fairly low-tech boats. I think there's a little front coming through, day after tomorrow. Let's plan on a couple hours of sailing when the wind is blowing. Leave a message at the club, and I'll be ready anytime you show up. This is my highest priority. Summer's nearly gone, and I don't fancy sailing south in the winter. Please get me on your schedule."

I got back to the boat around four. Fiona was finished with the forward cabin. It was spotless and neatly organized. Fiona was brilliant. "Wow, Fiona, great job. What do I owe you for today?"

"Oh, you don't owe me anything if I can keep what I swept up in the bilge!"

So much for keeping a low profile. By the next day everyone in Marblehead knew that I was a weed smuggler. And I didn't care. In fact, I was proud. No flash lifestyle, just a committed sailing vagabond. The Marblehead community adopted me. I added to the local mystique.

CHAPTER 18

KEY LARGO 1975

Maria was gone, and I knew damn well that I was going to need help in the boatyard. Kimo came to mind. Hmm, Kimo...Kimo... Kimo?

Kimo was an addict...of everything. But Kimo was smart, and more importantly, he was usually available if he could be found. He had been my boatyard crew in Key Largo for the year I completely rebuilt Misty, so he'd be a very useful shipmate to have around right now.

Kimo, Kimosabe, John Batistella, was from Texas, or at least I think he went to high school there, and maybe college. Slight build with large strong hands that were masterful at fingering his National Steel Standard guitar. Kimo would say that he could never forgive Chuck Berry for failing to learn to play the guitar.

Even in his early thirties his face (framed by shoulder-length, graying, black braids) displayed the ravages of alcohol and beatings survived. Kimo was smart, but not when he was drunk. When he was drunk he was clever, but not smart enough to keep his mouth shut–and the evidence for that was in his nose, broken many times, and the obviously broken bones below his left eye.

One night he was drinking for hours in the Caribbean Club, the famous bar in Key Largo that didn't have windows, just open walls on two sides with shutters that could be closed during a tropical storm, because the bar never closed. A rough-looking battleaxe of a woman, who was there with a big biker, stepped up to the bar next to Kimo. Before she could even order, Kimo looked right at her and said, "I don't care how ugly you are, I still want to fuck you."

She was shocked into silence. After a moment she yelled, "BUTCH, you won't believe what this asshole just said to me!"

In spite of the new face decoration, he walked out of that bar.

***

The year I met Kimo was the year I completely rebuilt Misty. Maria and I had sailed up from the islands after our first voyage south. We were heading to the do-it-yourself boatyard in Key Largo where a lot of well-respected, long-distance sailors built and refitted their sailing boats. Maria and I had now sailed Misty three or so thousand miles, so I knew her problems, but not exactly what to do about those problems. We'd hung out with some of the sailors who had worked in Key Largo; I knew there was a lot of expertise available there.

One afternoon found us sailing toward the Keys, almost

at the end of our long journey to Key Largo, and Maria was on her noon watch. Misty was slowly sailing through a mile-long patch of bright green sargasso weed.

TWANG.

The sound of the heavy monofilament jerking the running backstay startled me out of a sun-baked reverie. I looked up to spot a four-foot, iridescent mahi-mahi, leaping straight up out of the sea, thrashing his head about, trying to shake the annoying hook loose from his mouth. Handline fishing from a moving boat is tricky. I needed to keep the line firm, but pull it in smooth so as not to jerk the hook loose. The fish had gone back to hiding under the seaweed, and as I tracked his movement I noticed my fish wasn't the only thing hiding in there.

"Maria! Let the sheets loose. Get us stopped! I just caught a fish and there are three square groupers floating out there!"

There was so much marijuana coming into the Florida Keys then. A lot of bales went overboard in the Gulfstream during late-night hurried transfers to small boats. As well, a lot got thrown overboard when smuggling boats were ditching evidence while running from the Coast Guard or the Florida Marine Patrol. Smugglers would also toss bales from small airplanes flying low under the radar, to be picked up by a skiff on the water, to skirt the risk of landing a plane on U.S. soil with illicit cargo.

However these three square groupers ended up out here, hiding under a mile-long carpet of neon green sargasso weed, didn't really concern me. All that concerned me was putting an end to their ocean odyssey.

I quickly yanked the fish on deck, no longer caring if I accidentally pulled the hook loose, and killed it with a single blow to the head. Moving as fast as possible, I grabbed my mask, snorkel, and fins. Without thinking, I clutched a hundred meter coil of line and jumped overboard, swimming hard for the spot where I saw the bales of weed. It was a lot further than I thought. I guess we were moving faster than I figured, but I thought, Fuck it, I am going to get those bales. There's ten grand floating out there. The bales were wrapped in burlap. They're floating high. No marine growth. They probably went overboard in the last day or so. This is some serious luck.

Head down, I swam right into one, then quickly got a good bite on them with a series of hitches. Now I could drag the train of bales behind me. Excitement fueled me for the awkward swim back to the boat. The line was long enough that it wasn't necessary to tow them all the way back. Between gasps for air, I thanked Maria for having a halyard ready. Once the shackle was snapped to the line, Maria winched the bales up to the deck. They weighed something like seventy pounds each. We wrestled them out of sight down the forward hatch.

I took the time to cut fillets off the fish, but left the carcass on deck in case the law came along wondering what we were doing out there. We were instantly in LPL mode, getting the boat back to looking like a couple cruising the Florida Keys. The adrenaline was flowing. If the Monroe County Sheriff's Patrol or the Coast Guard were to find the bales, Misty would be impounded and one or both of us would do some prison time.

    I heard the clock ring four bells, two o'clock. Only an hour and a half since I hooked the mahi mahi and nothing in sight. We impatiently got the self-steering sailing us again. Now we could finally have a look at our floating treasure. I got the Ka-Bar combat knife out and cut into the first bale. The weed was wrapped in plastic under the burlap. It was weed... lovely Colombian Gold. The water had only penetrated about an inch and mold hadn't had a chance to grow yet. I figured they hadn't been in the sea more than a few hours. There was enough good marijuana in front of me to pay for Misty's entire refit. I continued sailing toward Key Largo while Maria stowed the bales and disguised them under a pile of sails.

    We got a good bearing on the Carysfort Reef Lighthouse during the night. This gave us a safe course to the airport along the access canal to the boatyard adjacent to the Holiday Inn. The next morning we safely passed Rodriguez Key and marvelled at the tiny airstrip surrounded by water on three sides. There were remains from wrecked aircraft on the fill along the approach end of the strip. I'm not a pilot, but it sure looked like a scary landing.

***

Before I continue, let me put you into that period in the Florida Keys with a story about one night at that airstrip. Misty was out of the water and I was welding a series of stainless steel pad eyes on the rail. It was a South Florida steaming late afternoon. I flipped up my face shield and looked around the 360° view from my spot fifteen feet above the yard.

I noticed five unmarked police cars moving slowly in a line toward the small airport. Two of the cars positioned themselves across the road, completely blocking any possible exit from the airport, then the drivers walked over to the airport to join their police colleagues. The other three cars pulled up to the airstrip, hidden by the big metal building. At least nine agents got out. None wore uniforms but all of them had on flak jackets and badges. They were definitely some kind of Feds.

Almost every sailor and worker in that boatyard was some version of outlaw, pirate, or smuggler, and every one of us could smell that something was up. Kimo joined me on deck with a joint and a couple of cold beers. All the sailors watched a spectacular sunset from various boats out of the water.

The Feds were starting to pace nervously. The evening's entertainment was about to begin.

The airstrip was isolated along the sea by a canal, but there were also a series of canals perpendicular to the airstrip, and each canal was accompanied by an undeveloped parcel of land with a stretch of road. The only access to these roads along the canals was from the highway. So it was more than a mile by road from the airport to the farthest adjacent canal. To get there from the airport road, you had to make a left onto a busy highway U.S. 1, then another left to get to the canals.

Around ten o'clock we all heard the plane. It was a hot,

single-engine turboprop, something like a Mitsubishi, with ultra-bright landing lights blazing. It flew in low, not to the airport, but straight at the canal road farthest from the airport road. The wheels touched down, and the engine was shrieking as the pilot fought to slow his fast (way too fast) aircraft. He was slewing back and forth, inches from careening off either side of the pavement, but finally made it to a stop at the very end of the road. As the pilot turned the plane around three pickup trucks pulled off the highway and up alongside the aircraft.

The Feds never saw this coming. They stood there in the glare of their headlights with their mouths open and blank looks on their faces, probably expecting the plane to crash into a canal, but wasting precious minutes before any of them moved. A few agents hopped into their cars parked at the airstrip, only to lay on their horns when they approached the two Fed vehicles that formed a blockade…now impeding their pursuit! The rest of the agents scattered, a couple of them running to unblock the road, a couple of them running to the edge of the canal, and the rest running who knows where. The lot of them helplessly scurrying about was downright comical.

All of us on the boats in the yard were cheering madly for the smugglers across the canals. It was amazing how fast those guys loaded the trucks then sped away into the night. By the time the Feds made it to the canal road the aircraft was just gaining altitude, headed out to sea.

Wild West? That was the Keys in the 1970s.

A Smuggler's Guide to Fine Dining

***

The first look at Redneck Ralph's boatyard on the canal that ended at the Holiday Inn docks was not a disappointment. I expected funky, and that it was. It had a concrete gantry where the travel lift picked up the boats to move down the yard, where Jimmy, the ex-Vietnam tunnel rat turned yard ape, propped them up with big timbers. Aside from the proper travel lift and haul out gantry, everything else was "au naturel." The canal was just a ditch with sailing boats, in all stages of repair, moored up to the coral rock bank. Rickety planks from the shore provided access to the boats, rafted three deep.

The power supply came from power cords of all lengths, run to various power poles throughout the yard. It was impossible that any of this was legal, but hey, this was the "Conch Republic," where everything was possible for a bribe. Or maybe the county officials were too busy supporting the drug smugglers to bother. During my stint in "Redneck Race Car Ralph's Largoland," the entire Monroe County Sheriff Department, along with most of the Monroe County Commission, were arrested and indicted for smuggling and related crimes. For two weeks there were almost no police in the Florida Keys, except the Highway Patrol.

Before Misty even came out of the water Maria and I became immersed in the local boatyard culture. This wasn't just any old boatyard; it was a veritable sailboat-construction commune.

At some point in recent history, a barbecue grill had

been constructed of concrete blocks and welded steel grills. Every night there was a communal dinner, featuring fresh fish, vegetables, fruits, yogurt, and even ice cream from the nearby Safeway dumpster. The yard apes had the employees from the store trained to put anything good (that was over the sell-by date) into boxes set aside the dumpster.

When the big fishing boat for tourists came into the Holiday Inn dock, a few of us would go over to clean fish. The tourists would pay us to fillet and pack up their catch, and we kept the wonderful pieces of cheek meat and fins to throw on the grill. Every day we collected five to ten pounds of filleted fish, caught just hours before.

This was one of those rare scenarios where a community of inspired individuals were all dedicated to a remarkable lifestyle, and instinctively I jumped right in, like I did in the early days of Haight-Ashbury and the climbing scene at Camp Four in Yosemite. These scenes exist for a short, vibrant flash, then disappear into legend.

We all sat around the barbeque, night after night, trading stories. Unlike many of the small sailing communities I've sown myself into, nobody there was handicapped by fear of the sea. Among this group of long-haired, ocean-going vagabonds were some of the world's most experienced long-distance sailors. None of them cared to be well-known. They were just living on the edge, "doing their own thing." Every argument and story told at dinner contained nuggets of precious information about unknown anchorages in far away places, how to behave in

A Smuggler's Guide to Fine Dining

arcane cultures, where to avoid pirates, navigation tricks, storm management technique, and more. I was in my twenties and had sailed enough to know how much I didn't know. These people really did know. They were mostly couples, and the women were just as proficient as their men, with their own skill sets. Maria fit right in, but she was determined to leave as soon as she got her third of the weed money. No matter how profound this small group of people was, Maria was not about to hang out in a filthy boatyard.

One of the reasons I decided to stop at this boatyard, in particular, was George Bond always going on and on about this genius boatbuilder, Joe Prinz, who lived on a fifty-foot steel schooner he had built in Tarpon Springs, up on the North Florida Gulf Coast. Unfortunately, Joe wasn't around when we arrived. However, there was a tall, dark, very handsome, and talented young farm boy (turned stoner) named Forrest, who was in the boatyard refitting his twenty-eight-foot Herreshoff. Forrest happened to be a good welder as well as a great guy.

Nobody there had a lot of money. They were there, first and foremost, because it was the cheapest do-it-yourself boatyard in South Florida, and because the vagabond lifestyle there attracted a lot of sailors with great expertise. I figured I could hire someone to do the steel working jobs that needed to be done. It looked like we could sell our weed for at least $20,000.

One night, after the evening fish dinner, I asked Forrest if I could hire him to do the fabricating and welding on my boat.

Forrest sighed, "Look, man. Nobody here has time for

Kenny Ranen

(Top) Ranen freeing jammed Halyard on Joe's Dugong.
(Bottom) Kenny in Key Largo boatyard

a big job like what you want. Everyone here has their own big project to finish before they can get back to sailing. But what I will do is make a list of equipment you should buy. I'll teach you how to fix your own boat."

"Seems fair," I answered. "Thanks, Forest. I'll trade you some of that weed we found floating." I could see there were no secrets in that boatyard.

"Don't sell it all. Keep some of it. It's better than money here. Working in the yard is easier when you can bust out a J for the grunt work. Speaking of J's, light one up then let's take that Zodiac of yours out to the reef this evening and grab some lobsters."

A few days later, Maria and I caught a ride up to North Palm Beach where I had parked my 1965 El Camino when we left, seven months ago, for the Bahamas. We drove down to Misty, threw the weed in the bed, covered it with an old inflatable boat, and then drove to Atlanta to sell it. We stayed at my old friend Scott's house. He liked to be on the edge of these things. Scott put us in touch with the guy he bought weed from who took it all. He must have thought we were a gift from the great weed god, Panama Red.

Then I hit the pawn shops with Forrest's list in hand, and bought a Lincoln 220v welder, a big grinder, an entire oxy-acetylene cutting rig with long hoses, a set of torch tips, and a sawzall. At the welding supply store I picked up the other stuff on the list: 200 feet of flexible welding cable, a box of grinding discs, various hammers, welding gloves, a couple of shields, and more. By chance, in the parking lot there was a big three-quarter ton delivery van with a for sale sign, "runs good–best offer." I bought it for $400, loaded everything into it, and drove it down to Key Largo. Maria followed me in the El Camino, and a few days later I dropped her at the Miami airport. Maria had no interest in spending months doing dirty steelwork in a dirty boatyard. As we kissed goodbye she smacked my butt and told me to get Misty back in the water soon.

    Ralph blocked up Misty close to the 220v power supply, and I parked the big tool van close to the boat. Forrest, true to his word, started teaching me to cut and weld. A trip to the scrap yard in Miami yielded a truckload of steel plate, pipe, and piece of heavy H beam, as well as various stainless steel shapes. The H beam, when welded to a truck wheel for a base, made an excellent anvil on the ground between the boat and the van. I used an old mainsail, stretched between Misty and the van, for shade over my makeshift shop. I started by fabricating simple parts. The mooring cleat on the foredeck was the first piece I made after practicing for a few weeks.

    And then, right when I was about to dive headfirst into the brunt of the steelwork, Joe Prins, the legendary outlaw boat builder, showed up in the boatyard, as if right on cue.

    Joe was five years older than I, but seemed much older, maybe because of his prematurely balding red hair. He had suffered a lot of loss in his life, so maybe it was that. 5' 10" and really lean, Joe was a dropout renaissance man with a Minnesota work ethic. Because he was highly organized, my short attention span drove him nuts. His obviously high IQ led him to abstract thought. Often I couldn't follow his explanations, either because he interspersed his very dry sense of humor in with his flow of ideas, or because they involved obscure intellectual analogies.

He enjoyed instructing by criticizing my work. His brilliant but restless mind loved problem-solving. I had a beautiful, thirty-year-old boat with a lot of problems, and he couldn't resist coming up with creative solutions. Forrest had taught me the basics, but Joe refined my techniques, and his rambling discourses revealed time-saving advice. For example, he taught me to let whatever shapes of steel I had collected determine the design and fabrication of my work. He taught me how to fabricate curves, to avoid distorting my work by overheating, but most importantly to avoid building in future problems.

Prins had built himself a steel sailing freighter that he sailed down islands during all seasons. He had that analytical mind and had built his schooner, Dugong, while working under the eye and mentorship of George Sutton, an old revered Florida steel-boat builder in Tarpon Springs.

In the beginning Joe worked on my welding techniques for different types of welding rods and steel, including stainless. I'm pretty sure he didn't like my reckless sailing style and somewhat arrogant attitude. He didn't get that I was into "fake it 'til you make it," and if I admitted to my ignorance I would never have the courage to do all the voyaging that I so wanted to do. The same principle applied to this refit. Joe was a natural builder with a midwest old country work ethic. He just didn't get that I had to fake an attitude to get this monstrous project finished.

Joe gave me the ideas, the knowledge, and the courage to start cutting Misty apart. I cut out windows, the entire cockpit, and the cap rail. To accomplish all this I had to remove most of the interior cabin. After two months of constant work she looked like a chopped-up derelict.

Just at that point, an old friend from Steamboat surprised me by showing up in the boatyard one day. I killed my torch, rolled up a reunion joint, and gave him a grand tour of all the plans I had for "my beautiful sailing boat."

Afterwards he insisted on taking me to the Caribbean Club for a beer. I had no idea he was about to stage an intervention.

When we had our beers in hand and were totally relaxed, he fixed me with a solemn stare and said, "Kenny, that is not a beautiful sailing boat. It is a fucking wreck. I know this is hard to hear right now. I'm sorry I have to say this, but you're not a welder, you're not a shipwright, and you're going to get yourself killed if you ever take that hunk of fucking mangled steel into the ocean. You need to pack up and walk away from that thing."

I was totally focused on my vision of what Misty was going to be. He couldn't possibly see what I was seeing. Then there was the issue of my appearance. Cutting apart a steel boat is filthy work. My work wardrobe consisted of four pairs of white bib overalls, and a pair of army surplus boots. Within minutes of my arrival in the yard, those overalls were various shades of

(Top) Misty "Before"
(Bottom) "In Slings," Misty after Refit

black. By appearances I could have fit right in with any homeless community. I guess I can't blame him for thinking that I was losing it.

All my life I've had people tell me what I'm doing is impossible and doomed to fail. From various smuggling plans, to learning how to rock climb in the Rockies, to learning how to sail the many seas, to writing books. There's always someone, sometimes with good intentions, sometimes out of pure incredulous jealousy, who has insisted that I can't just jump in like I already know what I'm doing.

But jumping right in is all I've ever done.

***

During the year in Key Largo, I became a competent steel fabricator and a pretty good yacht painter. After a few months, I bought a more sophisticated welding machine. It was a Miller DC stick welder and generator. A few years later I used that same generator to build my house in the Rockies, but that's a story for another time.

I was standing in my little open-air shop, staring up at the bow, trying to figure out a way to keep the anchor from slamming into the bow as it came out of the water. Then Forrest, Joe, and Lightning Florida John were all standing beside me. We pitched ideas to each other until we came up with a plan that satisfied us all: I would fabricate a little bowsprit, extending two feet beyond the bow, with stainless steel rails, so the anchor couldn't chip my paint. Bingo! I had the design. Whenever I faced a problem, someone would show up to lend a hand or an idea.

Kimo was my only paid helper, and he lived on a little sailing boat moored in the canal. He wasn't exactly reliable, but at least he was handy. George Bond rented me a bedroom at his tiny house two blocks from the yard while Misty was dismantled.

We all had a lot of fun that year in the boatyard, taking the Zodiacs out for reef diving, lighting bonfires, and partying after the evening meals.

None of the girls in the yard ever wore makeup. None of them needed it. I was attracted to all of them (who wouldn't be), but for my whole stay in "Largo Land" I might as well have been one of the girls as much as one of the guys.

Toward the end of my stay in Key Largo, when Misty was reassembled and ready to sail away, I organized a huge, wholesale, natural food order with Sue Viano (Lightning Florida John's partner) , Forest's sister Ginny, and his partner Connie. "Why don't you all come with me to Miami to pick it up?" I asked the girls. "I'll buy you ladies an elegant lunch at the Galleria. Do any of you have dresses?"

Forest's tall blonde sister glared down at me and said what all the girls were probably thinking, "Fuck you, Ranen. Why don't you do something about that shrub growing out of your head you call a hairstyle? Do you even own anything other than all those filthy overalls? We don't want you embarrassing us."

We had a great day in Miami, arriving at the Galleria

around eleven, and strolling over to Versace just after they opened. The obviously gay salesperson looked up to see three striking, uniquely-stylish women walking in like they owned the store. These girls could have been fashion models except for their sun tans and ultra-buff bodies. They were accompanied by a small guy wearing clean jeans, red high top All Stars, a Jimi Hendrix tee-shirt, and long wild curly hair who promptly (and loudly) asked, "Have you got any wine here?"

A young woman came out of the back, "We've some champagne in the fridge. Will that suit?"

"Perfect," I answered. "Let's look at some outfits." It was our private fashion week in Miami, and my three pals were knockouts on the catwalk. Connie, Sue, and Ginny were really hamming it up in their sexy thousand-dollar dresses. The sales people loved us: their other customers were also drinking champagne, and, infected by our enthusiasm, were buying. Versace was electric that day.

We left the Galleria and drove over to Coconut Grove for lunch. By late afternoon we stopped by the food co-op to pick up our provisions for three boats: sacks of rice, oats, granola, cases of crackers, nuts, and cans of beans. There was a lot. It filled the El Camino's bed.

I moved out of Bond's house. It was time. George and I had become bad for each other. His boat, Restless, was out of the water. We were working but doing a lot of drugs…all kinds of drugs. Anything that came around, and in the Keys those days everything came around. Kimo was an addict, George was an addict, and I was an addict. But my drug of choice wasn't available in the boatyard. You couldn't buy adrenalin in Key Largo. For that I needed to go sailing. George was looking like a ghost, and I had no interest in following George Bond down his suicidal path.

Misty was ready to go. Perfectly white, every detail neat and efficient, six months of food stashed away, all gear onboard, anchors rigged and stowed. She looked good, but she always looked good. Now I knew she was good. I had her name painted as small as I figured was legal on either side of her canoe stern. Her North Carolina registration number was painted even smaller on both sides of the bow.

Maria was still in California, and Kimo was hinting around that he wanted to go to the Bahamas with me. I needed a crew more than ever, now that I hadn't really sailed since we pulled in here a year before (or was it two years before? I smoked so many strange joints, and welded so many steel joints, I can't honestly recall however long it was). The fact was that Kimo and I had been getting too high way too often. I just didn't have it together enough to stay out of trouble. If you're not at the top of your game, there are plenty of ways to wreck a boat between Key Largo and Nassau.

(Top) Misty Ready to Leave. John and Sue Fitting the New Awnings. (Bottom) Kimo Later in Life

CHAPTER 19

CRAWLING AWAY FROM KEY LARGO, 1976

Kimo and I sailed Misty the twenty miles down to Islamorada a couple of days before Christmas just to prove I could get out of Key Largo. We raided the grocery store to secure the last fresh food, motored out to the anchorage off the town, then stowed the Zodiac and the outboard.

With everything stowed for going to sea, I got Kimo started hanking on sails, organizing the various lines, and lashing equipment we wouldn't immediately need on deck. Meanwhile, I covertly searched every millimeter of space in Misty for any form of alcohol. I didn't want Kimo drinking. Kimo was an alcoholic. Thing is, I was a professional sailor that sailed thousands of miles every year regardless of the seasons, and I needed hardcore crew. Kimo fit the bill except when he was drunk or drinking, which in his case were synonymous. I found half a bottle of rum buried in Kimo's gear.

He blinked at me when I stepped onto deck with his bottle, and squawked while I poured it overboard. "Jesus, Ranen! It was for medicinal purposes."

"There's a Bacardi distillery in Nassau, Kimo, but 'til then I need you awake and focused. We're gonna be dodging ships and coral reefs for the next few days. Tonight we'll be crossing the Florida Straits. If we can avoid getting run down by a ship and really stay on top of keeping our course, I believe, in spite of the tricky Gulfstream current, we can make a landfall in Bimini. It's fucking stressful to figure our position if we don't pick up that Bimini light.

"You have the first watch. I'm going to get my head down for a nap. It's eight so wake me when the clock rings eight bells[17]. That's midnight. But I want you to wake me if you even suspect a ship is within our course. I want to make every decision when it comes to avoiding ships. You just don't have the ocean-voyaging experience to make the calls, and we both know you don't like responsibility. So make sure you wake me up. I'll only get mad if you don't wake me." I really drove my points home as I lined Kimo out for his first night watch, because I could tell that all of his focus was still on whether or not he could manage to get a couple drips out of the empty bottle still in my hand.

Over the years, I had absorbed a lot of knowledge from my screw-ups at sea. There was the night when Maria was sleeping below while I was on watch. I had been tracking a small ship crossing in front of us. I watched it closely, because it was really lit up with mast lights and a big spot light. Its port (red) navigation light was showing which meant that it was crossing from my right to my left. I was prepared to pass it astern when I could see its white stern light. Something was nagging my brain about the situation as I closed on his wake. All those lights were in a vertical line on his wheelhouse, three white lights right on top of each other. I yelled down for Maria to bring up the navigation rules book. Misty was really close to passing the stern when I saw a cable spring out of the water in front of us. At that same moment the ship lit a spotlight, and casted the bright white beam onto a huge ship following behind the ship, which I could now see was an ocean-going tug. I barely had the time to turn Misty to starboard away from the deadly cable, which would have stopped us cold so the towed vessel could smash, bury, and sink us.

The point is, Kimo was intelligent and he was arrogant about it. That arrogance made him confident that he could rely on his intelligence instead of deferring to my experience and knowledge. I often had that problem with male crews. The smarter they were, the more likely they were to think they could ignore my orders. So I always slept lightly with Kimo on watch.

Kimo called down to wake me at eight bells, midnight, local time, then crawled into his sleeping bag as soon as I was up and making hot chocolate. I went up on deck, had a look around, read the Walker Log, then went below to put a position on the chart.

The first step was to enter the time and log reading. As I entered the time, I noticed that Kimo had left a long rambling note:

Merry Christmas. I keep seeing a blinking red light, then it becomes a blinking green light. I'm sure it's a Coast Guard chopper following us. IT'S SANTA COPS!

I thought, What the fuck? He's drunk but where did he get the alcohol? I was still a little bewildered by what Kimo could have possibly gotten into while I recorded the new details into the logbook: the time (UTC), compass course and distance covered, which sails were up, wind direction, speed...

...and "drunken prunes" materialized in my mind.

Constipation is a known sailor's curse, because of the lack of vegetables on long voyages. I stocked only whole grains and flours, but that didn't always do the trick. One of my alternative cures was my big pickle jar packed with a pound of prunes and filled with port wine. I immediately looked in the bin and the jar was empty.

Looking down at Kimo passed out on the settee gave me great pleasure. The punishment for the crime was built in. I woke Kimo and laughed, "That buzz is going to cost you, Kimosabe."

Kimo spent his next watch doubled over with diarrhea cramps or hanging over the side with the runs. At least now I knew without a doubt that having Kimo as a day worker and party mate was way different to having him stand watch in the Gulfstream. No real sleeping with Kimo on watch and only a guess what he would get up to in foreign harbors...scary thought.

The following morning Kimo spotted an island on the horizon, but it took us a few hours to get close enough to identify Bimini, one of Ernest Hemmingway's favorite hangouts and the locale of his final novel, Islands in the Stream.

It is more or less a hundred miles from Bimini across the

A Smuggler's Guide to Fine Dining

Great Bahama Bank to Chubb Cay, a small fancy yacht harbor where I chose to clear into the Bahamas. The winds were light so the plan was to sail east from Bimini. Although the Great Bahama Bank has a depth of seven feet (Misty needed only five) there are some sand bars and a few rocky shoals to avoid, so sailing at night was not a smart call. Probably okay, but why take chances? When it got dark, we could just anchor behind a sandbar.

As it turned out, we saw the NW Channel light just as it got dark, and right over there, I figured, was the Chubb Cay light. Why anchor when all we had to do was sail up to it and use the channel markers to get into harbour?

And that's when I made a classic navigation error: navigating by what I thought I was seeing, instead of plotting it all on the chart.

I wonder if I was exhausted from being out of sailing condition, then doing this two day voyage with very little sleep. I was breaking all of my own rules to get into a safe harbor: navigating by sight at night, without a position on the chart, and without keeping a dead reckoning position. I had learned the hard way (by running aground) that what you think you see with your eyes isn't necessarily what you are seeing.

I don't know why, but I was so sure we were heading toward the Chubb Cay beacon that I quit navigating on the chart in anticipation of easily motoring through the clearly marked channel.

Except what I thought was the Chubb Cay light was

actually a light off Andros Island.

As I approached the light that I thought was Chubb Cay, I saw a brief flash of light in the water where Chubb Cay channel should have been, and alarm bells went off in the lizard part of my brain. My conscious mind discounted the clue–convinced myself it wasn't even real–however, my lizard brain correctly identified the foam of a wave breaking in a place where there shouldn't have been water shallow enough to cause even a small wave break.

Without further hesitation I took down the jib, let go the mainsail sheet, slowed to just drift and wait for daylight. Call it intuition, if you like, but I believe in the school of thought that intuition is our unconscious brain collating a lot of information scattered throughout our mental hard drives.

Sure enough, daylight revealed that Misty was just a mile from running aground on the rocks off Joulter Cays, north of Andros Island. I wasn't even looking at the compass! Otherwise I would have surely seen we were sailing in a southerly direction instead of east-northeast toward Chubb Point on Frzer's Hog Cay. It turned out that the Chubb Point light was out. Still, that doesn't excuse my foolish navigation errors.

A wave of nausea swept over me when I finally identified the light I was saling for and put our correct position on the chart. We were minutes away from destroying the boat that I had spent a year or so rebuilding. Minutes from throwing away the thousands of dollars and the months I had spent doing the work. Life before GPS…

A Smuggler's Guide to Fine Dining

* * *

Late afternoon found Misty comfortably moored to a floating dock in the very clean, very fancy Chubb Cay Marina. Within the hour, Bahamian Customs and Immigration saw our yellow "Q" flag, stopped by the boat, and cleared us in. As the two officials walked off the dock, Kimo and I were right behind them on our way to the open-air bar and grill. Kimo ordered a bottle of Tennent's, and I asked for a Coke in a pint glass full of ice.

There were a couple of college girls, probably off Daddy's yacht, having a beer at the bar. I nudged Kimo gently in their direction, hoping to distract him from the wet seductress clutched in his fist, but much to my dismay the only curves he cared about were the curves on his bottles, beer after beer after beer. I guess he was determined to get his blood alcohol level up to his usual .8%. Right then it occured to me that I had never been in a situation where it mattered to me what Kimo got up to. However, now he was signed in as my crew, and under international maritime law I was responsible for him. As in any damages he might commit, debts incurred, and a ticket home if he was expelled.

"Kimo, how about going over to Misty, get the engine started and get her ready to leave. I'll pay the bill and be along in a few."

It must have been more than a few minutes, because Kimo lurched up while I chatted with the girls. "What's up,

Ranen? I untied all the strings and she's ready to go!"

"You drunken asshole!" I mumbled as I sprinted to the dock. There was Misty, floating away. I took a running leap and just got a grip on the rail, feet in the water, did a pull up, and got to the tiller before my little steel sailing boat could gouge one of the super yachts. One scratch on those girls' daddy's ship and we would have to trade the boat, and everything on it, to pay for just the paint job.

Kimo yelled from the dock, "Come around and pick me up, Captain."

"Swim out, you dickhead," I answered. I resolved right then to get him boarded on the first flight out of Nassau.

* * *

I sailed all night down the Northwest Channel to New Providence Island.

By ten the next morning, I shackled my mooring chain to the ancient ship anchor just off the Paradise Island Lighthouse and immediately went below for a few hours of sleep. Kimo was lighting a huge spliff in the cockpit as I disappeared through the forward hatch.

It was still early in the day when Kimo politely woke me by setting up the wind scoop over my head.

"Okay, okay, I'm getting up. Get the outboard on the Zodiac and get her ready for town. We'll need the chain, lock, and a couple of paddles, not the good oars. We can go to the lighthouse for a wash up before we head for town."

Kimo gave me an off look.

"Oh yeah. I forgot you haven't been to Nassau with me before. The lighthouse has an unlimited supply of good fresh water. We can stop back here to change into our city clothes. Who knows, we might get lucky tonight. It's Friday, the cruise ships should be in this afternoon. We can stop by the Chalk's ramp on the way to town and get you booked on the seaplane flight to Miami on Sunday."

Kimo and I hadn't previously discussed his departure date, and if he got belligerent on the topic I was ready as hell to tell him exactly why he was shipping out before the weekend was over. But he was still so stoned he just nodded along with everything I said and got to work on the outboard.

It was sunny and hot on the beach, but not too hot at the lighthouse. We dipped buckets into the big underground water catchments, bathing and washing our hair, then went for a stroll in the blinding sunlight of Paradise Island Beach, looking for tourist girls.

As beaches go, Paradise Island has one of the most spectacular on earth. It's about half a football field wide and sloping down to the bright teal waters of the Northwest Channel. The brilliant white sand has a pink hue because of countless conch shells pulverized by the pounding surf of thousands of storms over the span of thousands of years.

As we strolled, Kimo lightly chatted up a sunbathing beauty who coldly ordered him to "Fuck Off."

The tide was out so I walked near the water's edge, looking for seashells.

Suddenly a vision pulled me from my reveries. There, right before me, abandoned by the previous breaker, was a lone, perfect, shiny helmet conch lying on the wet sand. This was one of those unforgettable moments that explain the attraction to my voyaging lifestyle.

The moment passed. I left the shell where it lay, thankful for the epiphany. "Kimo! Let's head over to Nassau for a couple of rum drinks at the Pirate Cove Bar."

"Good idea, Mon Capitan, but let's stop at the hotel bar over here for a beer. It's happy hour. Maybe they still have some free conch fritters."

"Okay, but one beer," I answered. "I don't want to spend our first night in Nassau at a big hotel full of American tourists. I've got a lot of friends in this town, none of whom are to be found in a Paradise Island hotel bar."

Two days later, I motored over to the seaplane ramp and put Kimo and his cloud of alcohol fumes onto the plane. We had a lot of fun drinking and smoking weed with my friends all over Nassau. The Bahamians loved Kimo, and it was all I could do to pry him out of there.

I was still a little drunk and feeling wasted. Next stop was a local restaurant in Nassau for a big bowl of fish and grits, a classic Bahamian fisherman's hangover breakfast consisting of a clear fish broth with onions, lemon, hot ghost peppers, and big chunks of grouper meat served with a side plate of corn grits swimming in butter and a big chunk of white quick bread.

Maria was slowly making her way back from Santa Cruz. She was probably at least another month away. Meanwhile, I was spending time with young Bahamian guys from the out islands who were into smuggling, diving, and treasure hunting. A lot of us from the boatyard in Key Largo were very connected with our counterparts in the Bahamas.

CHAPTER 20

THE PIRATES AND THE EAST COAST YACHTING ESTABLISHMENT

I was going to need help and didn't know anyone in Marblehead, Massachusetts. For all of his drunken self-destructive behavior, Kimo was capable and knowledgeable. And Kimo was a lot of fun to have as crew. He was never negative. Never, even after a day of grinding steel welds over his head with a heavy grinder or during a gale in the Gulfstream. As I said, he was the only one I could think of for this situation. Having made the decision to hire him, how to find him? No cell phones, no internet, I had to track him down by calling friends, most of whom were also living on boats off the grid. Fortunately, Lightning Florida John had just left Boston for Maine, and Jeffrey had John's phone number there.

John did have an address for Kimo. And surprisingly, it was an address in New York City. Turned out that Kimo's Grandmother lived there. It seemed that Granny was a retired, well-known NYC attorney who was the first woman to graduate from the NYC Law School. She staked him to an apartment in

Greenwich Village. I caught a train to New York the following day.

Somehow the navigation to Kimo's ratty apartment building in The Village did not defeat me, although the NYC subway system did its best. The unlocked entrance to the old building opened into a filthy hallway. No trash, just dingy grey walls and a tile floor that hadn't seen a mop in years. Number 3 was at the end of the hall. I hit the door three times with the side of my fist. The door flew open to reveal a shocked Kimo. "If it ain't the Ferro Ferret! Is Misty in New York?

"No, she's up near Boston. About to go into the yard. They need you in Marblehead. That place is way too straight. They've never seen anything like us." I took a step inside. "You'll love Little Harbor, it's the coolest boatyard ever, it'll be fun. Listen, I'm starving. I haven't eaten today. Let's get a sandwich."

He clipped a massive key collection to his belt.

I asked, "What's with all the keys and junk?

In one fast move he had the clip in his hand and swung the mass of metal against the wall cracking a big chunk of plaster loose. "It's illegal to carry a weapon in New York City, but a set of keys? ...not so much."

Kimo knew right where to go for lunch in New York City, a deli in Little Italy. We had an epic meatball sub with grilled peppers and onions on freshly baked bread and a plate of olives with fresh mozzarella. Blood sugar under control, we headed for Penn Station, stopping by his apartment to pick up all of his worldly goods: a daypack, a National Steel Standard guitar in a soft case, and a pig nose amp.

I was a bit worried about Kimo in the yacht club, but it turned out that the members were more fascinated with Kimo than they were with Ranen. The uptight Boston Brahmins couldn't get enough of Kimo's clever pithy comments on any and every subject that came up at the bar. He came from a sophisticated background and knew where the line was in rarified company. This was the club that refused membership to the Kennedy family. Nevertheless, I made sure that he was out of the club as the line came into view. Kimo knew where that line was, but I didn't totally trust him not to cross it.

Kimo was cheap, but he wasn't free. He had certain requirements. Kimo couldn't just hang out. He required action. Spending an evening reading was not on Kimo's agenda, and this was one of those times when there was a lot going on: there were two hundred pounds of Jamaican weed that needed to be sold. The refit with Hood Sails was feeling like more money than I had anticipated. Finally, life in Marblehead was becoming a kind of roadside attraction now that Kimo was added to the mix. I needed to keep the energy levels high. Kimo's need for action was just the required medicine.

All the while, the clock was ticking. August was half gone. Kimo and I took a couple of guys from the Hood loft out sailing one windy day. For two intense hours they kept us on the move sailing on different courses with different sail combinations. Jess said aloud to no one in particular, "We've got to see this boat out of the water."

They wanted Misty out of the water as soon as possible. Jeff had studied naval architecture at MIT. He was determined to improve our upwind ability by bringing her rigging into the modern world. They needed to measure the entire boat, including the keel. The Hood project had graduated to building a mainsail to fit a new higher aspect rig. New, taller mast and shorter boom. They wanted to get a young genius group of high tech riggers down in Bristol to design the rig. It was time to make some money to pay for all of this.

With that in mind, Kimo and I caught a train up to Kittery, Maine to see Jimmy the dealer. Jimmy had sold the last big load that Jerome, Maria, Jeffery and I brought in, two years before. Jimmy bought this little farm in Maine on the Massachusetts border. It had a big barn with a hayloft perfect for storing bales of weed. Jimmy was a pro. If he agreed to sell the load, I wouldn't have to participate. I could just come up to pick up cash, whenever. Plus, I really liked Jimmy and enjoyed his company.

Just when we got off the connecting bus, Jimmy's Volvo pulled up right next to me. A show-stopping, petite redhead rolled down the window, and a bright smile appeared in a cloud of curly red hair. "You're Ranen. Right? I'm Caroline, Jimmy's wife. Finally...I get to meet the famous Kenny Ranen."

"Hey, Caroline." I got in the front; Kimo in the back. "This is Kimo."

Caroline drove us to the farmhouse. When she got out, I realized that she was pregnant. Women with red hair never need makeup. They already come with all that color, hair, eyebrows, skin–usually with freckles–eye colors, but Caroline had the mom glow thrown in.

Tall thin Jimmy was waiting in the front yard. He kissed Caroline and gave me a huge hug. She headed for the house with Kimo in tow. Jimmy and I walked to the barn. "Jeffrey came by last night with all the weed. His and yours. Why didn't you come to me first?"

"Timmy was there in Jamaica with our friend Jeffrey the dick. Timmy had the contact. Anyway, this way you didn't have to do the unloading. He has a nice boat, perfect for picking up the weed. We needed Timmy for the unloading. It was my good luck he wasn't up to selling it."

Jimmy commented, "Well, their Jamaican loaded some pretty average weed on you guys. At least yours is better than Jeffrey's. I can sell your weed. Not sure about Jeffrey's, but that's not your problem. Is it?"

"Listen Jimmy, is your old Volvo running? I'm gonna need a car."

"Yeah. You can use it for the rest of the summer. That way we'll get to see more of you."

We left after a seafood feast. Caroline and Jimmy were a formidable couple. They had it all going on–a big garden, knew all the local fishermen, not to mention his whole weed sales business.

Life was a lot more intense in Marblehead now that I had Kimo with me. We went to the local restaurants and bars and chatted up every female. Kimo and I were attractive or probably just fascinating. I think these conservative women were intrigued by a couple of guys who lived off the sociological grid. We appeared to live a free life, and maybe we did. We were sleeping with their women; the men must have hated it.

A girl strode up while I was tying up the zodiac late one morning. "I've heard about you. You're Ranen, the guy with the sailboat out there. I'm Gina." Twenty-year-old Gina, uncombed, no makeup, no pretense. "I'm not working today, let's go get some food," she said with a smile in her voice but not on her face.

I can't say why, but I wanted to get closer to this girl. We were close to the same size, which is always a plus for making love. Gina took my hand and led me to a table in a little courtyard behind a small restaurant. We had lunch, and I asked for the check.

Gina slid a piece of paper across the table.

I asked, "What's this?"

She answered, "A check."

The paper had a check mark. "Look, I used to work here. These are my friends. Marblehead is too pricey for us normal people. I rarely have to pay."

Our heads were together laughing at the check. It was the right moment. I kissed her...or she kissed me...we kissed.

"Let's go out to my boat to see how we fit."

Gina answered, "Yes. Let's."

Gina was clearly into me, and we did fit. We made love for a couple of hours, and we were flying with satisfaction.

However, there was a point she didn't want to cross. She was uncomfortable talking about why. I was okay with not crossing her line, and she was sweetly thankful. There are lots of ways to make love.

The dynamic that Gina and I had was a common theme in my life. Younger, somewhat rebellious women were attracted to my lifestyle of dangerous freedom. Even if I didn't talk about smuggling, and, in Marblehead I wasn't talking about it, women like Gina were drawn to the idea (or was it illusion?) of freedom.

Gina took me to her mother's house for dinner. At some point that evening, Mom took me aside and thanked me for being respectful and careful with Gina. I answered. "Why wouldn't I? Gina is one of the best people I've met in ages. We have a lot of fun. I'm crazy about Gina."

Sadly, Gina left town for college soon after. She told me, "Thanks Ranen, for showing me I'm not crazy for thinking the Marblehead people are full of shit. I'm really gonna miss your magical kisses."

A memorable epitaph.

I returned from one of my forays to visit Jimmy in Maine to find that Kimo had a running partner. Karen was a Marblehead girl, born and raised in a working class family. It still amazes me that Kimo could attract a creative, intelligent girl like Karen. He was so wild in every way. Kimo had the ability to connect with all sorts of people, and Karen was not only able to keep up with Kimo but she fit right into the Misty crew. She also had a restraining effect on Kimo, which freed me up to take care of my non-sailing business activities with Jimmy up in Maine.

Jimmy was doing okay selling my weed even though the quality was not that good. From the beginning, I was coming back to Marblehead with much needed cash. We were selling it for about half of what I expected to get for the load, but such is the way the weed business goes. Marijuana is an agricultural product and has all the problems that come with that…quality issues, mold, and shelf life, to name a few.

The switch from Timmy to Jimmy was turning out to be a real break, because I was going to need money immediately to get my mast and sail started. Time was not on my side at that point, and Jimmy had selling weed down to a science. Another perk to having Jimmy was the farm in Maine to recharge away from the boat. Caroline, Jimmy and I had some wonderful feasts on my weekends at that farmhouse in Maine.

CHAPTER 21

HOOD SAILS 1977

Once I had money coming in, I was able to get serious about doing the rigging and sail refit. I went over to the Hood loft to leave Jess a thousand dollar deposit for the new sail. I wanted to make sure I was on their schedule and, equally important, to appear on the rigger's radar. It was time to dive into the elite world of bigtime high tech sailing.

Ted Hood, sailmaker and marine architect, was an icon in the sailing world. When I showed up in Marblehead, he had a lot of irons in a number of fires. He had designed a couple of seventy-foot sailing yachts that were being built in Taiwan. The first was expected at the Little Harbor Boatyard for the final sea tests.

He had won the 1974 America's Cup skippering Courageous. At the time I walked into Hood sails, Ted had sold Courageous to Ted Turner and designed and built another America's Cup boat, Independence. Hood was immersed in rigging and building sails for his new cup challenger. The rivalry between the America's Cup challengers was all anyone in Marblehead Harbor talked about, argued about, even fought about.

I appeared in the middle of all the intense sailing energy going on in Marblehead at Little Harbor and the Hood Sail loft. My timing could not have been better. Robbie Doyle was still Hood's golden boy while we were at Little Harbor. Soon after we left, he jumped ship to work with Ted Turner and beat Hood in the trials. That jump started Doyle Sailmakers and a huge career in sailmaking.

Jess wanted to have Misty out of the water immediately. He was unwilling to start any design until the Hood design team could see and measure the boat out of the water. Kimo and I would need to make a list of repairs and maintenance jobs and start organizing tools for those tasks.

Jess was brusque. "You two pirates have a small window. We've got a lot going on here at the sail loft, designing and building all the sails for the America's Cup Challenge, and we're expecting the new Little Harbor 71 in the yard. So we need to get started on bringing Misty into this decade of sailing technology. Plan on getting the boat out of the water later this week. We all like you guys, but honestly I'm not sure why 'The Boss' let Misty in this yard. Let's just keep your project moving and lend a hand around here when you can."

The next morning, the club manager stopped me coming out of the shower. "I hear you are going to haul Misty at Little Harbor. The Commodore wants to know where you and Kimo are going to sleep while the boat is out of the water. He asked me to offer you one of the rooms upstairs."

"Thanks John, I think I'll take you up on that. I've been so busy organizing everything that I didn't think about where I was gonna sleep. I guess nobody lives onboard at Little Harbor." I was in love with the idea of having "a room at my club," like an old English movie.

We hauled Misty out of the water and got her placed right in front of the sail loft. Jess was there as soon as the boat was blocked and supported, measuring and taking polaroid shots. Kimo and I wasted no time. We had the usual maintenance tasks to do, but our real purpose here was the crucial goal to improve Misty's performance. We got busy making friends at the loft. Making sails is an art. We wanted the people building our sails to have a personal interest in our project.

The Kimo/Ranen dynamic was kicking in. It was haul-out day and Kimo and I were, out of necessity, really wired. I didn't know how good the yard crew was, so we needed to pay attention. Sailing boats are not designed to live on the land.

By ten, Misty was solidly supported and the seaweed and slime pressure washed from the bottom. We were both still wired from too much coffee and excitement. Kimo lashed the ladder to the rail. We got the power cord run to the boat and started digging out the paint rollers and brushes.

At noon I made some peanut butter and jelly sandwiches. Kimo got out his National Steel Standard guitar and his little Pig Nose amp and started ripping out Sister Morphine, playing slide. We were connecting with music, with laughter, and tales of the sea, during the Hood Sails lunch break. Then we all went back to work with a buzz.

I always tried to replace at least one thru-hull fitting and valve during every haul out. When these fittings that are below the waterline fail, boats sink. There were also a lot of other tasks that had to be done with the boat out of the water, like replacing the zinc anodes and the shaft cutless bearing.

Kimo and I worked all day, but everyday at lunch and every afternoon at 4:50 Kimo got out the National Steel and played. The sailmakers came by and grabbed beer out of our cooler. Often we all passed around a joint and talked about sailing and voyaging. These get-togethers usually only lasted half an hour, but on Friday and Saturday they went on til the late summer sunset.

The Hood loft was full of young, very cool, intelligent energy. We fit right in. Everyone working at Hood recognized I was living a lifestyle to which they all aspired. They knew I was a weed smuggler and that I needed their sail technology to pull it off. All of them were becoming my smuggling partners and enjoying it. That first day in the yard blew open Pandora's box.

Jess actually said to me, "Listen, numbers on your sail comes with the deal, but you can put anything on it. The team wants to put a big skull and crossbones on the main." I was tempted but in the end, I declined.

Jess came by for a coffee meeting about our project, which seemed to be growing now that the design team had a handle on the keel configuration. There wasn't anything that could be remedied in Misty's antiquated keel design, but fortunately the mast was stepped on deck in the best possible position. The builders were right at the pinnacle of 1930's yacht design. What we could do was give her a taller mast and shorter boom, putting the center of effort up high where the air was clearer. The new main would be more efficient and more powerful.

Hood was talking to Eric Hall who had started Hall Spars down in Bristol with a couple of young rigging technocrats. Eric's second-in-command rigger, Phil Garland, came up to Marblehead to talk about rigging a new Little Harbor 70'. While he was at the loft, Jess and he put their heads together about Misty's new mast and boom.

It was a lot of fun to hang out in the elite racing/sailing scene. In the years that followed, I connected with that scene. Once in Nassau, another time in Palma de Mallorca. It was a hard-partying crowd. The sailors, tactitions, and most of the captains were professionals, and for the most part gave me the respect due a colleague. The owners and backers, not so much. The money guys were wealthy egomaniacs, in it for the fame and bragging rights.

A few days after my conference with Phil, Jess told me the rig design came from Hall Spars. There were some sail design conferences. We talked about how deep I wanted the reefs. It was helpful that I had been sailing Misty for a few years and thousands of miles before drifting into Marblehead to work with the big boys. In fact, I had put together the rigging we were replacing. So not only did I know what didn't work, but

A Smuggler's Guide to Fine Dining

I also knew what did. So when they asked about the reefs, I had a firm handle on how I sailed and at what point Misty was overpowered. We settled on three reefs, one very shallow, the second medium, and the third super deep for heaving to or to keep the boat moving in strong winds and huge seas.

Long distance sailing is all about consistently getting the most out of your boat. Too much sail upwind overpowers the boat, actually slowing the boat down. Obviously too little sail area underpowers the boat. Moitessier, the French single hander, was a proponent of keeping the boat moving in heavy weather. That deep third reef would provide just enough sail area to keep Misty moving, mostly under control, on big waves.

The party in the boatyard became a regular thing every lunch and every day after work. Mainly it was the younger loft crewmembers who showed up for beer, chips and rock music, but Robbie and Jess would stop by as well. When the big Little Harbor 70 showed up, the action out in the yard ramped up. The delivery crew were young sailors ready to get high and cut loose after the delivery voyage.

Hood and Doyle were down on the tarmac looking at the hull. Kimo and I volunteered to clear out the galley. I was on deck sorting out any provisions we could use when I spotted three cans of spray whipped cream. I loudly exclaimed, "Ready Whip!" and inhaled some of the nitrous propellant gas. "Anybody want some?"

The delivery captain said, "Sure. I'll have a hit." And he took a hit.

Doyle looked up and held up a hand to catch the spray can.

Ted Hood, looking a bit shocked, remarked, "I don't believe this." He didn't partake.

With the help of the delivery crew, the lunch party got serious. Kimo and the captain went for pizzas and more beer. It was Friday and when the sail makers came out Kimo turned up the volume. Everyone was drinking, eating pizza, and smoking joints. Friends were showing up from around town, and we were all getting high and dancing. Pretty amazing for Marblehead!

Allison, the loft boss, walked up, beer in hand, "Your sail design hit first layout today, but Jess and I think you might like to wait until the America's Cup cloth comes in. Nobody will notice if we use some of it for your mainsail."

"Oh yeah. I'll wait. Anyway, I won't be able to use it until after I sail Misty down to Bristol for the new rig. The new sails won't fit the old mast."

She answered, "Don't worry Ranen, we know you have to get out of here before the winter storms. But if you get caught, I promise your sails won't let you down. I'm sure Hall Spars will say the same. As soon as the cloth arrives we'll build your mainsail. We all saw Misty's sail plan, and everyone thinks you should also let us build you a heavy weather genoa. These sails are gonna be bulletproof!"

"Okay Alli, put it on the list."

Kimo was off with Karen every evening after the party. I stayed to put the tools away and meditate on what Allison told me. I walked down the quiet waterfront street toward a bar to get a drink and a burger.

A cop was writing a parking ticket as Kimo and Karen approached. I could see that Kimo was more than a little drunk. He shouted toward the cop, "Leave that car alone. The car was framed!"

The cop was quite pleased that he had someone to arrest on a boring night.

Karen gave me a ride over to the police station. The cop had already put Kimo into the lockup in the back. I asked the cop, "I know you saw me and that you knew he is crew on my boat, so why in the hell didn't you let me take him home?" I was visibly angry and shouting at him. That was when he arrested me for interfering with an officer of the law.

None of this was going the way I thought it should go. This young policeman clearly had a problem with us. I was thinking that I had misread the situation. Keep your mouth shut, Ranen. Maybe this guy doesn't like a couple of out of town hippies running with the local girls. Anything you say now is only going to make things worse.

He escorted me into the back of the station. Kimo came to the cell door. "Great that you're here to get me out, Ranen. Wait, what's going on?" I walked through the metal door into the cell.

"I don't suppose you've got a couple of get out of jail free cards, cuz that fucking cop arrested me as well. I'm surprised he didn't arrest Karen. I REALLY hate cops."

Kimo didn't answer. He was already asleep on the hard wooden bench. Unfortunately, I wasn't drunk enough to be comfortable. Nothing to do but wait for morning.

I wasn't worried, just annoyed. Hours and hours went by. There was no window in the little fifteen-foot square cell, only two benches and a metal toilet with no seat. A different cop came up and opened the door. He waved me out, "You're free to go."

I walked to the front desk.

Jess was waiting. He laughed, "I'm not sure if getting you out of jail is on the Hood list of services. I didn't check. Anyway, they're not charging you. Kimo had a half smoked joint in his pocket, but they're only charging him with being drunk and disorderly. Let's get out of here. Allison is meeting us. You owe us a big breakfast. Kimo has to wait until the Justice of the Peace shows up. Sounds like he really pissed off a cop last night. Let's go, Alli is waiting."

Kimo had to wait for another day to see the judge. Karen brought him sandwiches at the lockup. The judge fined him two hundred dollars and sentenced him to time served. As I said, Kimo couldn't keep his mouth shut when he was drinking. He was one of those who had inherited the gene that allowed his body to keep drinking and functioning way beyond the point at which everyone else becomes violently ill or passes out.

Problems with alcohol were a plague throughout my career. I needed sophisticated crew, and as my boats got bigger and my voyages longer, that need became more crucial. The fly in the honey was that anyone good enough to keep up with all the nuances of my smuggling program would normally have their own boat. So, it always turned out that guys like Kimo had problems with drugs and or alcohol. Addicts were really good at convincing me that they had it all under control. I couldn't resist believing in them, and they always were a disappointment with all of their fuckups in my wake.

What a week. Caroline left a message not to come up.

I called the number she left. "The feds raided the farm and found a ton of weed in the barn."

This came as a shock. "Jesus, Caroline, you have a child coming. What are you going to do? Have you got money?"

"Listen up, Kenny, don't even think of getting involved. The DEA doesn't know you exist. It would get worse for all of us if you get on their radar. Jeffrey won't come near us, but you want to help; I can hear it in your voice. Stay out of it. I have plenty of money and a great lawyer. My sister is here to help. Jimmy and I both really love you. I only called to warn you to stay away."

Jimmy wasn't going to give me up. I never, even for a moment, considered that. I was pretty sure that Timmy would have. I was mostly paid up, so I was lucky on this one. I could have been up there when it all came down, in which case I wouldn't be living it up in Marblehead. I would be in a federal prison with a grim future. A sobering thought. Fuck Ranen, you dodged a bullet. Smoke a joint and let it go. There's nothing you can do.

Now I was really ready to keep moving. Misty was ready to go in the water. All that was left were the sails.

The following Friday after work, I ordered four large pizzas, expecting the usual party animals from the sail loft and boatyard. This time everybody from Hood was there. Everyone. Misty's sound system was blasting some George Clinton.

More and more sailors were arriving. Allison and Doyle came up, each carrying a sail. Someone threw down a big piece of canvas on the tarmac. Allison unfolded the new mainsail. Jess pulled out a marker and signed near the tack: "To Ranen from Hood Sails." Everyone signed. Ted Hood stopped by to sign and drink a beer. As he signed he said, "I'm not sure how a hippy managed to get one of the best sails to come out of this loft, but good luck, Ranen. You'll need it, I'm sure."

Jess waxed sentimental, "Thanks, Ranen. All of us have really enjoyed having you and Kimo. It's been a lot of fun working with the Misty crew."

Allison signed the sail and produced a small sail bag. "Here are some goodies from all of us." She dumped out the bag onto the sail. A spool of waxed Dacron hand sewing thread, a packet of different color spinnaker cloth scraps for making flags, a packet of needles, and a well-used but serviceable leather palm tumbled out. There were a lot of high fives and hugs as the signing went on. I always have an impact. I like to think a positive one.

CHAPTER 22

RHODE ISLAND

We were gone that afternoon. Now that I had the new sail, I was dying to see it up. Hall Spars were organizing our rig and were expecting us. Kimo and I were loving sailing again. We had a fair wind for the Cape Cod Canal. We anchored near the entrance to the canal and were up early the next day. The engine didn't want to start. I managed to get the old Lister diesel going after cranking til my arm was ready to fall off. Still, the engine just wasn't running strong. We stopped at some village on the canal to call Phil at Hall. He found a Lister dealer in a town, not too far from Bristol. Hall wasn't ready for us for another week anyway. I called the company in Fall River which sold and serviced generators for commercial fishing boats. They were happy to rebuild Misty's little engine and they even had all the parts on hand. Apparently, the two cylinder Lister was still in use.

So we sailed up the Sakonnet passage to Fall River, a small blue collar industrial city on the Massachusetts Rhode Island border.

"Wow!" I commented. "There's a shitload of fishing trawlers in this harbor, and not one sailing boat. Fall River really is the exact opposite of Marblehead. We can anchor wherever we want. Let's drop the hook over by the fishing fleet and see if we can find a cafe for lunch. I'm not ready to pull out the engine. We can find the Lister dealer while we're in town. They specialize in marine generators. They must be on the waterfront."

We were already towing the dinghy. Kimo dropped the outboard on, and we were off to town. I tied the Zodiac to the closest wharf and when we climbed up to the street, there was our engine shop. There was no showroom or front office, just a machine shop with engines and gensets around. The boss was willing to either rebuild my engine, which was built in the 1940s, or he would sell us a slightly used, much newer and higher horsepower model for a really low price. Still hand crank, it would bolt right on the same mounts and the old shaft mount would fit.

"Pull alongside the wharf tomorrow morning, and we'll switch out the engines with our crane. I'll keep your engine for an antique." These guys had an industrial sentimentality.

We found a workingman's diner right around the corner. Kimo spotted some dock workers heading for the door of an ancient brick building hidden between a couple of old factories with broken windows. No name. The sign just said FOOD. We walked through a door straight into the 1950's. Slightly rusted chrome tables with aquamarine laminate tops and an assortment of not quite matching chairs.

Our waitress was a wiry older woman. She had freckles. Curly auburn hair was escaping everywhere from a couple of chopsticks struggling to keep it all contained on top of her head. She looked me directly in the eye and said with a strong Boston accent, "Hahya, Ahm Ahleen. You guys need to have the meatloaf. It comes with wicked good mash potatoes."

The food came and it was good.

For some reason, I was really attracted to Arlene. She had to have had thirty years on me, but I was always magnetized by skinny, flat-chested women. My eyes kept drifting to the freckles revealed where the top three buttons of her uniform were undone. I took a leap, "We just sailed in on my sailboat for a couple of days. You want to go have a beer with us after work?

"Okay. I'm gonna bring a friend Kimo heah is gonna love. I get off at nine. Meet us at that bah two blocks down around ten."

Kimo and I tied up the Zodiac right across the street from the bar. It was a workingman's bar but not a redneck hangout. We weren't the only longhairs there. Bob Seeger was playing on the sound system. I ordered a couple of long-necked Buds. We were into our second beer when Arlene appeared in a mini-skirt and tee-shirt trimmed in sequins. She had a cute, early twenties brunette in tow. Suzy was also a waitress at "FOOD," but these girls were dressed for a night on the town.

Arlene was charming. She had charisma and didn't miss an opportunity to touch me. Suzy was fascinated by Kimo. I always wondered what women saw in him. Maybe he exuded a potential for wild sexuality. Whatever it was, she was buying it. A shot of tequila and we were off to a bar that had a band.

Another bar in an empty factory. Loud guitars and a strong drum beat, perfect for dancing and drinking. Arlene and I were kissing on the dance floor. I was flattered that an older woman was attracted to me. Finally, I couldn't wait anymore. I was physically aching to get her into my bunk.

Arlene's lips were touching my ear. "Suzy's takin' Kimo home with her. I want to go to yoah boat."

As we walked out the door, the bouncers were a bit nasty, almost aggressive. "Ahleen likes young guys. Hey hippy, get her to take out her teeth for ya."

But I was okay with being seduced by an older woman. We walked onto the foggy, deserted waterfront. A couple of drunks arm-in-arm, I stopped now and again to embrace her hard slim body. She responded with passionate kisses. Her lips were red-hot. I thought, I don't care if I have bruises on my neck tomorrow, this is lighting me up!

The tide was out and Arlene was unsure about climbing down the concrete wharf to the dinghy. I went first and coaxed and coached her from below. Her high heels didn't help. In the end, she let go and we fell, laughing, in a heap onto the wooden floorboards.

Getting out of the dinghy and on to Misty was easier. Arlene took off her shoes and Misty was really low to the water. Without her heels it was all much easier. I could see from the look on her face that Arlene didn't have a clue that there was actually a place to live on the little boat. She tentatively followed me down the companionway ladder into the cabin. "Theah's a little house down here," she whispered in surprise, and in the same moment jumped me.

I think she wasn't sure whether to devour me or fuck me. We were driving down a mountain with no brakes. And she was so strong. That skinny body gripped me like a vice, unable to get enough of me.

We awakened early with a smile and the sun on our faces. I got out of the bunk and made us coffee. Kimo and I had an appointment to get a new engine. I handed Arlene a steaming cup and asked, "Do you mind helping me tie up to the wharf by that crane there?"

"Sure, if you tell me what to do," she answered.

The engine reluctantly started. I got the dock lines and fenders out and set up, then went to pull up the anchor. We approached the concrete wharf. I could see Kimo waiting to catch a line. Arlene must have been from a seafaring family, because she coiled up the dock line and tossed it up to Kimo. While our focus was preparing for the crane to pull our little engine, my sassy middle-age waitress climbed up the wall's rusty rungs into the recesses of my long-term memory...forgotten until now, when she emerges here, just as she was then.

I had come to appreciate the yankee work ethic. The two "old" guys, who were probably in their forties, that ran the marine generator shop got busy. Kimo and I just barely got the companionway ladder and engine cover moved before they stormed aboard. In the end it took longer to pay the bill than it did for them to switch out the engines. They connected the cooling hoses and the fuel lines and cranked the engine. It started instantly.

"This little engine is exactly the same as your antique, except for a better injection system, and a few more horsepower as well." He pointed up at the old engine. "It was a perfect design. This one lasted over thirty years. I'm guessing no one ever had to do any maintenance."

"Wow. It's only noon, we should be able to get to Bristol before dark, right?" I wondered aloud.

Kimo answered, "Let's get out of here. Suzy was fun, but I'm not sure I want to do that again. Sounds like you're there, too."

"Yeah, I'm sure Arlene doesn't see me as a keeper. But what about you? Are you thinking about going back to New York?"

"I am…thinking about that. I'm also thinking about going back to Marblehead. I guess I'll decide when I get to the train station."

"Okay. Let's head down to Bristol and find a place for Misty. I think it's time for Maria to come back."

I had serious mixed feelings about calling Maria. I needed her on a cellular level. Sex between us was somehow beyond mere physical attraction. Maria was so powerfully charismatic, and she was fearless as well as impossibly strong. The thing was, I knew that she wasn't good for me on an emotional level. On the other hand, Maria was the perfect smuggling partner. She had already killed that Colombian to save my life.

But like an addict, I knew we were intrinsically bonded. So who was I kidding? I missed her. I needed her skills, courage, and her company. That we had a lot of fun together was something I missed. Camaraderie is a thing. We always remember and miss the good things and tend to forget the bad. In any case, in the choice between Kimo and Maria, Kimo was the long-distance second choice. Kimo knew it and was okay with it. Whatever could be said about Kimo, he was well aware of who he was. Kimo was okay with who he was.

Hall Spars used the Sakonnet Marine boatyard to step masts. We anchored just out of clear view of the marina. Misty didn't have a toilet. No place for a head on a small thirty-foot boat, so bad manners to be close enough to include the public in our open bath arrangement.

I took Kimo to shore with his duffle and guitar, and a pocket full of cash. I had no idea when Maria was going to show. There was an open ticket waiting for her in San Francisco.

This solitary lull provided an opportunity to connect with Phil Garland who was my project manager at Hall Spars. He was close to my age and kind of an undercover dropout. These guys at Hall were building expensive, cutting edge, yacht rigging and needed to appear respectable and responsible.

I was upfront about why I wanted and needed a "hurricane-proof" rig, a discussion that proved to be fortuitous a couple of months down the road. As soon as he got that I was a long distance sailor/smuggler he was hooked. Phil was not in it for the ego like many of the high tech racing sailors. He was a serious sailor and very grounded. I got the sense that he may have done a run or two, but we never went there. As different as we were, Phil must have enjoyed my company, because he took me with him wherever he went during those weeks.

There was a lot of boat building in the area and Phil took me around to see what was going on. We stopped into Eric Goetz's shop to get a look at cutting edge sailing boat construction. This was a gift from Phil. Whether intended or not, I was getting an education as a way for me to focus on what was needed for the new rig. We talked about the all-important details: terminals for the rigging wire, replaceable Staylocs or more permanent swaged fittings, jiffy reefing systems, and how to avoid corrosion on the base of the mast.

Phil was married but no children yet. I often had dinner with him and his wife Caroll. Once again the coastal subculture support was there for a sailor.

More and more, I was certain that Phil was a member of the "Smuggler Brotherhood," mostly because he understood why it was crucial that we were configuring the rigging for single-handing Misty. He added mast hardware like hooks and stoppers so whoever was on watch could reef quickly without waking anyone up or changing course.

That voyage from Jamaica had me thinking I was a knowledgeable sailor. Working with Phil Garland put all that to rest. Phil really did know. The mast was ready. It was heavier gauge aluminum, a foot taller than the old wooden mast. The double spreaders were gone. The new masthead was fitted with

A Smuggler's Guide to Fine Dining

a tricolor light, a bright strobe, and a highly visible wind vane. I took the opportunity to watch and learn how to assemble the rigging terminals as well as Hall Spar's technique to achieve proper tension on the mast rigging.

CHAPTER 23

STORM

Maria was on her way. I took Phil's car to pick her up at the airport in Hartford. God! I was dizzy at my first look at Maria who appeared amongst the weary passengers headed for the gate. She was tan with two long braids, sun-bleached from days at the Beach in Santa Cruz. Just looking at her had my heart racing.

Every head turned toward the carefree girl with a radiant smile who was intently striding toward an embrace. At some level, everyone waiting in arrivals, both men and women, was fantasizing it was them. I never knew how it would go with Maria, but there she was, and we were fiercely locked in a kiss that had us spinning away.

We were into mid-November when we finally stepped the mast, and there was plenty to do before we left. Fortunately, Phil's wife Caroll took to Maria. Women either really liked her or were totally put off by her. She was a strong, independent woman during a period when our culture was changing. The women who weren't prepared to give up their traditional roles were resentful toward adventurous, free-spirited girls like Maria.

Caroll went out of her way to help Maria get us organized to leave. Fall was almost gone, and the temperatures were dropping. I was busy with the rigging and organizing gear. Maria was buried in "the book of lists," cataloguing the ship's stores to make sure we left the first-world with a full complement of peanut butter, evaporated milk, and toilet paper.

It had been a busy summer and when I looked around I could see that winter was upon us. Living on a boat in the New England winter was not a possibility. One of my main excuses for not leaving was waiting out hurricane season, but even though there had been a recorded hurricane every month of the year, the generally accepted end of hurricane season was November first, now long past. However, we had accepted an invitation from Phil and Caroll for Thanksgiving dinner.

I guess I was stalling. All I knew was that we needed to sail south…away from winter. Thing is I had no idea where to go next. I felt compelled to make some money to replace what I spent on sails and rigging. I just didn't have an inspiration. It was my policy not to do any illegal business until or unless I was inspired to do it, unless "it felt good." To ignore that policy was to court the possibility of falling into the clutches of some government or another.

The temperatures were around thirty every night. One morning when hot coffee with chocolate didn't help, and I had to run the engine to warm up the boat, Maria said, "I don't even have a warm coat. It feels like Telluride. And by the way, we are not geared up to go to sea like this. What if it fucking snows? If we hit a storm, it's gonna be a snowstorm!"

We had wool sweaters and jeans but no winter boots or

coats. My only shoes were my All Stars and flip flops. It looked like we were going to need winter gear. There was a K-Mart nearby where we bought foam-insulated "Moon Boots" that actually appeared to be waterproof. We also bought cheap warm jackets, socks and gloves.

"Let's move the boat closer to the ocean. Like down to Newport," Maria said over coffee. "As far as provisions go, I'm ready. The book is up to date."

"You're right. If we're in a marina in Newport, we can stow the outboard, lash down the Zodiac, and secure the anchors for sea. We'll fill the water and diesel tanks right at the marina. Phil and Caroll will give us a ride down there after Thanksgiving. All we'll have to do is put away the dock lines and hoist the sails. We can be on our way south within an hour."

We had a homey but elegant Thanksgiving dinner with the Garlands, spent the night with them, and got a ride down to the boat the next day. Even though we were ready to leave, Maria and I were reluctant to force ourselves into "going-to-sea-torture mode."

I was monitoring the weather from NOAA marine HF radio broadcasts as well as Coast Guard weather reports over our new VHF ship-to-ship radio. There was a cold front on its way, but it looked like it was at least five days out. It appeared as if we would be well on our way south when it got here. Anyway, it wasn't a deep low pressure system.

We splurged on a good dinner at the Black Pearl, an iconic sailor bar and expensive restaurant just across from the boat. Over her broiled cod Maria asked, "What's next? Where are we going next? Look. I know we're leaving, but we're going to need a course to steer. So? Where are we going?"

"I'm inclined to go to Provo and see if we can pick up a load of something. It's a good place to hang out until something turns up. We've got enough money to coast for a while. We're ready. Let's leave in the morning."

Eight a.m. came with mugs of steaming coffee and chocolate in hand, frost on the deck and moon boots on our feet, and we cast off. By noon we were well away from the land with winds from the NE and our new brilliantly white mainsail and medium genoa drawing well, propelling us toward warmer weather. But it sure as hell wasn't warm yet.

I was pushing to get east across the Gulfstream before a nor'easter could catch us. Storms in the Gulfstream are bad news for a couple of reasons. First of all, that river of warm water flowing north in the Atlantic Ocean increases the storm's wind speed. So a force 5 nor'easter becomes a force 6 in the Stream. On top of that, when a strong northerly wind opposes the Gulfstream's four-knot current, the sea kind of piles up, creating enormous, dangerously steep waves. I'd learned a few things smuggling along the East Coast all those years. Among them was to avoid the Gulfstream unless I needed to ride the current north, and we were headed south.

My watch the first night was cold, but with all my new clothing, and my "moon boots" I was not uncomfortable. The seawater was not freezing on the decks. Salt water freezes at a lower temperature than freshwater. In the hour before sunrise, it was so cold that all the canvas was covered in frost. However, Misty was sailing noticeably better with the new sails and rig, and that brightened my attitude.

It was cold enough that I didn't put out a fishing line, because I didn't feel like cleaning fish. Maria and I just hunkered down to the task at hand. We were making and eating a lot of comfort food. Maria's mac-n-cheese and my potato salad were on the menu. We were working hard and it was cold, which was why we were craving high calorie, high protein food. We were already into one of the big rounds of cheddar that were wrapped in vinegar and soaked rags in the bilge. Grilled cheese sandwiches hit the spot on lonely late night watches.

The weak northern winter sun was good to brighten the day but provided little warmth. It was good to crawl into a warm, Maria-scented bunk after a chilling watch. We were hard pressed sailing in the winter, and this was the extent of our intimacy. Yet, everything about sailing in these harsh conditions in our small vessel was intimate, especially getting into her warm, recently deserted bunk.

There were no stars on the fourth night. It felt like it might rain so I put the second reef in the main. I was on watch when morning came, revealing dark clouds. The wind was strong out of the northeast. Then came, not rain, but driving snow. Misty was really heeling to the point that solid water was sweeping the deck from behind. We were overpowered. I had waited too long to change to a working jib.

Maria was on deck in a flash.

"Get that halyard loose," I shouted, running to the bow and struggling to pull the genoa down and gather it up on deck.

We were flying off the wind and I sure as hell didn't want to drag that big sail out of the sea. Or worse if it disappeared under the boat, drag it out from under the keel. We each had two pairs of wool gloves, but they made it difficult to operate the snap shackles that clipped the sails to the forestay. Furthermore, changing sails in these conditions was very wet work with the sea running down the decks, sometimes a foot deep. So, no gloves for changing sails. Cold hands. Fuck it, just like ice climbing, I thought.

The good side of the bad weather was that we were heading south by east as fast as Misty could sail with the Gulfstream far behind us. Still, NOAA weather was calling for a cold front from the northwest heading for our neighborhood. It didn't seem to be a deep low-pressure system. I tried to draw out the isobars on the chart, but I was confused by what seemed to be another low-pressure system coming from the south. So far, there were no storm warnings for our sector of the Atlantic. There were only warnings for Nova Scotia, a thousand miles away. I figured that my somewhat sketchy weather analysis must be making me paranoid.

Just imagine us sailing at full speed out in the mid-Atlantic winter, wondering what the wind gods were cooking. Those were the early days of weather forecasting using supercomputers. Still, weather reporting was way better than previous decades.

The understanding of the effects of global warming was in its infancy. Even if the NOAA forecasters knew about the effects of the El Niño, they weren't talking about it. There were fewer weather satellites, and interpretation of their data was much less sophisticated than now. The global weather models that the big Cray computers used still didn't include scenarios that hadn't been recorded before.

In the 1970s, the latest scientific information was unavailable to me. Maybe the weather forecasters had a better understanding of climate change weather than I knew of. However that information didn't show up in their forecasts during this voyage.

I sure as hell didn't know from looking at my crude hand-drawn isobar chart that we were sailing into the first "perfect storm" of the twentieth century. Two moderate weather systems colliding in the North Atlantic Ocean. Actually, the southern low-pressure system was deepening into a tropical storm…so not so moderate. I guess the geeks at NOAA somehow overlooked it, way out there where nobody was watching.

That snowstorm passed, but it was still cold. We were getting accustomed to being wet and cold while maintaining our sense of humor. The wind was picking up from the west. I wondered about that, because usually a west wind means a low-pressure system is coming. So far, NOAA was not broadcasting any warnings, but the barometer was beginning to move.

Still baking bread, positive attitude, no complaints, Maria

was a trooper. Good thing, because high fast-moving clouds streaming from the northwest were telling me a story not even hinted at in the weather report. Nevertheless, I wasn't worried. After all, I was sailing Misty, the ultimate unsinkable, bombproof deep ocean vessel. Furthermore, when I look back to write these stories, it becomes obvious that part of our attraction to this lifestyle was the buzz. We liked the storms. 5.14[18] sailing.

    Pretty soon those clouds started piling up and the wind was picking up as well. But still no mention of any major weather on Notice to Mariners. This weather system was developing so slowly that we were barely aware that conditions were deteriorating. Maria and I were only thinking about staying warm and sailing the boat. Misty had been at her max speed now for two days, we were down to three reefs, and the barometer was steadily falling. We were eating up the miles in a southerly direction and just like that, I was no longer struggling to stay warm. Still wearing my moon boots though.

    "This front seems pretty strong, Ranen," Maria commented when I came on watch. "Maybe you should put up the high-cut working genoa. I don't think she's ever made 120 miles in one day before. And the wind is still picking up. It's gotta be force 7, maybe 8[19]."

    The wind was still northeasterly and getting stronger but just barely. Definitely force 8. I wasn't questioning the weather yet. We were under control with three reefs in our new

---

18 5.14 In rock climbing. This classification for a climb would indicate great difficulty.

bulletproof main and a high cut genoa.

Maria was concerned. I saw her tap the barometer and then she started baking bread and cooking up storm food to last for a few days. The next morning there was a full pressure cooker of red beans, rice and ham, three loaves of bread and a pan of corn muffins. The swells, marching down on us from the northwest, were big with white caps. So far, not steep enough to overcome the wind vane steering.

Maria and I switched into storm mentality. Not a big difference, we were just more serious. No flirting and joking, just sleep, eat, and steer. The weather was creeping up on us and still no weather warnings, even when I was thinking about digging out the storm jib tucked away in the forward cabin. There we were, inches above the surface of the sea, and the wind was still picking up.

The waves were now larger and northeasterly with a conflicting swell coming up from the south causing a confused sea state. At this point, the motion down below on Misty was uncomfortable, even boiling water became a chore. She was rolling and slamming, making standing at the stove or, for that matter standing at all, difficult. And the barometer continued to drop.

Another half day of confused seas and Misty was still lurching south. Then the wind really picked up from the east to a strong force 8, gale force wind. I think at this point the tropical storm coming up from the south and the big northeastern low-pressure system were about to collide. However, it was only later when the storm became famous that I could put this together. At the time I had no idea what was going on with the wind gods.

I had sailed in winds this strong, but this storm was all over the place. We weren't making any distance with the waves coming from everywhere. Finally, I just got weary fighting to make headway. I sheeted in the triple-reefed main flat and took down the jib. The effect was to keep Misty headed into the wind while stopping the forward motion. We were heaved to.

Around noon the following day a huge container ship came into view, bearing the company name in letters at least three meters high along the length of her hull. Now the new VHF ship-to-ship radio justified the cost. I picked the mic off its hook and called out, "Nedlloyd container ship headed northwest, this is sailing vessel Misty one mile off your starboard bow. Please respond, channel 16."

"Good Afternoon, this is Nedlloyd container ship Adelaide, switching and answering channel 10."

"Adelaide, this is SV Misty. I've been trying to make headway in increasingly bad weather for a few days. Do you have any local weather reporting, because in spite of being heaved to for twenty-four hours, NOAA weather is calling for moderate seas from the northwest?"

"Misty, standby. I'll fetch a recent local weather update. We have also been seeing some unexpected storm activity."

"Misty, standing by channel 10."

"Misty, this is Nedlloyd Adelaide. I've got the weather you wanted, but first, may I inquire how many souls are aboard your vessel?"

"What? How many souls? I really don't like that question. Let's go straight to the weather report. Over."

"Adelaide to Misty. Listen mate, this is only the far edge of this system. You won't be feeling the full force of this storm for another thirty-six hours. You're going to see force nine or ten winds and commensurate waves. It is our company's policy to enter this conversation in our log during a serious storm. Do you want us to inform the U.S. Coast Guard that you are out here?"

"Misty to Adelaide. Thank you, but no. We don't need the Coast Guard, and we expect the same. Misty was built for this sort of weather. We're gonna be uncomfortable, but we are going to sail out the other side of this storm, wherever it is. And... thanks for the warning. Have a safe voyage. This is sailing vessel Misty out."

The disembodied voice from the ship answered, "Good luck and safe voyage. Nedlloyd Adelaide out."

We were alone again...far out in the Atlantic Ocean, facing a big storm.

I turned to Maria, who'd come below during the exchange with the ship. "Did you hear him ask how many "souls" we had aboard? He doesn't know this boat is bulletproof."

Maria answered, "Right. Good thing we're on Misty. We don't have to worry about losing our lives...only our lunch. Seriously, Ranen, the wind and waves seem to have settled out of the northeast. Let's start sailing again. It'll be more stable once we're moving."

The rolling and violent lurching was really wearing us down. I answered, "You're right. If we put the wind on our beam our motion'll be a lot less violent. Maybe we can even sail away from this storm. But we better get our shit together because it's blowing a full gale out there, and we haven't moved out of the cockpit in twelve hours."

I got suited up to go on deck to get the boat moving again. When I slid the heavy steel hatch back to step over the drop boards into the cockpit, Maria was doing her best to avoid being flung into the sea by hanging on to the dodger and kind of leaning against the solidly sheeted-in boom.

The 360° view was stunningly chaotic...and noisy. Really noisy. There was water in all forms everywhere. The air was filled with wind-blown seawater. Foaming seawater was pouring down the decks, and waves were crashing over the bow. An endless march of thirty-foot walls of water towered everywhere.

When we heaved to, we just dropped the jib and lashed it to the rail. The main was still up, and the Aries wind vane was still engaged. All that needed to be done was unlash and hoist the jib. Maria got busy coiling up the jib sheets that had drifted down the deck as I organized the tasks in my head.

"Ranen," Maria called out, jerking on the supple Dacron line. "This sheet went overboard and I can't pull it back. It's caught on something."

One end of the line was tied into the clew of the sail that was still lashed to the rail up forward. The other end that she was pulling on disappeared into the sea but clinging tightly to

Misty's hull. There was no doubt in my mind that it was jammed into the space between the rudder and the hull or caught in the propeller or both. No way we were going to get underway until I retrieved that rope.

Although the mainsail was up, Misty was not sailing. The mainsail was only up for stability and to keep the bow headed into the wind and waves. I staggered up forward on the rolling deck to untie the line from the jib. We needed some slack in that line to work with while we tried unjamming it from different angles. First, I fixed the free end to a cockpit cleat. We definitely didn't want to lose the other end into that wild sea. Then we wasted half an hour trying to free up the line even though we could feel that it was jammed some five feet under Misty's stern.

Options gone, we both knew what had to happen next. I just started stripping off my foul weather gear and clothes down to a pair of cotton thermal pants.

Maria was looking worried. "Wait a sec. I don't think this is a good idea, Ranen. It's too dangerous."

"Just go down and get me my mask and snorkel. And get the K-Bar knife and my dive belt. We know the weather is only going to get worse, and we can't maneuver if it's got the rudder jammed or worse, if it's caught around the prop. I'm not worried about going in. It's okay. I'll be careful."

I have never been afraid of the sea. I was always afraid when climbing, which is why I was never very good at it, but never on or in the ocean. So I was able to focus without the distraction that fear brings. Neptune is my patron saint and has always protected me.

I put on the belt with a couple of weights and the big K-Bar combat knife, pulled my diving mask over my head, gave myself some slack on the jammed sheet line, then with a firm left-handed grip on the line and the snorkel between my teeth, slipped overboard into the frigid blue sea.

The adrenalin was keeping my young mind and body sharp. Misty's stern was lifting a good three or four feet out of the water as each wave approached, then she slammed back into the sea when it passed. It was a struggle to avoid having my head crushed by the wicked ends of the wind vane frame when the stern dropped from over my head into the water. When the stern lifted, I could see that the rope was caught under the rudder and wrapped around the propeller.

As the next wave passed, I started pulling myself down the rope under the water to the rudder. There was a narrow window to work while the next wave approached. On that first dive I managed to jerk the line free from the space between the rudder and the keel before the line hauled me out of the water. I guess I had moved my grip up the rope when I jerked the line free. Once again I just barely ducked out of the way of the Aries steering vane.

I didn't dare take a moment to rest when the boat dropped back into the water, just quickly went down the line hand over hand to the propeller. What a relief, it wasn't knotted or jammed. Shit! I forgot to get a good lung full of air.

There was enough air in my lungs to get one wrap off the

prop before I needed to pull myself up to the surface to get a breath of sweet air. Without even looking around, I immediately pulled myself back down to the propeller. I was getting exhausted from hanging on and working in those wild seas. For sure this was going to become dangerous if I couldn't free the line on this dive. I was still fairly relaxed and not using too much air. Two more wraps and it was done. Once the line was free of the propeller, I floated away from the boat.

Now I realized how fucking cold the winter sea was. After all, it had just been snowing a few days before. My hands were starting to cramp. I thought, C'mon, Kenny get back to the boat or you might die!

I was right at the boat but my hands were too cramped to climb the four feet up the rope. Furthermore, my hands were cramped around the line so I couldn't let go to get a grip higher up the rope or the rail even if I could reach it. My teeth were chattering so hard I couldn't even call out to Maria for help. Maria saw what was happening, got a wrap on the winch, and began winching me up to Misty. When she got me close enough, she grabbed my belt and with her feet against the rail used all of her hundred ten pounds to pull me onboard. We both tumbled into the cockpit.

I couldn't stop shaking. Maria wrapped me up with one of those wonderfully insulated, lightweight, Vietnam War poncho liners and went below to make me a hot coffee with lots of sugary cocoa. It didn't take long with a hot drink and dry clothes to get me motivated. In no time we had that small working jib

A Smuggler's Guide to Fine Dining

up and Misty was sailing.

The storm was getting worse. That was the bad news. The good news was that even though Misty was rolling from rail to rail, there was no more jerking and lurching. All this and we still hadn't seen the actual storm yet.

At this point we were four days into this weather system. Every normal movement was difficult. No. Every movement was downright hard work. In those conditions we had to force ourselves to do everything. We were exhausted, and cooking was intimidating. The waves were getting bigger, and the wind was increasing. Soon survival would be an issue.

Going on deck required strength and focus. It's not that, even for a moment, I entertained the thought that one of us would go overboard, but somewhere in the back of my mind I knew it was a possibility. In that same place was the knowledge that a brief break in focus coupled with a severe roll of the boat could result in being flung into that wild sea. Rescue was out of the question. Misty was at her maximum hull speed and even if one of us saw the other go overboard a rescue would require turning the boat around. However, the concept of a rescue was purely academic. Whoever went overboard would immediately disappear into that maelstrom, never to be seen again.

Relaxed sleep was impossible. Even when lying on the cabin sole between the settees, it was work to stay in place just to rest. I volunteered to grate the cheese if Maria would make mac and cheese. I was craving Maria's crispy macaroni and cheese casserole. High carb, high fat, and high protein food, good hot or cold, a meal to sustain and energize sleep-deprived sailors. If you can't sleep, Maria's mac and cheese will keep you going.

On day five I put up the storm jib. Not only were we overpowered, but the giant breaking waves were slamming into the high-cut working jib. It was pretty intimidating going out on that forward deck. Misty was sailing in deep canyons with dark blue walls. Those walls of water came roaring up and lifted Misty to the sky then suddenly dropped her down their faces as they flew on their way. The shriek of the wind harmonizing with the roar of the waves was so loud that Maria and I couldn't yell loud enough to communicate.

Getting that jib down must have taken close to an hour. Maria cranked in the working jib sheet so that when the boat rolled, the jib backwinded. At that point I let go the halyard, dropping the sail on deck. The boat was rolling in the huge waves; no way I could walk forward to change sails. Down on my hands and knees, I dragged the storm jib up the heaving deck and made it fast to a big cleat. It seemed like it took forever to get the working jib hanks unclipped from the shiny new stainless steel forestay and back in its bag. The whole time I was getting beaten and battered like riding in a carnival ride without the bar secured. One hand to hold on and the other to do the task at hand, clipping, releasing, tying knots.

Finally the storm jib was up. It looked like half a bikini top, but we were still flying south. At least, for now, the wind was no longer in control. However, if the wind got stronger, even the bikini would have to come down.

A Smuggler's Guide to Fine Dining

We were way out to sea in force 10, maybe 11 (more than 60 mph) winds. Twice I heard distant, scratchy, broken, "maydays" on the VHF radio. That there were other vessels in trouble out there was somehow reassuring...to know that we weren't imagining that this was worse than it was.

My hands were suffering. Constant soaking in saltwater in conjunction with pulling and coiling salt-hardened ropes and handling salt-encrusted sails was literally wearing out the skin on my hands. The salt dried out the skin and the work tripled the effect. The damage was mostly on my thumbs and forefingers. There were cracks opening on the tips of my thumbs and in the creases where my fingers bent. These cracks were so deep that gripping anything was painful. They were almost down to the bone. Before getting into my bunk, I slathered my hands with vaseline then put on soft wool gloves. When I woke I used cuticle scissors to trim the hardened edges of the fissures which hindered healing.

I was feeling that as the waves got larger, the likelihood of the boat rolling over was increasing. During the day when a big wave came up, I could jump to the tiller and sail the boat down the face of the wave. Now it was getting dark and I didn't want to risk steering in zero visibility. I sheeted in the mainsail and the jib and adjusted the wind vane to keep us headed into the wind. Once again, we were heaved to.

The darkness brought stronger winds and larger waves. I switched on the masthead strobe and the deck floodlights that lit up the boat. Staying out in the cockpit standing watch seemed pointless. Even at the top of the waves the visibility was down to less than 15 feet. There was so much water in the air. Because of the driving rain and the wind-blown spume, we couldn't even see the bow from the cockpit. We gave up trying and just went below, trusting Misty to take care of us. And she did. She fought her way up to the crest of the huge waves but some of those giants were too much for her. The really big ones broke right over her, knocking the length of her new mast down to the sea. Undaunted, Misty came up every time.

In the middle of the night the world got a lot more quiet. It was creepy. The waves were still roaring but the wind was gone. We both went out onto the violently pitching and rolling deck. It must have been the eye of the storm. We could see stars. There, less than a football field away, was a large, lit up, fishing trawler motoring up the same wave we were on. We could see the crew in the lighted forward wheelhouse. They were frozen in time, intently staring forward with worried looks on their faces. Maybe I was reading my own thoughts into the tableau, but the last look I had of them in the few minutes before the wind came back with a vengeance is still burned into my memory. The old prayer came to my mind in that moment, "God help sailors on a night like this."

Those fishermen in their big trawler with big hatches to the fish holds and large glass windows in the wheelhouse had a lot more to worry about than Maria and I in Misty with her tiny polycarbonate portlights and small steel hatches dogged down tightly. We might roll or pitch pole, even lose the mast, but we wouldn't sink. There was no way for the sea to get in. Miserable... but not gonna die.

Neither of us were up for going on deck to pee. It was just too wild on deck. It took both hands to hang on out there. Maria and I were using a paint bucket and emptying it into the bilge.

I don't know why we bothered to pop our heads out to look around. Even if there was a ship approaching, we had no maneuverability.

Exhausted and a little bit sea sick, day six of the storm was an unending bad dream. An old Carley Simon song was playing in my head:

But ain't it strange how life goes on

A storm can never rage forever

And darkness only lasts 'til dawn

On day seven, the wind eased to force 8 (more than 40 mph) and the torrential rain quit. The wild sea state and the noise persisted. The dark clouds were still scudding overhead. However, by late that afternoon we had to get the boat sailing again. There wasn't enough wind to keep us headed into the waves. I eased the sails to get us on a course that put the wind and waves just forward of the beam or the middle of the boat. Once again we were moving fast in a southerly direction.

And just like that, life got a lot better. Actual sleep was back on the menu. We slowly got Misty organized. It was amazing how much stuff was lying around, pencils, clothing, odds and ends from the galley and provisions that had never come adrift before.

Then I had a look at the chart. Oh shit! I thought. I have no idea how far we drifted in all those days. It's time to get serious about celestial navigation, I hate this but...

I needed to do my best to get an approximate position. In celestial navigation the closer you can get to a true position to start with, the quicker your sextant sights will get you an actual position. I got out the sextant and my watch and went out to the cockpit. Wait. I thought, and threw the moon boots in the trash.

The sun was out! It wasn't cold! I stripped off my stale, sweat scented, foul weather coat and the urine scented rubber bib pants I had lived in for the past week. Maria came from the aft deck, drying her lean body with a big blue towel. "The shower bag is up and the soap and bucket are ready to go."

I was actually able to walk (not crawl) to the stern and scoop a full bucket of sea water and dump it over my greasy head. We used cheap, super detergent shampoo for soap. It was the only soap that would lather in salt water. I soaped up and scrubbed with the wash cloth that Maria had left me. It took many buckets of sea water and a lot of the cheap shampoo to feel clean. The fresh water rinse from the shower bag hanging from the back stay left me feeling like a different person.

CHAPTER 24

DUE SOUTH TO PROVO

It took all day and three sextant sights to make some sense of where we were out there in the endless Atlantic Ocean. Now the positions would get better and more refined each day.

After the next day's noon sight was entered to the log and charted, I came up on deck and addressed Maria, "I am fucking done with this voyage. Plot a course to the nearest land. I WANT OFF THIS FUCKING BOAT. Maybe somewhere in North Florida? Or anywhere not at sea."

"Okay. I get it." She threw at me on her way down to the chart table.

I was still brooding when Maria's laughing face appeared in the main hatch. "Well. I really am sorry to be the one to tell you...that the nearest land is exactly where we were headed. Providenciales, Turks and Caicos Islands...about a week away if this wind holds."

I laughed out loud at the irony while I put out the fishing line. In that moment I shed the sticky veneer of civilization. I realized that the nightmare storm had cleansed us of the North American coastal soot.

That epiphany was punctuated by a major strike on my fishing line. Right there in the middle of realizing that life had moved into the good lane, a huge fish swallowed my 00 double hook and ran the other way. No, it swam straight out of the water pulling me with it. On my way overboard my body slammed into the stainless steel aft rail, backstay, and the big metal Aries Windvane. Both of my hands automatically seized the line with a death grip. I hadn't yet fastened the fishing line to the boat and I was not about to lose our fresh fish dinner and my precious fishing rig with it.

Maria stood frozen in shock as an iridescently shining, striped, two-meter long, torpedo-shaped Wahoo erupted fully clear of the surface, shaking its head in a vain attempt to free itself from the hooks embedded in its mouth.

During the storm we had been comfortably and uncomfortably alone in a hostile environment. Just myself, Maria, Misty, and whatever the North Atlantic Ocean threw at us. But we weren't alone. The commotion of the large wahoo striking and leaping had woke us out of our storm reverie and brought us back to the reality of where we really were.

"Maria. Grab the gaff." I called out. "I need both hands to get this fish in. Fresh fish dinner sure am talkin to me!"

She quickly unfastened the four-foot, gold, anodized aluminum pole with 3 plastic hand grips and a big stainless steel hook at the end. Maria reverently waited for me to play the powerful fish up to Misty's stern.

Handlining a game fish is different from using a rod and

reel. You have to maintain tension with your hands or to release line to give the fish a chance to run...but not too far. I made it difficult for my fish to run and he was becoming tired. He looked much larger when he reluctantly came alongside. Now came the tense moment. I pulled the struggling fish close to the boat, head up. The moment when the hook may pull free, Maria slipped the big gaff hook through the gill and out its mouth. It took both of us to get that big thrashing fish over the rail and on the deck.

I got a good left-handed tight hold on the lowest grip and twisted the gaff to pin the wahoo's head to the deck. Maria handed me the lead-filled billy club made from a cut off Zodiac oar. Three hard wacks and he was gone, the beautiful iridescent sheen quickly fading to dull grey.

Then I was skinning the wahoo, all the while thinking, Hmm. There's a lot of fish lying on this deck. Aside from some sushi or ceviche for lunch, I'm gonna need to cook all of this so it won't go bad. It was the first fresh fish since the dinner in Newport, and it just wouldn't have been right to waste any of this remarkable creature.

I went below to retrieve my fish cutting plank and the plastic handled, Dexter fillet knife. The keen edge rode smoothly along the wahoo's spine, leaving no meat on the bones. One long cut down the top half, then the second slice down the bottom from head to tail. There were two beautiful boneless slabs of white meat over three feet long. Quickly, I flipped him over and the other side yielded 2 more perfect fillets. I put aside the head and throat fins for the fish stew. The bones and tail went into the sea.

Two cups of credit card thin slices would be enough for some sushi hors d'oeuvres right away. Next came a bowl of slices three times as thick for ceviche, Mexican marinated fish salad. I called to Maria, "Bring up the small stainless bowl, a couple of plates, a couple of lemons, soy sauce, a box of those rice crackers, and wasabi. Let's have some sushi while I get the ceviche started."

We were only 12 or so days from Newport and still had lots of fresh food. Maria and I stuffed ourselves on the absolutely fresh sliced wahoo dipped in soy sauce wasabi. Meanwhile, we squeezed lemon juice, cut tomatoes, onions, and cucumbers into a stainless bowl with the chunks of fish to marinate until dinner time for a ceviche cocktail.

I still had a small mountain of fish to process. I cut large chunks of the fillets for the fish chowder. Maria was on watch when the storm passed and had started making bread, so I figured to fry up fillets for fish sandwiches. "Is the dough on the first rise?" I asked Maria.

"Yeah. Why?"

"If you'll make some buns, I'll make fish sandwiches for dinner."

I cut thick pieces for four sandwiches. Still, there must have been over four kilos of fillet left. I sliced it all into thin strips which I soaked in soy sauce and laid out on three cookie sheets lined with aluminum foil. On my night watch I would bake it slowly for hours until it was crunchy fish jerky.

Maybe King Neptune was throwing us a bone to compensate for a solid week of torturous storms. All the fresh fish, light winds, and sunshine was going a long way toward softening the memory of the past weeks. Snowstorms...really?

Maria and I shared a long leisurely meal, fresh fish sandwiches and french fries, under a spectacular tropical sunset, the first since...well, I couldn't remember when. Maybe just before she shot the Columbian.

She was wearing a very large man's pinstripe dress shirt, nothing else. Night had fallen but with no ambient light, the sheer mass of stars lit the boat. Maria stood in the cockpit both hands holding the edge of the spray dodger feet spread apart for stability, showing off her spectacular behind. It was an invitation I never thought to refuse. I stepped behind her, my feet wedged inside her feet, holding myself with hands closed on breasts that responded to my touch. I slipped inside her. After all we had been through, we both groaned as if this were the first time.

We made love slowly again, then again as the Big Dipper moved above us. We couldn't get enough of celebrating our existence...of being alive. No thought of what was next.

Meanwhile, we had a destination and so continued sailing through tropical seas in that direction. Both of us were eager to drop the hook behind the reef in Provo Bay and have a large Coke with lots of ice and maybe a few cold rum drinks with Tay and Linda at the hotel bar.

We could see our progress on the chart. Nevertheless,

after so much time alone and away from land, it was a surprise when we arrived off the Turks and Caicos barrier reef. We passed through the reef and dropped the anchor off the beach in front of the only thing that passed for a hotel in Providenciales. Right away we noticed that something was different, but we couldn't put our finger on what had changed.

The first clue was that there was actually another cruising yacht anchored along that beach. Not like us, who were only pretending to be a cruising couple. We stopped by to say hello. They were a middle-aged couple with a well-appointed, sensible cruising sailboat. I won't pretend that I remember their names, but I clearly remember them telling us about their voyage through the Bahamas. She asked where we were coming from in the Bahamas. Maria answered, "We were really busy in Rhode Island and left late." She threw her hands up. "Ranen always leaves it too late. So by the time we got through that storm we were pretty much here."

The guy said, "You know they are saying that was the worst storm of the century[20]. I saved the weather fax charts during that week. Have a look."

I really didn't need to see the facsimile. We sailed through it.

When we got to the dock, it became clear. Only eight months or so had passed since we were last here, but the ambience had changed. The dock was empty. No boats fueling up, not even a dinghy. No obvious smugglers around.

Linda was behind the bar making drinks for some tourist

couples at one of the tables. "Well, Maria and Ranen have made it home again! I thought it was you out there. Misty is one of the only boats that actually sails through the reef. Good to see you lot still on the loose."

I had to ask. "Linda, what has happened here?"

"Well, Tay thinks that all the American Coast Guard choppers discouraged the smuggling boats from stopping here to fuel up and reprovision. The weed smugglers just aren't stopping. The airport is still pretty wild west. Money is still flowing in to keep the airport supporting the cocaine flights.

"I...I hope you guys can hang around for a while. We need you. You're the only pirates we can relate to. Tay needs Ranen for feedback on his marketing ideas for his mariculture project. He's raising mahi mahi in the pond at Leeward Going Through. We've got buyers for the fish and it looks like we'll be selling mahi to restaurants in the States by next fall. But Tay will love to have Ranen here to drink and toke with, and I need a woman to talk to. What tourists we've been getting have been pretty boring."

Maria answered. "We just sailed for two weeks through a bad storm to get here. So yeah, we're going to rest and regroup. But I'm pretty sure we're heading for the Bahamas in a couple of weeks. Ranen wants to meet up with some friends in Georgetown. There's a cruising boat out there. Who knows? Maybe you'll start getting some yacht traffic."

Linda gave a wry smile. "If only those cocaine cowboys will keep their guns outta view...this place is getting a reputation."

Maria replied, "Come on, Linda. The weed smugglers have loads of money to spend, and we're a lot more fun than the straight yachties. We're the ones talking up this island."

I called out, "There's Dugong out there past the reef. Let's go."

We jumped into the Zodiac and zipped out past Misty to greet Joe and guide him through the winding channel through the barrier reef. I pulled alongside Dugong and grinned at Joe Prins, my welding mentor from the boatyard in Key Largo. "What's up Joe? Follow me through the coral."

I led him through the reef and into the anchorage not too far from Misty, and since he had a rowing dinghy, closer to the beach. I introduced myself to Joe's crew, the handsome young black American standing at the bow. "Hey, I'm Ranen. You can let the anchor go here. Tell Joe to put it in slow reverse."

"Hi. I'm Michael and yeah, I'm on it."

Dugong was a 50-foot steel schooner. When Michael dropped the big Danforth from the bow, the half inch chain clattered loudly over the roller. I immediately rolled out of the dinghy wearing my mask, snorkel and fins. Maria was driving the Zodiac. I looked up just as Michael was dragged overboard and into the sea. He must have stepped in a loop of chain as Joe was in reverse and the tension between the anchor and the reversing boat locked the chain around his leg. He was drowning and Joe was fifty feet away completely unaware this was going on.

I yelled at Maria, "Michael is caught on the chain. Tell Joe to go forward to put slack in the chain." I immediately swam down to try to get Michael loose. His face was a mask of panic as he struggled to get loose. I dove fast for the bottom, planted a foot on either side of the big anchor, and heaved with all my strength to flip the big Danforth out of the sand. Still not enough slack on the chain, but the tension was less. I finned hard for the surface to get a full lung of air then straight down to Michael. Between us, we got his leg loose. We swam to the surface together, and he got a grip on the dinghy rope as I swam down to set the anchor by hand.

We smoked weed, talked boats, and generally filled each other in on the happenings for the two years since Maria and I had sailed out of Key Largo. Eventually we got around to recent history. Joe was here waiting for his globe trotting, treasure hunter, renaissance girlfriend, Sue Hendrickson, to show up. Sue had a theory that she could track down the true story and shipwreck of the Niña. Treasure hunting with an historical twist was the kind of adventure Sue was good at, actually finding one of the ships in Christopher Columbus' fleet.

Joe finally got around to gossip about some of our pirate colleagues from the Keys. Some of the boats were hanging out in Long Island in the Bahamas. "Billy was there waiting to get some bales. Henry's cousin Peter has a thirty something foot Formula. I think he's fueling the Colombians and getting paid in weed, which is going to the States with our friends from Largo Land."

I paused before I climbed down to our dinghy, "Listen

Joe, you need to teach your crews how to lay out anchor chain so they don't get dragged overboard to their death. If we hadn't been there, Michael would have drowned."

Joe just waved me away. He was always a bit reckless.

Just what I wanted…a weed connection in the Bahamas. We made money with the Jamaican weed, but not nearly enough because the quality wasn't there. This time I would pick out my own weed. Now I could relax, knowing what our next move was. Joe and I spent a few hours every day spearing fish on the neighborhood coral heads. The air was warm, the sea cool, and the wind scoop blew the trade winds through Misty's cabin. A few days (maybe they were weeks) passed without any of us noticing. But one morning we did notice, and we left.

CHAPTER 25

NORTH AGAIN

It was just a couple of days to Salt Pond Cay on Long Island, Bahamas. No land, just open ocean to the deep water Crooked Island Passage between Crooked Island and Long Island. The passage was well marked with a 22 mi light on the north end of Crooked Island and a 12 mi light on the south end of Long Island.

I loved those Brits for all those lighthouses they built in the 19th century. There are all kinds of currents and hidden rocks to hit around those island passages, but with those bright lights you just needed to be close to get a position fix. In spite of all those aids to navigation, it was a lot of nervous hours dodging coral heads to get to the Salt Pond anchorage.

When I let the anchor go, I wondered if we were actually at Salt Pond because we were the only foreign sailing boat there. It seemed as if one moment we got anchored and the next Peter's Formula was tied up to Misty's stern rail.

Peter didn't waste any time. "Listen mon. I'm thinkin you an Maria shouldn't be hangin round. Billy was here for a night an gone. Let's do this now and I'll bring it around late tonight. No secrets here in Salt Pond, Ranen. Bettah no one sees too much."

He handed me a big spliff. "So fire this up. It's good."

I took a big toke and started violently coughing. For ten minutes I couldn't move and my mind was reeling. Finally I managed to talk, "Holy shit! Is it all this good?"

"Or better." Peter answered. "So how much you want? I got a lot of it but it be goin faast."

I instantly committed. "If it's packed tight, I want two hundred pounds. That's all Misty can safely take. And I'm paying for all of it tonight in hundreds, so I figure you can give me a better deal than you gave Billy. I just know you fronted him a lot of this stuff. You're not taking a risk with us."

We came to an agreement that was good for both of us. Honestly, I do not remember what we paid for the weed, but I remember that it was a great deal for us and that Peter was thankful that we came by to take it off his hands. A true "win-win." Some time after midnight he came alongside in his Formula and we quickly moved the eight burlap packages down below into Misty's forward cabin. I passed him the cash, and he was gone.

We had cleared the cabin to make Maria's job of "disguise and camouflage" easier and faster. Misty was ready for sea, so we took the opportunity to get a few hours of sleep. As soon as the sun was up we pulled up the anchor and headed across the Exuma sound to Georgetown, the port of entry on Great Exuma Island. Just as we were in sight of the town, Maria put a sheet of chocolate chip cookies in the oven. The smell of fresh baked cookies filled the cabin as we pulled up to the funky government dock where the mail boat tied up. The yellow quarantine flag was flying from the masthead showing that we were coming from a foreign country, nevermind we had just come from loading two hundred pounds of weed at Long Island. We called in at the customs office and the lone government agent was too busy to come by the boat. He stamped a visa in our passports, and we were in.

It was still early enough to pass the coral heads to sail up the Exuma Sound to our old hangout at Halls Pond Cay. I knew that I had just jumped at the golden opportunity to load up with Peter. The quality and price were as good as it gets. We were in the right place at the right time. When opportunity knocks, you open the door. But now I needed to think what to do next.

My overall thought was to merge into the fleet of sailing boats cruising the Bahamas toward the States, but it was too early in the year to get lost in the yacht traffic on the American east coast. It was still winter up there. The city of Nassau was used to seeing Misty anchored over by Paradise Island, so why not hide out in plain sight.

We were discussing a plan. The weather was good enough to anchor off Halls Pond Cay for a couple of days, go diving, look at charts and talk about what we were going to do with this cargo.

Maria opened, "You haven't really got any idea where we're going with this weed, have you?"

"Okay, I admit that I loaded us up without a plan. We need the money. You need the money. The weed was there as if we ordered it up. It just fell into place and I have been spending a lot of thought on places to unload. How about going up the St. Johns River from Jacksonville to central Florida to that little boatyard in San Mateo. We can take Misty out of the water for hurricane season. Buy a truck or something and take the weed to Atlanta.

"We can hang out with Hugo and Adrienne. We've got a lot of friends up there. It's pretty much backwoods in North Central Florida. The police aren't thinking smuggling. All the dope up there is made in trailer park kitchens."

Maria looked right into my eyes, "I think this is good, especially the part about making money, but the part about driving out of Florida is a little dicey."

"But that's why they call it smuggling," I answered.

Having had the strategy talk, we pulled up the anchor and headed across the Great Bahama Banks. Misty slipped into Nassau through the back door, and picked up our secret mooring under the lighthouse on Paradise Island.

Maria and I were pretty relaxed in Nassau. Maybe too relaxed. We rented a car one day to tour the island. We picked up the car at the big pink hotel in town and headed west out of the city toward the beach where the first James Bond movie was filmed. Just as we cleared the traffic I fired up a big spliff of the weed we bought down islands. As we came around a corner there was a uniformed traffic cop stopping cars for a funeral procession. I blew out a cloud of marijuana smoke through the open window...right in the cop's face. "Oops," I muttered.

A Smuggler's Guide to Fine Dining

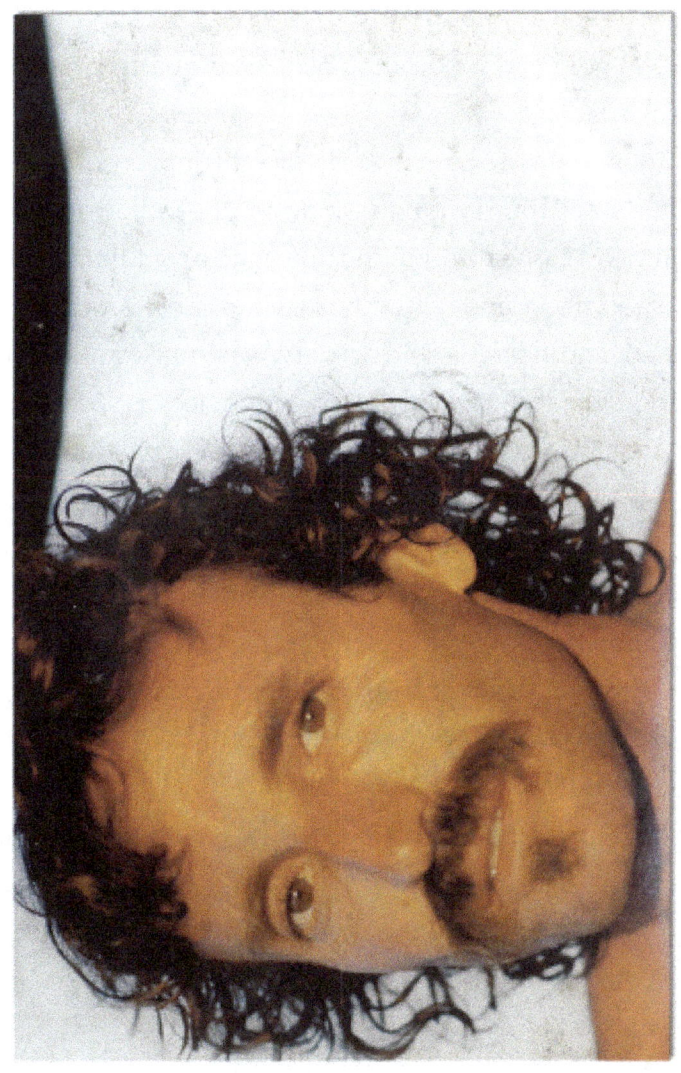

Swimming in a Storm

"Pull over there." He ordered. "Let's see your passports."

He looked through our passports and found the entry visa. I could clearly see that the visa rang an alarm bell in his head. "We goin to drive over to police headquarters." He got into the back seat.

Maria and I spent a half hour sitting on a bench at a table in a small room with no windows. The uniformed cop who brought us in came through the door with a middle-aged man in a pair of tan slacks and one of those white linen, South American, untucked, short-sleeve shirts. There was no mistaking the big gold and blue detective inspector badge he was sporting on his belt. At that moment, I had to suppress a rush of fear. We were being way too careless, and now we could be in serious trouble.

The detective looked hard at Maria, then gave me a hard stare. He turned to the policeman and asked, "What d' hell man? Why you bring deese tourists down hea?"

The policeman answered, "Look inspector, I know dey jus smokin some weed. Den I see they got a boat an I thinkin we should have a look."

The inspector answered, "Okay, but we ain' got time to mess with a couple of tourists on some little sailboat. Cut em loose." Then he gave me that hard look. "You two are too old to be misbehavin and breakin laws in dis country. Next time we catch you smokin ganja you goin to jail."

After our day at the beach turned to near disaster we went to the grocery store, returned the car, then returned to the boat.

A Smuggler's Guide to Fine Dining

Maria looked at me with a question mark in her face. "Is it too late to leave now or do we wait 'til first light? And...where can we go and not be noticed?"

"Let's get out of here in case they change their minds about us. I really don't think we have to worry, but starting now we're going to be a lot more careful. We cannot count on getting that lucky again. We can tow the Zodiac, but I'm putting away the outboard, tank and oars. Meanwhile have a look at the chart for a place to lie low, somewhere north of here. Berry Islands or some deserted reef between Andros and Bimini. We've got at least a month to wait. Nowhere that's a port of entry."

An hour later, Maria was raising the mainsail as I dropped the mooring chain. We sailed out of Nassau on the outgoing tide. Maria carefully scrutinized the Bahamas Guide and found us an empty anchorage in the Berry Islands. Night arrived two hours out of Nassau. No problem because we were sailing in the deep Northwest Providence Channel, a major big ship channel that was well marked by powerful lighthouses all the way. Lignum Vitae Cay, something like a hundred miles from Nassau, was a deserted island with a protected anchorage where Maria and I had holed up during a three-week storm on our first voyage on Misty in 1975. A perfect place to disappear, with a reef full of fish and lobster. "Good thinkin, Maria. I completely forgot about that anchorage. This is going to be fun."

We prudently hung around in view of the Stirrup Cay lighthouse until the sun was high enough to see and avoid hitting the coral heads.

I laughed.

Maria said, "I know just what you're laughing about. The first time we sailed in here. Right? God! I can't believe how unprepared we were."

"Now here we are laying low once again after another fuck up, but at least now we know how to sail this boat. Remember when I decided we were sailing in through this reef with no engine and broken rigging?"

"Yeah, Ranen. That was before you knew when to reef. Did you even know how to reef? Anyway, I was crying, because I was sure we were going to put the boat on the rocks.

"You said, 'Listen, we might wreck the boat, but we aren't gonna die. The worst that will happen is that we will grab our passports and money and wade ashore. We may lose our boat but not our lives.' That put it into perspective and put my panic to rest.

"This time you've got us a new engine and all new rigging and even better...we know what we're doing. Now we're through. Funny, I remember this inlet being a lot more scary."

She put her reverie aside and got down to business. "I'll steer and you drop the hook. Then you can dive us up some dinner. I wonder if the cruise ships still come in?"

When we were stuck here three years before, one of the perks was that a big cruise ship anchored off the lighthouse for half a day. They brought the passengers ashore for a fancy beach buffet. Suddenly, a deserted island beach became crowded with hundreds of florid-faced tourists lining up to fill their paper

MARIA'S CRISPY MACARONI & CHEESE

NAUTICAL KNOSHES

This high calorie high protein high fat recipe will keep you going through any three-day storm. I always bought big rounds of cheese then wrapped them in rags soaked in vinegar and stored them in the bilge. Also giant quantities of sundried tomatoes, olive oil, olives and capers when in the Mediterranean. They keep forever and add flavor to otherwise boring food.

Ingredients
- 3/4 package macaroni (spiral is my favorite)
- 3 Tbsp Olive oil and or butter
- 3 Tbsp whole wheat flour
- 3 cups of rice milk or other milk
- 14 ounces sharp cheddar and/or other sharp cheese…grated
- 1 cup of cubed ham (canned, cured, gammon…)
- 1 handfull of sundried tomatoes soaked in olive oil
- 2 Tbsp or more (to taste) Dijon mustard
- 1 good pinch each of salt, pepper, cayenne, paprika

Boil pasta till al dente then cool. Heat oil/butter in pan with ham then whisk in flour, no lumps. Slowly add milk continually stirring. Stir in mustard, tomatoes and ¾ of the cheese. Stir in any spices that sound good. Pour the cheese sauce into the baking dish or bread pans with the pasta. Sprinkle remaining cheese on top with paprika. Bake at 350° degrees until top is crispy.

plates with beautifully prepared food. Chefs in white coats and tall hats were tending big bowls of fruit, huge platters of meat, potato salad, and trays of freshly baked bread.

We arrived on Friday and sometime during Monday night a big cruise ship must have anchored off the Great Stirrup Light. Just before sunrise, I went on deck and, just like that, Las Vegas had seemingly appeared into the previously darkened neighborhood.

By ten o'clock the beach was peppered with umbrella tops and sun-soaked tourists. The crew from the ship was setting out a feast on tables set up in the casuarina pines. We were hoping to go unnoticed, just another couple in swimsuits and sun hats. But in the food line a woman, sporting a thick layer of bright red lipstick, seemingly applied in the dark, spoke to Maria. "Wherever did you get that suntan? Do you live in Florida? Or California?"

Maria turned, got a look at lipstick woman, pointed at me and answered in her best southern accent, "No ma'am, I live with mah boyfriend heah on that sailboat out thear."

"Oh my, this is like meeting a character from a book!"

Maria laughed as she reached for a deviled egg. "What? Like Dracula?"

We stuffed ourselves on rich cruise ship food but gave the sickly sweet rum punch a miss. I spent some time quizzing an officer about the day's weather report then swam back to Misty.

Misty was there for three of those cruise ship parties. I

really appreciated making love with Maria after the cruise ship buffets. Maria's concept of sexuality was so exotic compared to the women we met on that beach. Something about those encounters with people from the real world reminded us to explore new horizons of intimacy. I have fond memories of lonely anchorages where Maria and I shared unrestricted sex.

Although, especially after the Nassau fuck-up, we were aware of the two hundred barely concealed bales of weed in the forward cabin. At the same time we were ignoring it and most of the time...forgetting it. However, the northers weren't coming through anymore, and we were seeing sailing boats heading south from the States. It was time to head to the St. Johns River.

CHAPTER 26

BACK IN THE USSR

We were anchored ninety or so miles east of Florida and less than fifty miles from the Gulfstream which runs northerly along the American Eastern Seaboard. My plan was to stay far on the outside to the east of the "Stream," at least until we got far enough up the coast that we didn't appear to be coming from the Bahamas. It was tempting to jump right into the Stream and get a free hundred miles a day from the four-knot current, but once again the close call in Nassau kept me from taking the chance.

So we tacked out into the Atlantic on a six-day roundabout course to North Florida. There was one upside of going the long way: some of the best fishing in the world is in the waters around the Gulfstream in the Florida Straits. I caught the first Mahi Mahi as soon as we passed Grand Bahama Island. She was hiding under one of those mile-long rafts of sargasso weed, waiting for a flying fish to swim by. She was a perfect one-meal and ceviche fish, and we never even slowed to land her.

The next day as we headed east away from North America, the fishing line jerked so hard that I could actually feel the boat

A Smuggler's Guide to Fine Dining

CEVICHE

This Ceviche is a Mexican hors d'oeuvre that is a perfect recipe for a fish filleted directly out of the sea. It is a dish we always ate while preparing the various recipes for dealing with the large amount of meat we commonly pulled from the deep ocean. The Mexicans use fresh cilantro, which we rarely had onboard, but tomatoes, limes, hot peppers and onions keep well without refrigeration, and are garden staples throughout the islands of the world.

Ingredients
- 1 pound fresh fillet of firm fleshed fish cut into small chunks
- 1/2 onion thinly sliced
- 3/4 cup fresh squeezed lime (or lemon) juice
- 1 cup chopped tomato (tinned can be used on a long voyage when tomatoes are gone)
- 1 hot pepper without seeds finely chopped

Combine all ingredients and let marinate until fish is cooked. About 15 minutes.

stagger. I pulled the slack line in and found the monofilament was broken. Whatever was hooked, weighed more than one thousand pounds. Over the years I went to heavier and heavier fishing rigs. I really hated losing fishing gear.

Maria and I were so happy out there in the open ocean. Except for the U.S. Coast Guard, all the monsters were below, unable to eat us. The open ocean was our comfort zone, and we were just not inclined to hurry back to land and the suppressed anxiety associated with smuggling. Our profile improved as we sailed further east and north. After a few more days of sailing slowly, we were just north and a hundred miles east of Daytona Beach Florida. If we were noticed, Misty would look like a boat sailing south from North Carolina. We could have sailed directly west into the St. Johns River inlet, but that would involve sailing into a commercial harbor, passing right under the eye of the huge Jacksonville Coast Guard base.

Instead, I chose to aim for a little used inlet just south of Daytona, Ponce De Leon Inlet. Now we were heading in a southwestern direction, opposite of a direct course from the Bahamas. Sure, some smart Coast Guard officer might figure out that we had circled around to disguise our point of origin, but something would have to make that officer suspicious in the first place. Our safety lay in our entire profile and not giving anyone anything to be suspicious about, and this time we were dotting every "i."

Still, we took the time to appreciate life.

Maria and I sat on the cabin top intently watching the sun

lay huge on the calm horizon and slowly sink into the sea. We were waiting for the Green Flash–a rare and interesting optical phenomenon where a green spot or flash is visible at the top edge of the sun at sunset or sunrise, although I have only seen it at sunset. Sailors have been obsessed with this phenomenon probably as long as...well, forever.

    The horizon all around us was filled with the violent colors of an intense sunset. And the color didn't end at the water. The undulating sea was smeared with the reflection of all the versions of red and yellow. The sun stretched across a large piece of the canvas, getting larger just before it sank into the brightly colored sea. We were lost in the spectacle, our unblinking gaze fixed on the disappearing, burning orb. The heavens were going gray, but our eyes were fixed on that last piece of the sun that was flattening as it disappeared. There was no time to notice that it was gone, because there was a blip of intense emerald green in the middle of the yellow residue of sunlight. It only lasted a second, that Green Flash, and Maria looked directly at me as if to say, "That has to be a good sign!"

    The weather was settled with a light, southeasterly breeze. Luck seemed to be with us...not that we were making the mistake of counting on our luck. It took us two nights to get across the Gulfstream, then when I knew we were closing on the coast we heaved to for half a day to clean up our act.

    The Florida coast in the '70s was the hottest place to enter the United States with contraband. Maria and I were sailing right into the dragon's mouth. Having said that, there are two distinct hiding places: the inconspicuous hiding place and the conspicuous hiding place. I hate to beat a dead horse, but here we are back to profile. It was our profile that saved our asses in Nassau, and once again we were going to get Misty so clean that she sparkled. We also took the time to get the Zodiac inflated and tied up to the stern rail.

Once the decks were spotless and chrome rigging polished, we threw on our "yachtie" clothes we had folded in a plastic bag. Clean blue shorts, white shirts, trendy deck shoes, and just like that–we were unnoticeable. Still, I was hoping by sailing through Ponce Inlet that we wouldn't be seen at all. But if we were noticed, I trusted our carefully engineered profile to safely carry us through.

At nine p.m. the Florida coast was a vague shadow on the horizon. Now I had to figure out where the fuck Daytona was. I guess it's hard to imagine trying to make landfall before electronic navigation. Finding your way through the offshore sand bars and reefs to safe inland waters is tricky.

A couple of years before, I had nearly sailed onto Miami Beach thinking that a blinking red traffic light was the red navigation light marking the jetty entrance to the Port of Miami. Fortunately I had a nagging feeling that something was not right and waited for daybreak to enter the harbor. Following ships in was a method I used for finding harbor entrances. Picking one light out of the blinding smear of lights in coastal cities is difficult at best.

There are all kinds of ways to find the safe entrance, but

without an electronic confirmation you just cannot be certain. You can be almost certain. I chose Ponce because no one used it, probably because it was poorly marked and shallow with drifting sandbars. It had been days since we had a confirmed position based on an accurate noon sight, and I had been meticulous in my navigation since then, so I felt cautiously confident that we were close to the inlet.

During the night we finally started seeing the brilliant six blinks of the Ponce De Leon lighthouse flashing every thirty seconds. It could be seen for twenty-two miles, which gave us a good idea how far away we were from the inlet.

I watched Misty's ancient analogue depth sounder like a hawk looking at a mouse far below. The chart was open and I was comparing the depth sounder to the depths on the chart. Maria was glassing the coast with the binoculars, looking for buoys. We were in sixty feet of water and I wasn't about to come any closer until we saw entrance markers.

Maria was on top of her game. She had a pan of garlic and fish on the stove, as well as two loaves of bread ready to bake. The hatches were open with the wind scoop blowing fresh air through the cabin. When we sailed in, Misty was going to smell like dinnertime.

She spotted the first red marker. I carefully approached, leaving it to starboard until we could see the red "2" and heard the bell that positively identified this buoy as the entrance to Ponce De Leon Inlet. Focus Kenny, don't get distracted, I thought as we started finding our way. The murky green water roiled with the incoming tidal current.

We passed through the two prongs of the beach into the clearly marked Intercoastal Waterway. Maria had the binoculars up at the bow, identifying the channel markers, but there had been a lot of winter storms and there was a good chance that the channel markers were unreliable. I wasn't overly concerned. The tide was low and rising, the bottom was sand, and Misty was a steel boat.

We were all alone. Just our boat, a lot of sand, and light green water. There was a green marker that I left well to port. The boat bumped the sandy bottom then abruptly stopped dead. We both fell when Misty stopped under us.

The anchor was ready to set if we needed it to winch ourselves into deeper water, but first I wanted to take some soundings. I could see from the marker that we were aground IN the channel. I jumped into the Zodiac with a pole that I used as a depth sounder. My soundings showed us to be just out of the channel. We were almost floating and the tide was rising. I didn't even try to get us off; I decided to just wait until we floated off.

Then, out of nowhere, a twenty-foot rigid-bottom inflatable Coast Guard patrol boat came roaring up.

They pulled alongside and the Chief Petty Officer ordered his crewman to put a line on our forward deck cleat, "We'll pull you off. This channel has changed in the last few storms."

The shock of our sudden predicament made my voice croak. "We're barely stuck. Tide is rising." I quickly regained my composure and added in a more commanding voice, "Honestly, thank you, but we're almost floating now. Five or ten minutes should see us free."

"Well, we're here. We might as well pull you into deeper water. I've got to write this up and have a quick inspection."

I said, hopefully without a trace of panic in my voice, "Okay. Come aboard. We aren't goin' anywhere. I think Maria just took the bread out of the oven."

This was the worst possible scenario. Maria and I were looking into the face of a nightmare–losing our boat and our freedom, actual prison time. Everything hinged on maintaining our cool, but how to get a grip? If this Coast Guard officer really looked he could see burlap bales stacked in the forward cabin. They were visible from the cockpit. He wouldn't even have to go below to spot our cargo of contraband.

All that can be said is, "Never underestimate the power of adrenalin."

When he climbed over the life lines, my mouth went so dry from fear and panic that I could spit cotton balls. I'm sure Maria was on the verge of panic as well. However, we were no strangers to adrenaline. She must have pulled it together, because she popped out of the main hatch from the galley, blocking the officer's view down below to where the bales were stowed. She had put on her Southern Belle persona, and asked, "I jus' baked some bread! Would y'all like a coffee and a slice of warm bread with jam, Officah?"

"No thanks, ma'am. We're on duty, but it sure smells

good." His attention turned to me, "Where are you two coming from? Last port?"

I managed to summon enough spit to speak, "We are just down from the Carolinas." I artfully managed to avoid a specific port, so as not to get caught in a lie.

Before the officer could ask his next question, I volunteered all the information a yachtie would expect to provide to an inspector, fully committing to my role as an intensely helpful yachtsman. "The man-overboard pole is clipped to the backstay there, and the life jackets are down there in the forward cabin." I pointed right to where the life jackets were disguising the bales of weed. Before he could get too good a look, I picked up the conch shell under the spray dodger and blew a blast, making him jump in his starched suit. "This is our horn," I laughed incredulously, holding it out to him, as if a conch shell were some prized curiosity and we were just so clever for having it. He waved away my offer to inspect the conch, not hiding the fact that I was making him a bit annoyed, and I just continued on as if I were completely oblivious. "And down there is the manual bilge pump. I've always said, why keep a backup bilge pump for your electric bilge pump if you can just go with a manual bilge pump in the first place, wouldn't you agree!?"

All that adrenalin was exaggerating my manic personality, and it was making this boring Coast Guard officer severely uncomfortable. Suddenly, he wanted nothing more than to haul us off this sandbar and get us well on our way. He checked off some things on his clipboard and fled to his boat.

The rising tide had nearly floated us off so the instant he powered up those two huge, high horsepower outboard engines, the tow line to Misty went taut, and we were instantly off the sandbar. I pulled his line off the cleat, coiled it up and tossed it into their cockpit with a jaunty salute.

Just like that, the patrol boat roared away, and it was done. At least for now.

> Don't anticipate outcome.
> Await the unfolding of events.
> Remain in the moment.
> —William Gibson

I have always lived by that; it's how I survived the smuggling lifestyle. For the moment we were safe, thank Neptune. But there was no time to relax or celebrate. We had to focus on another chokepoint right in front of us…moving toward the St. Johns River and through the Port of Jacksonville.

Misty was just another boat on the Intercoastal Waterway, that man-made river that ran down the American east coast, connecting all the rivers and waters inside the barrier islands. The Army Corp of Engineers maintained the bouys and mostly kept it dredged for commercial traffic, like barges and fishing vessels, as well as private vessels that for one reason or another wanted to avoid going offshore. Maria and I were relaxed. We were just another car on the freeway, not much chance of being stopped again until Jacksonville.

A Smuggler's Guide to Fine Dining

We weren't sailing, just motoring from marker to marker. We arrived along Daytona Beach that evening. Daytona has a ton of corners to drop an anchor, lots of places in deep water, not in the front yard of houses overlooking the Waterway.

The release of all the suppressed tension of a close call results in a kind of euphoria. I think maybe it flooded our brains with dopamine. Everything was brighter; colors were more vivid. We were somehow ecstatic.

Maria was letting out the anchor chain at the bow. When I leaned over her to gauge how much chain was out, the scent of her skin tasted of sunshine and sweat. She turned her head to look up at me and our lips met. That kiss was so sexual that we swooned. Somehow I managed to get the chain secured while our lips searched out places to absorb each other. Her hands were all over me at once. We just couldn't get enough of each other. It was all so electric.

Out there in that empty anchorage, the hours passed unnoticed while Maria and I explored the places where the dopamine led us. Morning came. I cranked up the little engine and, coffee in hand, we continued on our way to Jacksonville.

We arrived at the St. Johns River after sunset. Jacksonville's ambient light was like daylight. We motored up the river into the city. For once, we decided to spend the night in a glitzy marina in the recently gentrified downtown. Hot showers and a nice bar and restaurant. Once again our best option was to hide in plain sight.

Both of us were feeling comfortable having passed a

Coast Guard inspection two days before. However, we still had another hundred miles and two drawbridges to go. At first light we were off. No sails, just the chug-a-chug of the Lister diesel. Unlike voyaging at sea, motoring up the St. Johns River required paying attention.

I have always enjoyed sailing through industrial cities. Jacksonville was a good one. Lots of big shipyards, and lots of big deep-ocean tugs. There were ships of all sizes and types.

Up at the bow, Maria called out, "Ranen, look over there. Aren't those two barges over by the cranes exactly like the abandoned unlit barge that almost killed us when we sailed out of the Bahamas a few years ago?"

There was a large barge terminal across the river. Barges the size of football fields and six big ocean-going tug boats. "Oh yeah. We should go in and give 'em some shit. But I've got a feeling that tug captain was fired when he arrived in port without his cargo. Weird. It's still scary seeing those monsters there...even safely put away."

The wind was steady from the north. The river is really wide, and since we already had the mainsail up, I hoisted the genoa and shut down the diesel. We slowly made our way up river. With the wind right behind us, there was nothing to do but steer. No tacking or pulling lines.

Maria hailed the drawbridge on the VHF radio, "Interstate 95 drawbridge, this is sailing vessel Misty requesting opening. Standing by channel 10, over."

"Misty, this is the Interstate 95 bridge. Do you kids have

some kind of motor on that Dinky Toy? 'Cuz if you think I'm gonna open and take a chance on the wind quitting and you kids getting that mast hung on MY bridge you got another think comin'. No way I am gonna be held responsible for stopping traffic on one of the busiest highways in the freakin' world. Take down those sails and I'll open the bridge. You can put 'em back up after you pass."

We passed more bridges and the river turned south. The St. Johns River flows north some three-hundred miles through Lake George to Jacksonville. It passes through serious wildlife rich wilderness. The bird population is something like the Amazon. Reptiles abound from alligators and snakes down to the tiny skinks. Bears, lions, and all kinds of animals can be seen from the boat. Of all the wildlife, the most common introduced non-native species is the North Florida Redneck.

We continued south through wilderness interspersed with very small towns and a few larger ones, our wake disturbing huge sleeping gators and nasty poisonous cottonmouths lazily swimming near shore. Each night we looked for a wide spot in the river to anchor far enough out of the channel where the huge tugs towing big oil barges to Orlando couldn't run us over.

Maybe it was a river legend, a wives tale, but we heard the most bizarre story about a tug that took out a sailboat when its barge swung out and ran it over. The sailboat ended up buried deeply in the mud, only to be found by a fisherman who hooked a piece of the wreckage. They say the tug captain never even knew the incident happened and the couple onboard were never found...buried in the black muck of the St. Johns River bottom. In some ways the voyage up the Saint Johns River was a little creepy around the edges of our awareness.

One morning a few hours after a very early start, we pulled over to have breakfast. As we quietly sipped our coffee, an elderly woman in stylish church attire sporting a floppy-brim hat strolled by walking her pekingese on the well-worn path along the river. We thoughtfully observed her deep south, old white woman's haughty demeanor, when, silently, an enormous owl swooped down out of nowhere and grabbed the dog in its talons. We watched in horror as the owl slowly gained altitude across the river, dog yipping in terror, leash dangling, and disappearing into the green canopy.

Maria dryly remarked, "Jesus! This place is straight out of a horror movie. Let's leave. NOW."

I cranked up the engine and Maria pulled up the anchor. We drifted out into the current, leaving the woman on the path, screaming her dog's name and slinging her anguish into the open sky.

Misty headed toward a tiny boatyard in an un-village with a post office and the name 'San Mateo, Florida.' No real community, just the post office and the name.

We spotted the travel-lift gantry as the light faded. The boatyard was small, the size of an American baseball diamond, with a small shack that served as an office for the dapper, white-haired ex-airline pilot who ran the yard. When Misty neared, the old man was standing on the bank above the river dressed in knife-edge creased khaki trousers held up with suspenders, a white shirt, and a U.S. Navy officer's cap. Odd, but he seemed to be waiting. Did the "gator telegraph" warn him?

He pointed to a canal that ran alongside the boatyard. There were four or five anchored sailing boats in the lily-choked canal. As we entered he shouted, "The canal is dredged to six and a half feet."

I shouted back, "Perfect. We draw five." I knew we would fit because I already had this secret little yard in my catalogue of potential illegal landing spots. It was as tucked away as I remembered, a little black hole in the boating world.

CHAPTER 27

HUGO AND ADRIENNE

Our old friends, Hugo and Adrienne, lived on an island not twenty miles from our perfect little hiding spot.

Adrienne was George Bond's girlfriend back in 1970 when he planted dynamite in Steamboat. I had never met Hugo before, but he was an old friend of Bond's, so I'd heard plenty of stories about the man. I figured Hugo had likewise heard enough stories about me to make us acquaintances by association. Somehow, Adrienne and Hugo had met up and become sailors, and by the mid-seventies H and A were living on an old wooden schooner anchored off Peanut Island in Riviera Beach, and tying up their dinghy at the end of the dock where I had recently bought Misty.

There I was, sitting on the deck of my sailboat, back in the same exact place from where I'd purchased it, and I still felt like this thirty-year-old steel sailing boat was brand new to me. I realized in that moment that I knew nothing–nothing about sailing, about navigation, or about anything else, really.

In my moment of doubt, insecurity, and panic, Adrienne happened to be tying her rowing dinghy to the end of Misty's finger pier. She approached cautiously once she saw my hunched form, and she recognized I was having a moment.

Adrienne spoke out from the pier, "Hello Ranen, maybe you remember me? I'm Adrienne, I was living with Bond when you and Nancy were living in Roly's pickup out in our driveway, during that bitter winter in 1970. You guys just disappeared one day, and now, after all these years, you show up as the new owner of the beautiful Misty." She kneeled and placed a hand on Misty. "Everyone knows this stunning little jewel."

I responded, "Ever since the day I bought this boat, I've been getting different versions of resentment from local sailors, that I own Misty…dismissive looks and catty remarks from dock passerbys. Tough shit. It was for sale, I bought it and intend to get it organized, then leave here to do some serious long-distance sailing. Trust me. I won't look back. End of story." I guess my insecurity was showing.

Adrienne just shrugged, "Right. Well, Bond asked if we knew a boat called Misty? I told him we knew the old owner, but some hippy bought it. He said, That hippy is Nancy's brother, Kenny. Go say hello… So. Hello."

That was Adrienne. Very dry. It took years to learn to appreciate her taciturn, sarcastic style.

Hugo, I found, was the complete opposite. He nearly fell over himself, extending his hand, "Hey! Hugo Smith. Friend and old shipmate of Bond. No idea how he knew you were here, but he told Adrienne to keep an eye out for you, and here you are!"

Everything about this encounter was more than a bit

unreal. I finally met Hugo, and although I'd known Adrienne from a previous chapter of my life, our circumstances then weren't exactly cozy.

Years ago George let me camp my pickup in the driveway of his house, while he was out of town, but while Adrienne was living there, who was not even remotely friendly. I agreed to Bond's terms to avoid her at all costs.

She was working as some sort of medical assistant for a local MD, so it was pretty easy to stay off her radar. In the end it became way too cold to live in a truck, even with two snow dogs and lots of sleeping bags. I just borrowed some gas money and moved to Telluride, opening a whole new subchapter in my life.

A series of random events led me to end up buying Misty at that tiny marina in Riviera Beach. Still, I was there a couple of months before that day that Hugo and Adrienne finally figured out who I was. Probably George ran into my sister Nancy in Aspen or Telluride. It was very strange that suddenly all these ghosts from my Steamboat Springs past showed up on boats. This whole encounter was becoming more and more awkward, but I pressed on anyway.

I knew from the local sailor gossip that Hugo was a very knowledgeable sailor and an accomplished smuggler. During my forays around the local shipyards, I'd seen Hugo and his partner Shannon perform magic on older motor vessels. They were master shipwrights.

"Listen, Hugo, I don't have much navigation experience aside from putting in dead reckoning positions. So, I'm guessing you've sailed a lot of miles. Will you teach me how to use a sextant to chart celestial positions? I'll pay you for your time."

Hugo shrugged and said, "I can do that." He needed the money to help keep that hundred-year-old wooden fishing schooner afloat. He jumped below to the chart table and wrote out a list of things I needed: a sextant, the book, Celestial Navigation for Yachtsmen by Mary Blewitt, a current maritime almanac, the sight reduction tables, a reliable time piece, dividers, and parallel rulers, etc.

Hugo became my navigation mentor. It was the beginning of a friendship that lasted for years.

I bought Misty in August and used the summer and fall hurricane season to refit my new boat. Although the previous owner was meticulous about how she looked, he never pushed her hard enough to reveal her real problems. Everytime a gale passed through, I took her out into the Gulfstream to see what would break and to find her leaks. This was the real beginning of my lifelong love/hate relationship with yacht repair.

There was a skilled mariner and professional diver who had an impressive Columbia 50 in the marina. Mike was doing a complete refit on his yacht and took pity on my bold ignorance. Between him and Hugo, I had plenty of knowledgeable project management.

I discovered another resource in the neighborhood. Perry Submarines was just down the harbor. They were designing and building some high tech small subs, maybe for oil rig maintenance. I didn't ask or care. I just liked to wander down there and entertain the geek engineers with smuggling and climbing stories. They were always a big help when I needed a custom built, stainless steel mounting bracket for my reefing system or some rigging part. Sadly, one day the shop foreman came by the boat to deliver a part they made for me. He told me that the Feds were "uncomfortable" with my visits to their facility. Apparently, they had secret government military contracts. The Feds objected to my being there. Pity, the guys at Perry were a good resource.

***

Maria arrived in November, right around the time Hugo left with Sailmaker Rick to pick up a load of weed from Columbia. By the time Hugo returned, Maria and I had left for Nassau. The next time we met up was a year or so later when we showed up in Key Largo to refit Misty. They had already sold Hugo's old schooner and bought the house and land on Lake George.

    The hideout at Lake George was a big factor in our being here. Now that we had Misty tucked away in an invisible canal in the middle of nowhere, it was time to map out the logistics for getting our product to market. For a change, we had a most excellent product. But we were nowhere near home free.

    First of all, we needed a vehicle to move a couple hundred pounds of weed to Atlanta where I had contacts in a thriving market. However, there were a bunch of state lines we had to cross. Getting out of Florida was fraught with danger.

A Smuggler's Guide to Fine Dining

The highways north from San Mateo were as hot as a two dollar pistol. Every mile north of the Georgia line was a mile further from the smuggling coast. Police awareness would diminish as we moved north and west.

I called Adrienne, told her we were nearby, and soon Hugo came by in his not-so-old Chevy pickup truck. Maria and I piled in, and we drove ten or so miles to Crescent City to buy groceries and pick up a couple bottles of gin and three bottles of wine before heading for the Drayton Island Ferry. The ferry across the river was a barge big enough to hold three or four trucks or cars.

Eddy, the ferry captain, greeted Hugo in his slow North Florida drawl as he jumped into the open aluminum jon boat with a Johnson fifty hp engine that powered the barge.

"Eddy, this is Ranen and Maria, old sailor friends of ours."

We drove off the ferry onto a sandy rutted road through scrub palmetto palms and huge ancient live oak trees draped in moss with air plants nestled in the massive branches. In less than a mile, we turned down a drive through a citrus grove. The trees on both sides were heavy with oranges, grapefruits, lemons, and even kumquats.

Three athletic looking, scruffy mutts ran out to greet us as the truck emerged from the grove into the bright sunlight reflecting off Lake George. Hugo parked the truck between his big pole barn shop and the two-story house with the big front porch. Maria and I carried the paper grocery bags through the back door into the spacious country kitchen. Adrienne was having a gin and tonic at the table. Hugo arrived in a cloud of noisy dogs and deposited the bottles of wine and various spirits on the table.

Adrienne put together a big dinner. Pot roast and vegetables from her garden. We were all pretty drunk by the time Adrienne's key lime pie, made from limes off her trees, arrived.

Early the next morning, I wandered out to Hugo's shop feeling a bit rough and looking for a machete. And there one was, an old razor sharp machete, hanging on the outside wall. The perfect solution for all the poisonous snakes living everywhere on the property. It was also the solution to my alcohol dehydration.

I was off on a fruit safari, starting with the pink grapefruit trees. Seven cuts and the peels were gone. My mouth was so dry that the juice from the first one never made it to my throat… instantly absorbed by my parched mouth. The dogs were with me, hopefully running off the horrible cottonmouth snakes and alligators. Hugo was smart to keep everything mowed. "Snake in the grass" is a Central Florida nightmare reality. I remember he had some kind of industrial bush hog to do the mowing.

Everyone was drinking coffee when I walked in with a burlap bag of fresh fruit. "Plenty of fruit here for breakfast and rum punch," I announced.

Meanwhile, that cargo languishing on Misty was burning a hole in my brain. We desperately needed an appropriate vehicle to get it out of Florida to market, and I needed H and A's help to find a truck or some other invisible ride.

"So, there's a lot of weed ready to go north. You guys got a line on a pickup with a shell?"

Adrienne looked over at Hugo and said, "What about that Jap pickup over in George Sodder's yard?"

Hugo stood up, poured himself another coffee and said, "It's a long bed Nissan. Never saw it running, but George never turns down money. Let's go over there and see him."

We all filed out of the kitchen and down to the path along Lake George. We could hear the deep throated diesel roar of George's crane echoing off the lake. I really wasn't looking forward to buying anything from "Salvage George." He was a hard, sixty-year-old ex salvage master and tug captain who had a lifetime resume of hard bargaining. We all walked up to the cab of his crane. He stopped working but kept the engine running.

I got right into it. "Hey George, I need a pickup. Any chance you'd sell me that old Nissan that's been parked in the field for years?"

"Sure. You got a thousand in cash?"

"C'mon George, four flat tires, paint fading? It's a four hundred dollar truck at best! IF it runs."

"Tell you what Ranen, you help me set these pilings and I'll give it to you for four hundred. It was running when I parked it three years ago."

"Done. How does this work?" I answered.

"You wade in and I'll lift the pilings while you jocky them

into position. Just stay out of the way when I start pounding them down. Watch for cottonmouth snakes. I've got a shotgun up here. I'll kill 'em. They don't like being disturbed, but don't worry. I never miss."

"That's comforting," I muttered as I waded into the tepid water of Lake George.

I spent the rest of that day and most of the next setting pilings for Salvage George's new pier. True to his word, he killed three vicious and deadly cottonmouth snakes before they got close. He even used his compressor to inflate the pickup's tires and loaned me some compound to revive the paint job. The battery was still good and it started right up. It was a ten-year-old truck with a six-foot bed and a camper shell. Just another cheap Japanese pickup truck on the highway. It even had Georgia plates. Florida plates were a red flag to Georgia State Patrolmen in those days, maybe still.

We spent a couple of nights at H and A's while we got Misty organized for long-term storage. We moved all of our personal stuff off the boat to hide the weed that we stowed in the forward third of the Nissan bed. If you looked in the camper window all that could be seen were boxes of clothes. I had a technique for hiding weed in a pickup. We wanted any cop to think we were a couple moving to another state. When a cop wanted to open the gate for a look, he'd find three bicycles with greasy chains and pedals locked in spokes. Impossible to untangle without getting grease on his uniform. Policemen don't have to pay for their uniforms but they do have to clean them.

    When we drove away from Misty, we didn't know that we would never sail her away from that boatyard.

    That this was the last time we would ever see Misty.

CHAPTER 28

MARKETING

I tucked my hair under my cap, jumped into the truck and we headed north. We were driving to Atlanta where I knew we could safely stay at an old friend's house. We didn't take the Interstate. Instead we drove on the old Highway 75. More local police but I felt it was less predatory. The police in North Florida were looking for dope and illegal money both coming out of and going into the south. Confiscated money and vehicles propped up a lot of poor counties in Florida. But the major heat was on the interstates, the freeways.

    I had some ideas about where to sell this weed. We needed a safe place to think and make calls. An old friend was living in suburban Atlanta. He had nice, upper middle class digs not far from I-75N in Marietta. We drove the back roads, staying off the Interstate until we got halfway through Georgia. In the seventies, no one took those Japanese pickup trucks seriously. That old faded black Nissan just didn't look like something a drug runner would use. Once again Maria and I were relying on profile instincts. And we passed plenty of local cops, none of whom gave us even a passing glance.

A Smuggler's Guide to Fine Dining

Maria had put together a cooler full of pot roast sandwiches with horseradish, oranges, and a big jar of fresh grapefruit juice so we didn't need to stop for food. Too bad in a way. There were some tempting small town diners that looked like they might serve up some great fried chicken, mashed potatoes, and fresh pecan pie. But we were on a mission, and it just wouldn't do to park a truck carrying bags of weed on a small town street where some local cop might smell it. The close call in Nassau was a lesson I didn't need to repeat. So we continued on toward Atlanta...and Scott's house.

Scott was a radical human disguised as a successful business executive who chose his house for the wooded yard on a deadend street because it was discreet. His disguise was perfect, because he really was a successful business executive. The radical part was why I could pull into his driveway just before midnight with a truck full of illegal drugs without calling first. In fact, I hadn't even talked to him in a year. There was a moment of panic that he might have moved, but there was his Porsche, just visible through the garage window.

We walked around and banged on the back door. The doorway was suddenly filled with the wide shouldered, imposing figure of Scott holding a .45 automatic down by his leg. "Finger off the trigger, wild man! It's just us."

"Well, I haven't heard from you in a year and wasn't expecting a strange truck in my driveway. Where in the hell have you been? Where'd you guys leave Misty? Come on in."

Scott's laughing, very slim, very beautiful, California,

curly-haired wife Connie shouted from the kitchen, "God, Scott. I don't think it's legal to shoot unexpected visitors in Georgia…or is it?" Connie flew to the door to give Maria a crushing hug.

I collected my hug from Connie, and Scott led us into the front room and started rolling a few of his buds.

I tossed him an old cigarette pack with some buds of our weed in it. "Try this. I've got a couple hundred pounds of it in the pickup. Let's see what you think. By the way, it's gonna take a few days to get rid of this stuff. Where can I leave the truck?"

An hour later in the kitchen, Scott pronounced our weed "most excellent" as he finished off half a cherry pie. "Listen, Ranen, it would be better if we move your truck tomorrow out of my driveway and especially out of Cobb County. My old warehouse is empty. You can lock it up in the loading bay. And even better, it's in Fulton County. I'll follow you over there tomorrow."

I took out enough for sales samples and stashed the truck. Now that I didn't have to watch over the weed, we were free to organize the least fun and most dangerous part of this odyssey. Thing is, I came here because I knew a lot of stoners in Atlanta. After all this was the city where I grew up. Over the years I'd become a sort of pied piper for the alternative lifestyle of the late sixties. Ranen was kind of an icon amongst the local hippies. I was one of the first stoners, and then I left. So the legends grew, many of which were only vaguely based on fact.

In fact, Kenny Ranen was the source of a lot of great weed that appeared in Buckhead over the years. Even before I became a sailor, I would buy weed in the late fall when good weed was plentiful and cheap. Bagged well in plastic in a trunk, it stayed in reasonably good condition until it was time to ship to Atlanta during the dry summer when weed was scarce and very expensive. For a couple of years I sent the padlocked trunk to Georgia by train. Before UPS there was Railway Express!

Scott had to work, so Maria and I cruised around with Connie in her dark blue hot rod Camaro. We all had a lot of fun stopping by to visit friends' and dealers' houses to smoke weed and give out samples all over North Atlanta.

David Reeves was an old friend who had sold a lot of my weed over the years. He figured that he could sell it all. I didn't doubt he could, but David was a junkie at times, so he never had any cash to buy anything. I sure as hell wasn't going to trust him with any amount of weed he hadn't paid for. It was looking like I would have to sell this weed a kilo or two at a time and charge more. That weed was damn good. So once David got started, I was sure it would fly out his door. I wasn't big on hanging around while the Atlanta Police started wondering where this new weed came from, and David understood that principle as well. Hopefully, he could find someone to buy it all in one go and we could be done with it before the cops followed it back to him.

It took a nervous week before the market responded, and a bigger dealer in fine weed wanted it all. David told me it was Pete that wanted the entire load. I knew and trusted Pete. He had been selling weed for years and was flying well under the radar. David agreed to let me work directly with Pete to arrange the transfer, but I insisted that he be present when it went down. If he was going to make money on this, I insisted that he share the risk. Anyway, I wasn't worried. All these players had been selling drugs for many years.

Pete had a house on a wooded acre out Peachtree Dunwoody past the ring road. There was an 8-foot high fence around the property. He had a very aggressive Doberman who wouldn't let us out of the truck until Pete came out. We all carried the bales into the house and smoked a few joints.

Pete handed me a paper grocery bag and said, "Listen boys, I've got to be somewhere in half an hour. There are six hundred Benjamin Franklins in the bag. Count 'em."

They were all there. I counted out ten for David, folded up the bag, and put a big rubber band around it. Pete chained up the dog, and we left. I dropped David at his house then headed back to Scott's house in Marietta.

Maria saw the banded paper sack and nodded as I walked through the door.

Scott asked, "Did you get paid?"

"Have you got any champagne in the fridge?" I asked in response. "We're going to try to leave soon, and I'll leave you some weed, but tonight let's go for some classic Atlanta junk food at the Varsity."

"A chili dog will sound better after a couple glasses of this French wine." Scott replied.

Connie added, "I really don't get what you see in that place."

"It's an Atlanta high school nostalgia thing" was Maria's comment.

The chili dog wasn't anything close to what I remembered. However, I did remember why I left Atlanta the day after my high school graduation. In something like ten years, Atlanta's population had grown from two hundred fifty thousand to millions without any regard for accommodating the infrastructure problems that come with that kind of growth. I had never seen gridlock before that trip. The Chattahoochee river was an urban sewer. Even to this day, Atlanta is the benchmark of how not to run a city.

In the morning, Connie made us all eggs and biscuits for breakfast. Maria and I started west just after Scott left for work. We were headed to my hundred acres in the Idaho Rockies.

CHAPTER 29

A ROCKY MOUNTAIN HIDEOUT

As far back as the late sixties in my City College of San Francisco days, I thought about having a house and land in the west. I guess I was part of the back to the land movement that caused the original Hippy exodus from Haight Ashbury. Or maybe it was a fantasy derived from childhood television: Kung Fu, Have Gun Will Travel, Maverick. Hard to say how much of our thinking is media-based.

The move out of San Francisco was an earthquake in my life. I had it pretty together in "The City." Lots of friends in and out of the famous Haight Ashbury District, a comfortable and cheap apartment on the upper edge of the Mission District, two doors from Dolores Park, and I had a high-paying job as a non-member extra at the SF Longshoreman's Union. The Vietnam War was in high gear so the union just couldn't find enough manual laborers to load ships down at the wharf. Just show up at five in the afternoon and work all night for the highest wages anyone was making in SF.

I needed to be enrolled in college to avoid being drafted into that war and was attending City College, but I was still thinking about getting a degree. For the degree, I transfered to San Francisco State. A few photography courses and a history class fit the bill.

At SF State a new student government had been elected, all drawn from the influx of radical thinking, anti-war students. After the election the new government promptly took half the student funds out of the sports program to fund a volunteer organization to tutor inner-city children. Young Americans were waking up to the horrors of a pointless war and inequality in American culture, but I was waking up to all the possibilities of the life in front of me. These were changing times. Anything seemed possible.

The Board of Regents freaked out about the new student government defunding the sacred cabal of sports, and promptly took the funds back, then dissolved the government. The student body called a strike, peaceful demonstrations ensued, and Ronald Raegan, as the Governor of California, quickly appointed the right wing S. I. Hayakawa President of the college.

Ronald Reagan was from the beginning a puppet of Carl Rove, who has been the shadow figure behind the Republican Party and the Vietnam War (as well as the many, many wars since). These protests were a problem for Rove and his Republican Party. The protests were threatening the flow of money into the massive U.S. war machine. Fortunes were being created on every level. And then, as now, the "military-industrial complex" had no interest in peace.

I questioned, right at the beginning of the Reagan campaign for Governor of California, how a B-movie actor ended up with so much support. He was a good speaker as long as he stuck to prepared speeches. However, he made stupid gaffs when asked questions for which he had not been prepared. At a public meeting, Governor Reagan was asked why the new Redwood National Park was so small next to thousands of acres of clearcut redwoods, Reagan's reply was paraphrased by the then governor, Pat Brown: "If you've seen one redwood, you've seen them all."

At the behest of Reagan, the freshly minted President Hayakawa called in the newly formed San Francisco Police Tactical Squad. Until this moment, American police wore blue uniforms and carried small-caliber pistols. The new "Tac" squad arrived in black military combat gear, armed with M16 assault rifles. In this new millenium we're used to militarized cops, but at that point it was shocking. The police, who had always been the enemy of anyone not white middle class, were now a threat to the newly aware members of the white middle class who were opposed to the status quo.

Aside from showing up at a few rallies, I didn't get involved. I was anti-war and anti-U.S. Government but not really an activist.

It was morning, and I headed to the photo lab with an armful of photo developing gear when I walked straight into a crowd of students running from the campus. Having worked

A Smuggler's Guide to Fine Dining

all night at the wharf, I was oblivious of the danger that I'd stumbled into. A running cop dressed in black combat gear tried to arrest me when we collided. He grabbed my shirt with one hand, trying to get a grip of my arm. Good luck for me, he was also swinging a long night stick with his other hand. He lost his footing for a moment on all the boxes and books I had dropped. The moment he stumbled, I spun out of the shirt and ran, shirt buttons flying everywhere.

I kept running...until passing a bus stop with a bus door opening. Breathless and still a bit shaky from the adrenaline, I made my way home. That evening, my neighbors in the back apartment of the flat were thrilled to take over my digs. It was time for me to leave city life behind.

A week or so later found me on the road to the mountains. Three young guys in an older car stopped to pick me up on Highway 50 somewhere in the hills east of Vacaville. The guy in the back lit up a joint and passed it to the driver. By the time it got around to me, they were all laughing hysterically. I took one hit and was instantly hallucinating. The rain-deprived hills along the road were on fire and it was electric green flames then, electric blue.

"Need to get out." I squeaked in a voice I didn't recognize. The guy driving lurched onto the road side and said as he drove away, "Enjoy the trip. You'll be back in half an hour." Sitting on the roadside leaning on my pack, in some little corner of my mind a voice told me that the joint was DMT and that the only thing to do was enjoy looking at the cactus-like ice plants and their neon pink flowers until it was over. Already the green wildfire was gone.

Those were the times…stoners giving away trips. Gifts from the Universe. Psychedelic kindness.

I was hitchhiking to South Lake Tahoe where Carole and Mickey were living with Adam who was one-year-old. At that moment, Carole was three months pregnant with Timmy. Mickey had rented a big fancy house up a hill from Highway 50. They had plenty of room, and I was a big help to Carole since Mickey had a sales job that took him out of town a lot.

In those days the population of South Lake Tahoe was 500 year round residents, not enough residents to fill out the Tahoe workforce, so there was no problem finding a job at Heavenly Valley Ski Area. A lot of Mickey's friends worked at Heavenly, and Mike Powell took me to the first lift meeting just before opening day. I showed up with my hair tucked under my ski cap. I told Frank, the lift foreman, "Oh yeah. I can ski."

Frank was relieved to hire a guy who he could put at the top of the mountain, a job no one wanted because it was boring and the lift shack was too far from the lodge to get away for a lunch break. Aside from the part where I lied about being a skier (I could do a snowplow and that was it), it was the perfect job for a twenty-year-old stoner straight out of the SF hippy scene. Just sit in the lift shack at ten thousand feet, smoke joints, listen to tunes on my transistor radio, and enjoy the 360° view of all the mountain peaks surrounding the bright deep blue Lake Tahoe. The work involved watching the skiers and pushing the stop button if someone fell or got hung up or didn't get off. The top of the Sky Chair duties also involved a lot of shoveling to keep the ramp and shack clear, no small task since sometimes it snowed a foot every hour.

But the best part of the job was all the skiing I was able to get in, except for the first week. That first week was somewhat of a nightmare. Skiing up the two lifts in the morning to get to number four wasn't too bad. My snowplow skills slowly got me there but skiing down had me worried the entire first day. I knew that I had to ski down with the "sweep." The ski patrol had to be the last skiers off the mountain to make sure there was no one injured or lost, left to die on the slopes.

At three-thirty, a couple ski patrolmen got off the lift and stopped at my shack. It was Tim and Grant. "You saved us each a joint right?" Tim asked.

I handed each of them a big fat one and said, "Listen. I lied to Frank to get this job. I told him I could ski, but really I only know how to do a snowplow. Sorry, but you guys are gonna have to teach me to ski if you want to get to the bar before it closes."

Tim said, "This is going to cost you many drinks until you learn, but Grant and I'll have you up to speed this week."

Grant and Tim were getting high and really laughing in anticipation of watching me struggle to get off this mountain in one piece.

Tim said, "You can follow me down the Ridge Run. Just do exactly what I do. You're gonna learn a stem christie turn. It starts with a snowplow. This is your first and last lesson. Sink or swim, man."

That was also the year I learned to climb. By the end of the ski season, my old friends Beach Rat, Noel, John, and I were living in an apartment over a shed in an industrial big truck junkyard. Noel was a craps dealer at Harrah's club. Beach was out every night at the casinos, drinking heavily, gambling, and winning! By the end of the summer he was banned from playing at all the Casinos. Apparently the casinos don't like winners.

During the summer, Beach and I were both collecting unemployment checks each week. Beach from his time in the Army and me from being laid off from the ski area. Occasionally we were sent out on a job. On one of those jobs we worked next to a guy who asked if we wanted to go rock climbing. We jumped at it. For me it was my chance to really get up into these mountains.

Smoking weed all winter up in my lift shack at the top of the Sky Chair, I was obsessed. My childhood dreams of living on a frontier that hadn't existed since the advent of cattle ranching had now evolved into living in the high peaks.

Refining that dream would take five more years of wandering before I actually bought the land in Idaho. I had a lot of exploring in the mountains to do before I could even approach my childhood fantasy of having a mountain home.

***

In the early seventies, my sister Nancy and her boyfriend

followed an exodus of their Colorado friends to Idaho. There was a large segment of the "ski bum" subculture that was tired of searching out, finding, then being forced out of cool mountain towns by big money tourism. One particular group of friends from Telluride and Steamboat migrated to the Salmon River Valley.

Nancy and Rolly bought ten acres in an upper corner of an old ranch north of Salmon, high above Tower Creek. It was one of the last pieces of private land before the National Forest leading to the big peaks on the Continental Divide. They picked up a bunch of four by four timbers and built a "log" cabin. There were no power poles up that far, so without electricity, using hand tools, they put together a cozy home. Rolly did have a chainsaw, and he was an artist with that chainsaw. They carried their water from a spring just above the cabin. Heat was provided by an Ashley wood stove, and the west-facing deck just out the front door was a lovely spot to watch the sun set into the mountains across the Salmon Valley.

It was a bit rough, but their act had a certain elegance. The outhouse, with its sheepskin covered toilet seat and open view, transformed our morning constitutional into a transformative experience. During my early years in the Caribbean, Nancy's cabin was my vacation "getaway."

Maria and I had just made a pile of extremely hard-earned money on a smuggling trip with Jerome and Jeffrey. We were wasted both mentally and physically and in desperate need of rest.

She and I flew from Switzerland to New York. There, in a terminal at Kennedy, all the tension of the past months culminated in a huge yelling match. We were both furious, and I could see she was about to punch me, but I at least had the presence of mind to leave before one of us got arrested.

I spent the night in a motel in Newark and we took separate flights to Missoula, the closest airport to Salmon. We met up the following day and laughed at yesterday's violence.

We couldn't get through to Nancy and Rolly so we just started hitchhiking from the airport, which just happens to be on Highway 93, the road to Salmon. We stuck out our thumbs. An older chevy pickup flew by, and the driver stood on the brakes slewing all over the road to a sideways stop in the middle of the highway. We threw our packs in the open bed and jumped onto the bench seat.

Maria was sitting in the middle, straddling the long gear shifter that curved up over the seat. The driver was a Native American in his late twenties, sporting long, greasy black hair. There was a vague whiff of alcohol in the air around him.

Long Feather was artfully navigating traffic through Missoula to the highway south out of town. He was sipping from a half pint bottle and driving fast. I wasn't too concerned; he was keeping between the white lines.

Maria gave me a look now and again when he would miss the shifter. "I'll be glad to change gears if you have trouble finding the shift lever," she said in her most stern voice. Maria could be pretty harsh when she needed to be. After all, she was the one who shot the Columbian, but that was later. Long Feather mumbled an apology.

We stopped for gas in Darby, a little Montana mountain community two hours from the Tower Creek road. While I filled the tank, Long Feather went into the casino to pay and buy a bag of chips and a fresh bottle of cheap whisky. From Darby, Highway 93 was a narrow twisting road that ran along a river then up and over Lost Trail Pass. Since then the pass has been completely upgraded, but at that time the road was so narrow that there were no guardrails (because there was no room for them) and so steep that no big trucks would take that road in the winter. Even in the summer semi-trucks only used 93 over Lost Trail if they had no other choice.

Long Feather was driving faster now as both the new bottle of whiskey and the traffic diminished. We hit the top of Lost Trail running hard, the wind whistled through the cab, and Johnny Winter's slide guitar blared out of Long Feather's tape deck. I had a moment of panic but realized there was nothing I could do. I took a couple of deep breaths, relaxed my mind and body, and accepted our fate.

The North Fork Store appeared around a curve. I shouted with released tension, "This is our stop, Long Feather. My sister works here."

He stopped barely long enough for me to grab our packs out of the bed. I turned around to say thanks, but he was already burning rubber onto 93 South.

We walked through the store to the restaurant. I poked

my head through the waitress window to greet Nancy who was rolling out pastry dough for her famous pie. "What's up, Sis?"

"Hey Bro! How'd you get here?"

"Maria and I made it here from the Missoula Airport in one ride…2 hours."

"Two hours, really? Were you hitching outside the Smoke Jumper's hanger?"

"No, Maria got us a ride with a drunk Indian in an old Chevy pickup. When can you get out of here?"

"I can't leave 'til these pies come out of the oven. You and Maria can hang out here in the kitchen with me, drink coffee, eat cherry pie, and tell me what trouble you two have been up to since you were last here. Seems like two years? Where's Misty?"

"Misty's in a little boatyard near Adrienne's house in North Florida."

On the road up to their cabin, Nancy told us that there was one hundred acres for sale behind their place. She was being a bit pushy about me buying it, because if I owned that land they would never have neighbors. I was resisting buying that property, because it wasn't right up in the big walls.

Nancy was losing her patience, "Listen Brother, there is no such thing as a perfect piece of land. This piece is as good as you're gonna find. Never any neighbors, close but not too close to a town, great ski area that's never going to be a giant nightmare, be sensible. If we had stayed in Telluride, we couldn't afford to live there."

A Smuggler's Guide to Fine Dining

***

In the end, I bought the land and now that three years later, it was finally paid up, Maria and I were back here up Tower Creek to pick a building site.

We decided not to stop at Nancy and Rolly's cabin. We just drove the truck very slowly past the end of their steep two-track road and up a couple of football fields of overgrown pasture, avoiding giant hidden boulders, looking for a place to build a house. The clearing closed out where the aspen trees met the big doug firs at the base of the south ridge. I drove through an opening in the trees and arrived at a spot well below the spring, just where the terrain leading toward the Continental Divide became steep. There wasn't an actual flat spot anywhere on my 110 acres, but with a few hours of bulldozing it would be perfect.

I got out of the truck. "Well, we can't drive any further from here. Great view to the west but protected from the winds off the peaks above, and it cannot be seen from anywhere, not on my land. I think I'll build the house here."

Maria got out and did a slow 360. She scanned a clearing the size of a track field surrounded by two hundred year old pines and firs.

"Okay. This spot really is magical..."

EPILOGUE

BEYOND 1979

Maria - When I began writing this story, I was conflicted about including the incident that occured with Maria in the Southern Bahamas. I hadn't had any communication with her in many years and was not in contact with anyone who might know her. Finally, I did an internet search and up came her obituary. So it turned out there was no reason to withhold any part of the story.

Misty - In 1983 I realized that I needed and wanted to do longer voyages. I had been sailing American waters for far too long. I had reason to believe that I was becoming known. Thing is, I needed a bigger boat to make money on the larger world canvas. It was time to retire Misty.

I left her in the boatyard in San Mateo, Florida then sailed away to the Indian Ocean. Sometime during my many years in those waters, a guy from Aspen bought her. Alas, he liked working on boats, but not sailing them. Misty had a distinguished sailing career with Ranen at the helm and sadly, I dropped her like a girlfriend I had tired of.

Nancy - My younger sister divorced Rolly in the 1980's. She lives in Sedona these days.

Carole - My sister Carole is living in Minnesota.

Hugo and Adrienne - Hugo succumbed to the grim reaper at the millennium, but Adrienne still lives on their little citrus plantation on Drayton Island.

George Bond - Died of liver disease from substance abuse in the 1980's.

Mickey Thompson - Killed in a drug deal gone bad in Belize in the late 1980's. But really, Mickey always flew too close to the Sun.

Fred Thomas - I heard he had died in the late 1980's.

Smitty - Last I heard Smitty lives in Norwood, CO.

Summer and Spring - These magical twins are even more magical. Summer has Grandchildren and continues to celebrate life, art, and nature, living in the mountains of California. Spring has a kite-boarding school in Hood River, Oregon and winters in Baha.

Peter Szymanski - Living in the Denver area.

Paul - Paul is a well-known and respected marine biologist.

Noel - You'll have to wait for the third book...no spoilers here.

Jeffrey Richardson - Thank the gods I have lost touch with Jeffrey.

College Jay - No idea where he is, but one can only hope that his karma caught up with him.

Scott - Retired and living up in the mountains outside of S. Lake Tahoe.

Two Italian Sisters - I have since returned to Boston and couldn't find a trace of the "Sisters."

Kimo, Kimosabe, John Batistella - Kimo had a daughter with Karen. He sobered up to become a better father. Karen and Kimo separated, and Kimo bought Bond's house in Key Largo. At some point, after their daughter was out of college, Kimo began to drink and take opioids. He ended up shooting himself in Key Largo.

Redneck Ralph - In the late 90's Ralph sold the boatyard and moved to central Florida. I wonder if Jimmy the tunnel rat went with him.

A Smuggler's Guide to Fine Dining

Joe Prins - I introduced Joe to my sister Carole in the early 1980's. They were partners until he died in 2017.

Forrest and Connie - My welding teacher and friend Forrest and his wife Connie, who was one of the "fashion week" girls, moved to Crescent City Florida. They have two grown children and an excavating company. Ginnie, Forrest's sister, also lives up there.

Sue and Lightning Florida John Viano - They lived in Maine for quite a few years. John bought Joe's Dugong.

Jimmy and Caroline - I hope my readers will forgive me for my light treatment of Jimmy's bust. Even thinking about them all these years later is difficult. Frankly, I feel as though I abandoned Jimmy. I know there was nothing I could have done. He had Hepatitis C, and the stress and bad prison lifestyle gave the virus the opportunity to destroy his liver. I heard that he couldn't get any treatment inside and the courts weren't going to let him go. I don't know how it ended for that lovely family, and I have lost touch with everyone who might know.

ABOUT THE AUTHOR

In 1971 Kenny Ranen was living in Telluride, climbing and skiing. Then he was gone...

For over three decades, no house, no address, no phone. Sailing the oceans of the world and smuggling to pay the bills. Today Ranen's podcasts tell endless stories from the days when he was sailing ten to twenty thousand miles a year without GPS and without a care, notwithstanding sharks, pirates, monsoon storms, medical emergencies at sea, and the Guardia Civil.

In 1995 Ranen stopped in Charleston, South Carolina to rest before crossing the Atlantic to Europe. It was there at Charleston City, Marina that he met his future wife. Soon after, she joined him on Sara in Palma de Mallorca. Elizabeth was not interested in becoming an international criminal, but Ranen had a backup plan. He had been thinking for many years that a live documentary of his lifestyle would be popular. The two of them spent the next two years sailing the Mediterranean and the Red Sea, shooting video of their adventures and producing episodes, some of which can be seen on Ranen's website: https://asmugglersguide.com.

In 2002 Ranen sold his last boat, Sara, and left the sea to live in his house in the Idaho Rocky Mountains where his son was born. Nowadays Ranen spends his time writing, skiing, and traveling with his teenage son. They backpack, bag peaks, visit friends, and sell books up and down the length of the Rocky Mountains.

ACKNOWLEDGMENTS

Thanks to my editors—Cody McFadden, Angie Stone, Marty Himmel, and Mark Mendel—for their work and support.

A big shoutout to Tracey Fedor in Albuquerque who designed all the images including the recipes and the covers of all the Smuggler's Guide Series. It was Tracey's idea, starting with the title, to make this a cookbook.

The discovery of Lara Helmling, Forest City Publications, saved my butt. I was at a loss as to book design until she agreed to produce this book.

My amigo and traveling companion, Josh Manzer, came up with the ending to this book.

Aldea Coffee in Grand Haven, MI provided the espressos that fueled my writing these stories. The baristas also were my friends, my muses, and my enablers. Thanks to Chloe, Anna, Jenny, and Brittany.

A Smuggler's Guide to Fine Dining

FOR YOUR NEXT READ...

A Smuggler's Guide to Good Manners

by Captain Kenny

A True Story Of Terrifying Seas, Double-Dealing, And Love Across Three Oceans

AVAILABLE NOW AT MAJOR BOOKSELLERS

amazon   BAM!   BARNES & NOBLE   AND MORE!

COMING SOON!

A Smuggler's Guide to Jail Break

by Captain Kenny

The adventures continue...from Columbian prison breaks to high sea romance to more unforgettable characters...and the best part is, the stories are real.

FOR EVEN MORE PICTURES, STORIES, AND INSIDE INFO GO TO ASMUGGLERSGUIDE.COM

www.ingramcontent.com/pod-product-compliance
Lightning Source LLC
Chambersburg PA
CBHW071952070526
44583CB00015B/1155